Essentials of Microeconomics

Essentials of Microeconomics is an excellent introduction to microeconomics. It presents the basic tools of microeconomics clearly and concisely. It presents a vigorous treatment of all relevant introductory microeconomic concepts, and emphasises modern economics – game theory and imperfect markets. Each chapter is self-contained and includes the required key mathematical skills at the start.

Now in its second edition, this updated textbook includes:

- Expanded lecturer resources, including detailed lecture slides, sample exam questions and updated test bank multiple choice questions
- An additional section on Economics in Practice, focused on policy, econometrics and behavioural economics

This book is ideal not only for introductory microeconomics courses, but its level of analysis also makes the book appropriate for introductory level economics taught at postgraduate level. With the emphasis on strategy, this text is also well suited for use in business economics courses.

Bonnie Nguyen is an Honours graduate from the University of Sydney in both Law and Economics. Bonnie's research interests include an economic analysis of litigation and the internal organisation and ownership structure of firms. She has published research in the *Journal of Institutional and Theoretical Economics* and the *Australian Economic Review*. Bonnie has previously taught microeconomics at the University of Sydney.

Andrew Wait is a Professor in the School of Economics at the University of Sydney. He has a PhD from the Australian National University and a Bachelor of Economics (Honours) from the University of Adelaide. Andrew's research interests include industrial organisation and organisational economics. Andrew has published in the *RAND Journal of Economics*, the *International Journal of Industrial Organization* and the *Journal of Law, Economics and Organization*. He is the co-convenor of the Annual Organizational Economics Workshop.

"One of the standout features of this textbook is its clear and concise writing style, which effectively conveys complex economic principles in an accessible manner. The authors have succeeded in presenting the material in a way that is engaging and easy to understand for students with varying levels of prior knowledge."

Kadir Atalay, Associate Professor,
University of Sydney

"Without the clutter that sometimes chocks introductory texts, this book allows students to focus on the core intuition and analytical tools. This book presents the essentials of microeconomics. It provides an excellent platform for further study in economics. This textbook will stand the test of time. I recommend it to instructors teaching any principles or introductory microeconomics course."

Alexander Matros, Professor of Economics,
Moore School of Business, University of South Carolina

"Good economic analysis requires understanding of how to apply models to the world. This book strikes the right balance between technique and economic relevance. The authors lead students through just enough analytical tools to be able to understand and then apply economic models to real economic problems. By focusing on the essentials this book makes economics accessible to students from all backgrounds. Its strength lies in the brevity and clarity of its exposition. At no point is there anything extraneous, yet all is covered."

Guillaume Roger, Associate Professor (Research),
Monash University

"The second edition improves on what was already an outstanding introductory microeconomics textbook. A particular strength of the book is how the presentation of the material highlights the power of economic models for helping us understand the world around us. The new chapters on policy and applications show students how to apply what they have learnt. There is nothing extraneous in this book. A mastery of this content will provide students with almost all of the microeconomics tools of analysis they will need for the rest of their academic and professional careers. I recommend this for any introductory microeconomics or business economics course."

Kieron Meagher, Professor,
Australian National University

"Economic thought is vital to understanding individuals and their interaction within societies. This textbook provides a set of tools for students to understand markets and analyze the decisions made by consumers, businesses and governments. The exposition is concise and precise, presenting fundamental techniques and insights in a way that is accessible to students new to the discipline, giving a good balance of mathematical rigour and verbal explanation. I used the first edition to great success and will use this new edition too. I highly recommend it."

Jonathan Newton, Professor,
Kyoto University, Japan

Essentials of Microeconomics

Second Edition

Bonnie Nguyen and
Andrew Wait

LONDON AND NEW YORK

Designed cover image: © Getty Images

Second edition published 2024
by Routledge
4 Park Square, Milton Park, Abingdon, Oxon, OX14 4RN

and by Routledge
605 Third Avenue, New York, NY 10158

Routledge is an imprint of the Taylor & Francis Group, an informa business

First edition published by Routledge 2016

British Library Cataloguing-in-Publication Data
A catalogue record for this book is available from the British Library

Library of Congress Cataloging-in-Publication Data
Names: Nguyen, Bonnie, author. | Wait, Andrew, author.
Title: Essentials of microeconomics / Bonnie Nguyen and Andrew Wait.
Description: Second edition. | Abingdon, Oxon ; New York, NY : Routledge, 2024. |
Includes bibliographical references and index. | Identifiers: LCCN 2023034859 (print) |
LCCN 2023034860 (ebook) | ISBN 9781032453675 (hardback) |
ISBN 9781032453668 (paperback) | ISBN 9781003376644 (ebook) |
ISBN 9781032647289 (ebook other) | Subjects: LCSH: Microeconomics.
Classification: LCC HB172 .N446 2024 (print) | LCC HB172 (ebook) |
DDC 338.5–dc23/eng/20230727
LC record available at https://lccn.loc.gov/2023034859
LC ebook record available at https://lccn.loc.gov/2023034860

ISBN: 9781032453675 (hbk)
ISBN: 9781032453668 (pbk)
ISBN: 9781003376644 (ebk)
ISBN: 9781032647289 (ebk+)

DOI: 10.4324/9781003376644

Typeset in Times New Roman and Helvetica
by Newgen Publishing UK

Access the Support Material: www.routledge.com/9781032453668

Contents

Illustrations

Tables

PART I

Key concepts and tools

Key economic concepts

1.1 Introduction

Economics is the study of choice under scarcity. Typically, consumers want more goods and services than they can afford to buy. Similarly, businesses face constraints in relation to the funds and resources they have access to. Governments and countries also face the same type of problem: a government might want to tackle a large number of social problems but only have limited resources to draw on. Economics is about understanding how a party (that is, a consumer, a business, the government of a country and so on) deals with the fact that when they use their resources to pursue one option, they cannot use those resources to do something else. And so, a consumer may have to choose between a new pair of shoes or a textbook; a firm may have to choose between developing a new product or launching a marketing campaign; and a government may have to choose between improving education or targeting crime.

To help understand these issues, economics has developed a set of analytical tools. This book provides an introduction to these tools. They can be used to help understand economic problems wherever they arise, be it businesses understanding the markets they compete in, governments trying to develop social policy, or families trying to manage their households. These tools are not meant to capture everything that is occurring in any given situation. Rather, they are designed to simplify (or to model) complicated and potentially messy real-world issues into a tractable form that can provide valuable insights.

Given that resources are limited, the key questions that an economy needs to 'decide' are: (a) what to produce; (b) how to produce it; and (c) who should get what is made. In modern economies, the answers to these questions are largely determined by the market – that is, through the interaction of sellers and buyers.[1] Sometimes, however, the government also helps determine the

DOI: 10.4324/9781003376644-2

answer to these questions by regulating or intervening in the market. Consequently, our focus in this microeconomics text will be on the behaviour of individuals (consumers, firms and governments) and their interaction in markets.

This chapter provides a few key concepts that underpin the analysis in the rest of the book, as well as economics analysis in general.

1.2 Scarcity and opportunity cost

As noted above, it is usually the case that resources are limited, so not all wants can be met. We call this situation **scarcity**.

Scarcity also means that consumers, firms and governments face tradeoffs; by choosing one thing, a person must give up or miss out on something else. For example, if a consumer uses their money to buy product X, they cannot then use that same money to buy another product.[2] We use the concept of opportunity cost to capture this tradeoff; the **opportunity cost** of any choice is the value of the next best forgone alternative. In the example above, if the consumer buys product X, and the next best thing they could have done is buy product Y, the opportunity cost of buying X is forgoing Y.

Individuals also face opportunity costs in terms of their time – that is, if a person spends his time doing one thing, he cannot also spend that time doing another.

> **Example.** Suppose Elizabeth prefers to spend her Saturday afternoon walking. The next best thing that she could have done is to sleep, and her third best choice is to go swimming. Therefore, if Elizabeth goes for a walk, the opportunity cost of going for a walk is not sleeping, as this is her best forgone option. The option of swimming is not relevant here because it is not the next best option.

Opportunity costs include both explicit and implicit costs. Explicit costs are costs that involve direct payment (or, in other words, would be considered as costs by an accountant). Implicit costs are opportunities that are forgone that do not involve an explicit cost.[3]

> **Example.** Suppose Stephen decides to go to university, and his next best option is to work at a construction site and earn $80,000 over the year. The explicit costs are those that Stephen must directly pay to go to university, such as student fees, the cost of textbooks, and so on. The implicit costs are the opportunities that Stephen must forgo – in this case working at the construction site and earning $80,000.

It is important to note that the opportunity cost only includes costs that could change if a different decision were made. The opportunity cost does not include sunk (or unrecoverable) costs. **Sunk costs** are costs that have been incurred and cannot be recovered no matter what. For example, if Katrien spends the weekend reading an accounting textbook, no matter what she does (such as whether or not she decides to continue studying accounting), she cannot get that time back. Similarly, if a business spent $100,000 on an advertising campaign last year, regardless of what they decide to do this year, that money (and effort) cannot be recovered.

1.3 Marginal analysis

Typically, we assume that economic agents are rational and act to maximise the benefit they receive from any economic transaction.[4] For example, consumers seek to maximise their benefits from consumption and firms seek to maximise their profits from production. One way that economic agents can solve this maximisation problem is by considering the additional benefit or additional cost of any action. This sort of analysis is referred to as **marginal analysis** and it is a recurring theme both in this book and in economics generally.

For instance, consider a consumer faced with the decision of whether to buy one more unit of a particular good. That consumer might consider the extra benefit he derives from buying that extra unit; this is referred to as the **marginal benefit** of that extra unit of the good. The consumer will also consider the additional cost of buying one more unit; this is referred to as the **marginal cost** of purchasing another unit, which is typically the price of the good. In making their final decision, the consumer will weigh the marginal benefit against the marginal cost of buying that extra unit. For example, if a consumer is considering buying another cup of coffee, and the marginal benefit is $5 and the marginal cost is $3, the consumer will be better off buying the extra coffee.

Each of the marginal terms noted above, and many others, will be discussed at length throughout the book. What is crucial to note is that the term 'marginal' simply means additional or extra. That is, we are interested in what happens if we increase something (such as the number of coffees bought) by a small amount.

1.4 *Ceteris paribus*

The notion of *ceteris paribus* is also an important foundation of economic analysis. As noted, because the real world is complicated and messy, it is necessary to simplify real-world situations into tractable economic models, in order to better analyse them. Thus, in order to determine the impact of a particular event, economists tend to examine the impact of one change at a time, holding everything else constant. This is called *ceteris paribus*, which roughly means 'other things equal'.

For instance, suppose we are interested in how a change in price will affect the quantity demanded of a good. In reality, demand for a good can be affected by a number of other factors, such as changes in the tastes or income of consumers, or the availability or price of substitute goods. Therefore, in order to isolate the effect of price on quantity demanded, we need to hold everything else constant. This is not to deny that in the real world multiple changes can occur at a time – they often do. Rather, to fully understand the relationship between price and demand, it is essential to isolate that relationship from other events that might also be occurring. For example, a firm might be interested in the effect of advertising on demand for its product. To understand the impact of advertising, it is crucial to remove other factors that could affect demand, otherwise advertising could be attributed too much (or too little) influence, which could lead to poor decision-making by the firm regarding its next advertising campaign.

1.5 Correlation and causation

Another factor to keep in mind is the difference between correlation and causation. **Correlation** refers to a situation in which two or more factors are observed to move together (or in opposite directions). On the other hand, **causation** refers to a situation where a change in one factor brings about, or *causes*, a change in something else. To make statements about causation requires an economic theory about how the world works – without a theoretical framework telling us why one factor causes another to change, we are just observing a statistical relationship between several variables.

Sometimes when we observe a correlation between two variables, A and B, it is because the movement in one variable causes the other to change. Sometimes, it is because a third factor causes changes in both A and B (like a tide coming in can cause two boats to rise in their moorings). Sometimes, there is no connection between the two variables and it is just by chance that we observed the change in both variables at the same time. Without a theory about how a change in one variable affects the other, it is not possible to say which option it is in any particular case.

1.6 Concluding comments

This chapter provided a very brief introduction to some key economic concepts. In the next chapter we outline some of the mathematical tools that we will use throughout the book.

Notes

1   By 'market', we simply mean a place where buyers and sellers of a particular good or service meet, such as a traditional bazaar or an online trading site.
2   It is common to hear people refer to the 'economics' of a particular situation. This colloquial statement really means that, given the limited resources available, a choice had to be made and something (possibly worthwhile) could not be done.

3   Sometimes, economists distinguish between 'economic costs' and 'accounting costs'. **Economic costs** is just another term for opportunity costs, and therefore include explicit and implicit costs. **Accounting costs** refer to explicit costs only.

4   We are not suggesting that, in the real world, consumers are always fully rational or that firms do not sometimes have other objectives. Rather, we adopt this simplifying assumption because it allows us to analyse the behaviour of economic agents in markets. This type of analysis will be fairly accurate, provided that on average individual consumers and firms act more or less in their own interest.

CHAPTER 2

Key mathematical tools

2.1 Introduction

Even at an introductory level, the analytical nature of economics requires us to draw upon some mathematical techniques. This chapter outlines some of those basic tools. Specifically, we cover: the formula for a straight line; understanding the slope of a line; simple differentiation; and solving simultaneous equations. In the next chapter we outline some tools that are useful for thinking about economic environments in which the interaction between different participants is important. All of these techniques will be useful in dealing with the material covered in this text.

2.2 Equations

Often we are interested in the relationship between two variables, x and y. Sometimes, it is convenient to express that relationship using an equation. In this section, we will cover straight lines and briefly discuss equations of curves.

2.2.1 Straight lines

The equation of a straight line can take the form

$$y = mx + c. \tag{2.1}$$

In this equation, x and y are the variables whose relationship we are interested in; m and c are parameters.[1]

DOI: 10.4324/9781003376644-3

When graphing this equation, we might want to know where the line intersects the axes. Along the y-axis, x takes the value of zero, so we can solve for the y-intercept by setting $x = 0$ (in equation 2.1, the y-intercept is $y = c$). Similarly, y takes the value of zero along the x-axis, so setting $y = 0$ yields the x-intercept (in equation 2.1, the x-intercept is $x = -\frac{c}{m}$).

> **Example.** Suppose we are interested in the relationship between the price of a good (P) and the quantity demanded of that good (Q). We might represent this relationship using the equation $P = 100 - 2Q$. Here, Q and P take the places of x and y, respectively. The slope of the line is -2 (see the next section). The line cuts the P-axis at 100 and the Q-axis at 50.

2.2.2 The slope of a straight line

Note that, in equation 2.1, if we increase x by 1 unit, y must increase by m units. Thus, the parameter m determines how a change in x affects a change in y (recall that this relationship is the focus of marginal analysis – see Chapter 1). The parameter m is also known as the slope or the gradient of the line; it tells us how steep the line is. That is, if we graph equation 2.1 with x and y on the horizontal and vertical axes, respectively, for every 1 unit we move horizontally (along the x-axis) we must also move m units vertically (along the y-axis). Note that if an increase in x results in an increase in y, the slope is positive. Conversely, if the increase in x results in a fall in y, the slope of the line (by definition) is negative. It is the fact that the slope is constant that makes this the equation of a straight line.

2.2.3 Determining the equation of a straight line

When we are not explicitly given the equation of a straight line, we can determine that equation from any two points on the line. First, we need to determine the slope, m. Recall that the slope is simply the change in y for a one-unit change in x. Therefore, if we have two points on a straight line, (x_1, y_1) and (x_2, y_2), the formula for the slope m is[2]:

$$m = \frac{\Delta y}{\Delta x} = \frac{y_2 - y_1}{x_2 - x_1} \tag{2.2}$$

In other words, the slope of the line m is the change in y (Δy) given a change in x (Δx). As we have calculated the slope m, it can be substituted into the general equation of a straight line, $y = mx + c$, so as to find c. To do this, we use the fact that the equation must pass through the point (x_1, y_1), so we can substitute these values into our equation to determine c.

> **Example.** Suppose a line passes through $(4, 3)$ and $(5, 1)$. Applying equation 2.2, we can find the slope, $m = \frac{3-1}{4-5} = -2$. Recall that the general equation of a straight line is $y = mx + c$. Substituting in $m = -2$ and $(4, 3)$ yields $3 = -2 \times 4 + c$, so $c = 11$. Therefore, the equation of the line is $y = -2x + 11$.

2.2.4 Curves

Some economic relationships are represented by equations that are not a straight line. For example, we might think that total cost (TC) is related to output (q) in such a way that $TC = q^2$. Plotting this curve (for $q \geq 0$) does not yield a straight line; rather, the slope of the curve becomes steeper and steeper. The key thing at this stage is to remember that the marginal relationship between two variables does not need to be constant. When this is the case, we can use differentiation to determine that marginal relationship, as will be discussed in the following section.

2.3 Differentiation

Sometimes, when we know the equation that connects two variables x and y, we want to find what happens to y when we change x by a very small amount. In these cases, we can use differential calculus. Differentiation is similar to finding a slope in that it shows how y responds to changes in x (in fact, for a straight line, calculating the slope and differentiating both yield the same answer). The difference is that calculus is concerned with very small changes in x, whereas slope is usually concerned with whole-unit changes. Differentiation is a useful tool because economics is often concerned with marginal changes; in particular, we will make use of it when discussing elasticities (Chapter 10) and determining marginal revenue for a monopolist (Chapter 13).

2.3.1 A simple rule for differentiation

For our purposes, we need one rule of differentiation. Take a function $y(x) = Ax^n$. Here, y is written as a function of x. A and n are parameters. By differentiating a function once, we get the **first derivative**, which we can write as $\frac{dy}{dx}$ or $y'(x)$. The rule of differentiation that we need is:

$$y(x) = Ax^n \Rightarrow \frac{dy}{dx} = n.Ax^{n-1} \tag{2.3}$$

This rule can also be applied to each individual additive component of a function, as shown in the example below.

> **Example.** Consider a function $P(Q) = 10 - Q^2 + 3Q^{-5}$. We can apply the rule in equation 2.3 to each individual component (10, $-Q^2$ and $3Q^{-5}$) separately. Note that 10 is really $10Q^0$, so after differentiation this becomes 0. Applying the rule to the next two components of the function yields $-2Q$ and $-15Q^{-6}$, respectively. Thus, the answer is $\frac{dP}{dQ} = -2Q - 15Q^{-6}$.

Like slope, the first derivative of a function tells us how steep a curve is at a particular point. If the first derivative is positive (resp. negative) the curve is rising (resp. falling), and if the first derivative is zero, then the curve is flat.

2.3.2 Finding minima and maxima

Differentiation is also a useful way of finding the maximum or minimum of a function. Notice that when a function reaches its maximum or minimum, the slope of the function is zero (that is, the curve is 'flat' at that point). Therefore, by setting the first derivative equal to zero, we can find the maximum or the minimum of a function. Of course, we will need to know whether the point we have found is a maximum or a minimum. There are ways to do this (for instance, by checking the second derivative), but graphing the function is usually a good check.

> **Example.** Suppose we want to find the maximum of the function $P = 100Q - Q^2$. Setting the first derivative equal to zero yields $\frac{dP}{dQ} = 100 - 2Q = 0$. Solving this equation yields $Q = 50$. We can graph the function to confirm that this is a maximum.

2.4 Elasticity

Another thing we might like to know about the relationship between x and y is how responsive y is to changes in x. That is, when we increase x by a certain amount, does y change by a small amount or by a large amount? We can measure the responsiveness of y to changes in x using the concept of **elasticity**.

We can calculate elasticity (ε) by dividing the percentage change in y by the percentage change in x:[3]

$$\varepsilon = \frac{\%\Delta y}{\%\Delta x} \tag{2.4}$$

This tells us what the percentage change in y will be, given a 1% change in x. As you can see, the larger the absolute value of ε is, the more responsive is y to changes in x; conversely, the smaller the absolute value of ε, the less responsive y is to changes in x.

We will discuss the methods of calculating elasticity and the economic applications of elasticity further in Chapter 10.

2.5 Simultaneous equations

In some cases, we will have multiple equations that link our variables. In the simplest case, two equations link two variables, x and y. If we want both equations to hold, we will need to find values of x and y that satisfy both equations. One way of solving this 'system' of equations is to rearrange each equation to have y on its left-hand side, and then equate the right-hand sides of the equations.

Example. Suppose we are given the following two equations that link P and Q:

$$P = 100 - 2Q. \tag{2.5}$$

$$P = 3Q \tag{2.6}$$

(These two equations could represent demand and supply, for instance.) First, note that P is on the left-hand side of both equations. Therefore, we can equate the right-hand side of the equations, giving:

$$100 - 2Q = 3Q$$

Solving this gives us $Q = 20$, which can then be substituted into equation 2.5 or 2.6 to find $P = 60$.

2.6 Concluding comments

Mathematics allows us to make explicit assumptions and solve and analyse complicated models. This chapter outlined some of the mathematical tools that we will use repeatedly in this text. The next chapter outlines some of the conceptional techniques used to analyse strategic interaction. Taken together, these tools form the foundation of how the models in this text are constructed and solved.

Notes

1   Here, 'parameter' simply means that the values of m and c are fixed and do not depend upon x or y. m and c are sometimes called 'constants' because their value does not change. For example, c could equal 2 and m could equal 5; importantly, this will be the case regardless of the value of the variables x and y.
2   In this equation, Δ simply means 'change', so Δy means 'the change in y'.
3   Here, $\%\Delta$ simply means 'percentage change'.

CHAPTER 3

Key strategic tools

3.1 Introduction

As we have previously discussed, economic agents try to do the best they can for themselves; in other words, they try to maximise their wellbeing subject to the constraints that they face. Sometimes, it is sufficient to consider a consumer or firm's maximisation problem in isolation. But at other times, the strategic interaction between parties is important. In these situations, what an individual chooses to do can depend on what other parties choose to do. In this chapter, we outline a few basic tools that are useful in analysing these situations. We will later look at applications of these tools in Chapters 5 and 15.

3.2 The essentials of game theory

Strategic interactions between economic agents can be analysed using **game theory**. This requires the relevant strategic interactions to be represented in the form of a **game**.

For most people, the word 'game' brings to mind card and board games or sports. However, in economics, the term has a specific meaning. In particular, a game has the following elements:

- Two (or more) players.
- A complete description of what actions each player may take.
- A specification of each player's payoff associated with the actions taken.

For now, we will assume that each participant in the game has full knowledge of these things. That is, each player knows who the other players are, what actions each player may take, and the payoffs that each player receives if certain

DOI: 10.4324/9781003376644-4

actions are taken. Note that this does not imply that each player knows what actions are *actually taken* by the other players.

As you can see, the economic notion of a game is different but related to the everyday understanding of what a game is. In fact, the economic definition of a game would probably include most card and board games and sports, but it also embraces a wider variety of situations. Consider the following examples.

> **Example.** Annie and Kat are working on a group project together, and their final mark depends upon how much effort they jointly put in. Let us say each person has the choice of putting in effort or not. If both of them put in effort, they will get a mark of 100%; if only one of them puts in effort, they will get a mark of 70%; and if neither of them puts in effort they will get a mark of 0%. This situation has all the characteristics of a game: there are two players (Annie and Kat), we know what actions each player may take (effort or no effort), and we know each player's payoff associated with the actions taken (their marks).

> **Example.** Fran and Maxwell are playing soccer, with Maxwell as the goalkeeper. Fran can kick the ball into the left or the right side of the goal and, at the same time, Maxwell can dive to the left or the right. If Fran kicks the ball to the opposite side that Maxwell dives, she will score a goal. If Maxwell dives to the same side that Fran kicks the ball, he will save the goal and prevent Fran from scoring. This has all the characteristics of an economic game: there are two players (Fran and Maxwell), we know what actions each player may take (left or right), and we know each player's payoff associated with the actions taken (the score).

3.3 Simultaneous-move games

In this section, we will consider games in which the players have to choose their actions simultaneously or without knowledge of what the other player has chosen. We will consider how to represent and solve these games.

3.3.1 Representing simultaneous-move games: the normal form

It is often convenient to represent a simultaneous-move game using the **normal form** of the game. In the normal form, the elements of a game are represented in the form of a table (or matrix).

To see how this is done, consider the following example: Two firms, A and B, are selling an identical product in the same market. At the beginning of the day, each firm must choose to set its price high (p_H) or low (p_L) without knowing what the other firm has chosen. If both firms set a price of p_H, both firms receive a payoff of \$4. If both firms set a price of p_L, each firm will get a payoff of \$3. If firm A sets a price of p_H and B at p_L the payoffs are \$1 and \$5 to A and B, respectively. On the other hand, if A chooses p_L and B chooses p_H the payoffs are \$5 and \$1 to A and B, respectively.

	Player 2	
	p_H	p_L
Player 1 — p_H	(4,4)	(1,5)
Player 1 — p_L	(5,1)	(3,3)

FIGURE 3.1 The normal form of a game

This information is represented in the normal form in Figure 3.1. Firm *A* and its choices are represented by the rows, and firm B and its choices are represented by the columns. The payoffs associated with these choice combinations are depicted in the four boxes of the matrix; firm A's payoff is the first number in the box and firm B's payoff is the second number in the box.[1] Together, A and B determine the set of payoffs that are realised. Suppose A chooses p_L and B chooses p_H. A's choice of p_L puts us in the bottom row; B's choice of p_H puts us in the left column. Hence, it is the payoff in the bottom left box that is realised (that is, \$5 to A and \$1 to B).

3.3.2 Solving simultaneous-move games

Let us now turn to the question of what the outcome of a simultaneous-move game will be. We can solve (or predict the outcome of) a game by assuming that each player is only interested in maximising his own payoff. In particular, we assume that each player does not care about the other player's payoff; that is, he is not interested in minimising or maximising the other player's payoff.

Dominant strategy equilibrium

Sometimes, it will be possible to solve a game using dominant strategies. A player has a **dominant strategy** when the action that gives him the highest payoff does not depend on what the other player chooses.

For example, consider the game depicted in Figure 3.2. In this game, Player 1's dominant strategy is to choose T as this will yield a higher payoff no matter what Player 2 chooses to do. To see why this is so, consider the game from Player 1's perspective:

- If Player 2 chooses L, Player 1 can choose T for a payoff of 4 or B for a payoff of 2. Therefore, Player 1 should choose T in this case.

	Player 2	
	L	R
Player 1 — T	(4,8)	(3,6)
Player 1 — B	(2,7)	(1,5)

FIGURE 3.2 A game with a dominant strategy equilibrium

- If Player 2 chooses R, Player 1 can choose T for a payoff of 3 or B for a payoff of 1. Therefore, Player 1 should choose T.

As can be seen, no matter what Player 2 chooses, Player 1's best choice is T. Similarly, it can be shown that Player 2's dominant strategy is to choose L:

- If Player 1 chooses T, Player 2 can choose L for a payoff of 8 or R for a payoff of 6. Therefore, Player 2 should choose L.
- If Player 1 chooses B, Player 2 can choose L for a payoff of 7 or R for a payoff of 5. Therefore, Player 2 should choose L.

When both players have a dominant strategy, the game has a **dominant strategy equilibrium**. That is to say, the outcome of the game will be one in which both players choose their dominant strategy. In the example above, the dominant strategy equilibrium is (T,L).

Note that the equilibrium of the game is expressed in terms of the players' strategies. It is important to express the equilibrium in terms of the strategies adopted, not the payoffs. While the payoffs help determine the best strategies for each of the players, as economists we are interested in the players' choices and actions. Another way of thinking of this is that each player needs to give instructions to a subordinate about what to do, and what to do in any situation that could arise. Here, the instructions would be to play *T* or *L* for each player; instructions that stated '4' or '8' could be confusing.

Nash equilibrium

Sometimes, neither player will have a dominant strategy; for example, consider the game depicted in Figure 3.3. In such cases, we will need another solution concept in order to solve the game. Because neither player has a dominant strategy, each player's choice of action is dependent on what he or she thinks the other player will do. We say that an action is Player 1's **best response** if that action gives him the highest possible profit, given Player 2's choice.

To see how this operates in practice, consider the game depicted in Figure 3.3 from the perspective of Player 1:

- If Player 2 chooses L, Player 1 can choose T for a payoff of 5 or B for a payoff of 8. Therefore, if Player 2 chooses L, Player 1's best response is to choose B.

		Player 2	
		L	R
Player 1	T	(5,2)	(7,4)
	B	(8,3)	(6,1)

FIGURE 3.3 A game with two Nash equilibria

- If Player 2 chooses R, Player 1 can choose T for a payoff of 7 or B for a payoff of 6. Therefore, if Player 2 chooses R, Player 1's best response is to choose T.

Let us also consider the game from the perspective of Player 2:

- If Player 1 chooses T, Player 2 can choose L for a payoff of 2 or R for a payoff of 4. Therefore, if Player 1 chooses T, Player 2's best response is to choose R.
- If Player 1 chooses B, Player 2 can choose L for a payoff of 3 or R for a payoff of 1. Therefore, if Player 1 chooses B, Player 2's best response is to choose L.

A **Nash equilibrium** exists if each player's choice of action is their best response to every other player's strategy. For a two-player game, this means that Player 1's choice of action is his best response to Player 2's choice and that Player 2's choice of action is also her best response to Player 1's choice.

In the game depicted in Figure 3.3, there are two Nash equilibria: (T,R) and (B,L).[2] Let us check each of these in turn:

- (T,R): If Player 1 chooses T, Player 2's best response is to choose R. If Player 2 chooses R, Player 1's best response is to choose T. This is a Nash equilibrium because both players are choosing their best response, given what the other player has chosen.
- (B,L): If Player 1 chooses B, Player 2's best response is to choose L. If Player 2 chooses L, Player 1's best response is to choose B. This is a Nash equilibrium because both players are choosing their best response, given what the other player has chosen.

A corollary of this is that, in a Nash equilibrium, no player can unilaterally deviate (that is, switch his choice of action, holding constant the strategies of all other players) and increase his payoff. This is because every player is already choosing his best response and making the maximum payoff possible, given the other player's actions. It is the fact that no player has an incentive to deviate that makes the outcome an equilibrium. Note that often a convenient way to check whether an outcome is a Nash equilibrium is to ensure that no player would like to make a unilateral deviation in order to make herself better off – often referred to as a **profitable unilateral deviation**.

To see this, let us check the possibility of profitable unilateral deviation for each of the feasible outcomes of the game illustrated in Figure 3.3. First, take the outcome (T, L) – are there any unilateral deviations that make a player better off? Holding Player 2's action fixed on L, Player 1 can continue to choose T and get 5 or can make a unilateral deviation to B and get 8 – Player 1 has a profitable unilateral deviation, so (T, L) cannot be a Nash equilibrium. Similarly, consider the outcome (B, R). Holding Player 1's strategy constant on B, Player 2 would want to deviate and play L, improving her payoff from 1 to 3. Consequently, (B, R) cannot be a Nash equilibrium. On the other hand, if we consider either of the two other possible outcomes – (B, L) and (T, R) – each player has adopted their best response to the other player's strategy. As a consequence, there are no profitable deviations, and both outcomes are a Nash equilibrium.

Finally, it is worth noting several other points regarding Nash equilibria. First, a dominant strategy equilibrium is always a Nash equilibrium. In a Nash equilibrium all players have chosen their best response to the strategies of all other players. This is true in a dominant strategy equilibrium. Consider the game shown in Figure 3.2. Player 1 chooses T – this is his best response to whatever Player 2 is doing. Similarly, Player 2's choice of L is also a best response. This means that the dominant strategy equilibrium of (T, L) is also a Nash equilibrium. Note that while all dominant strategy equilibria are Nash equilibria, the reverse is not necessarily true – a Nash equilibrium need not be a dominant strategy equilibrium. For example, consider the Nash equilibria in Figure 3.3. The players in this game do not have a dominant strategy, so no dominant strategy equilibrium exists; there are, however two Nash equilibria as outlined above. Second, depending on the possible actions and payoffs, a game could have one, two or more Nash equilibria. If a game has only one Nash equilibrium, it is often referred to as a unique Nash equilibrium.

3.4 Some types of simultaneous-move games

In this section, we describe some of the 'classic' simultaneous-move games.

3.4.1 Prisoner's dilemma

The **prisoner's dilemma** is perhaps the most canonical simultaneous-move game. In this game, two criminals are being separately questioned about a crime and they have no way of communicating with each other. If both criminals stay silent, there will only be enough evidence to convict them of a lesser crime with a sentence of one year each. The police offer each criminal the following deal: if he gives evidence and his partner stays silent, he will go free but his partner will be imprisoned for three years. However, if both criminals confess, each will get two years in prison. This game is represented in Figure 3.4.

This game has two important features. Firstly, there is a **dominant strategy equilibrium**; the dominant strategy of both parties is to confess and hence the equilibrium is (Confess, Confess). Secondly, **surplus is not maximised** in equilibrium – that is, there is another outcome that would make both players better off. If both players confess, each spends two years in prison. A better outcome could be achieved if both

		Player 2	
		Silent	Confess
Player 1	Silent	$(-1,-1)$	$(-3,0)$
	Confess	$(0,-3)$	$(-2,-2)$

FIGURE 3.4 The prisoner's dilemma

players stayed silent. However, this is not sustainable as an equilibrium because each player has an incentive to deviate; given that the other player stays silent, he will go free if he switches his choice to 'confess'. It is these two features that allow us to characterise a game as a prisoner's dilemma.[3]

The prisoner's dilemma has a number of real-world applications, outside the rather limited scenario outlined above. For example, it can be used to explain why firms in an industry do not collude and charge high prices to consumers, even though this would increase their profits (see Figure 3.1). It could represent an industry with two firms (department stores or supermarkets for instance) that choose to advertise, even though they would be both better off if they could commit not to do so. It has also been used to explain the arms race during the Cold War; both the USA and the USSR would have been better off if both parties had chosen to disarm, but there was a fear that if only one party chose to disarm it would be vulnerable to attack by the other party.

3.4.2 Coordination game

Another important game is a **coordination game**. In one formulation of this game, two drivers meet on a narrow road and must decide which way to swerve in order to avoid colliding with each other. If both execute the same swerving manoeuvre, they will avoid the collision (with a payoff of 1 each); however, if they choose different manoeuvres, they will crash (yielding a payoff of 0 for each driver). The normal form of this game is depicted in Figure 3.5. The feature that makes this game a coordination game is that there are **two Nash equilibria**, and the parties are trying to coordinate on which of those two equilibria is realised.

A variant of this is a game called **battle of the sexes**, in which Jay and Daisy are trying to organise a date. Jay would prefer to go to the opera, whereas Daisy would prefer to go to see a boxing match. However, both would prefer to be together rather than alone. The normal form of this game is depicted in Figure 3.6, with its associated payoffs. The distinguishing feature of this game is that the two parties would like to coordinate, but have opposite preferences as to which of the equilibria is chosen – that is, Jay prefers (Opera, Opera) whereas Daisy prefers (Boxing, Boxing).

Another variant is the **stag hunt**, in which two hunters have the choice of hunting stag or hunting hare. If either chooses to hunt hare, he will be guaranteed to catch a hare. However, successfully hunting stag requires both hunters, and catching a stag yields a higher payoff for both hunters. This game is depicted in Figure 3.7. Again,

		Driver 2	
		Left	Right
Driver 1	Left	(1,1)	(0,0)
	Right	(0,0)	(1,1)

FIGURE 3.5 The coordination game

Jay \ Daisy	Opera	Boxing
Opera	(2,1)	(0,0)
Boxing	(0,0)	(1,2)

FIGURE 3.6 Battle of the sexes

Hunter 1 \ Hunter 2	Stag	Hare
Stag	(2,2)	(0,1)
Hare	(1,0)	(1,1)

FIGURE 3.7 Stag hunt

this game has two Nash equilibria, but the distinguishing feature is that both parties prefer the same equilibrium (Stag, Stag).

Finally note that the game depicted in Figure 3.3 is also a coordination game with two equilibria, (T, R) and (B, L).

3.5 Sequential games

In this section, we consider games in which one party (the leader) chooses their action first. The other player (the follower) observes the leader's choice before selecting their own action. We will consider how to represent and solve these games.

3.5.1 Representing sequential games: the extensive form

As before, we can represent sequential games using the normal form of the game. However, it is often convenient to represent sequential games using the **extensive form** of the game. This involves drawing out the order of the choices in the form of a 'game tree'.

To see how this is done, consider the following example: There is currently one firm operating in the market (denoted 'I' for 'Incumbent') and there is one other firm that is contemplating entry (denoted 'E' for 'Entrant'). The game proceeds as follows: First, the Entrant chooses whether to enter the market or not. The dot here – or the *node* – represents the point at which the Entrant can make a decision, with her possible choices being 'enter' or 'not enter'. If the Entrant does not enter, the Entrant receives a payoff of \$0 and the Incumbent receives \$20. Alternatively, if the Entrant enters, the Incumbent observes this choice, and then decides whether to accommodate or punish the Entrant. If the Entrant enters and the Incumbent accommodates, each firm makes a profit of

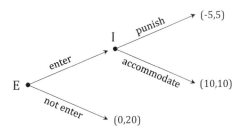

FIGURE 3.8 Extensive form of a game

$10. Finally, if the Entrant enters and Incumbent punishes, the profits are −$5 and $5 to the Entrant and the Incumbent, respectively.

This information is represented in the extensive form in Figure 3.8. The left-most decision point (node) is labelled 'E' to signify that the Entrant's choice is made first. The branches originating from this node denote the two actions that the Entrant may take. The node labelled 'I' and the branches originating from that node denote the Incumbent's choice of actions. The choices of the players trace out a path along the game-tree, and the payoffs associated with these choices are shown at the end of each path.

3.5.2 Solving sequential games

We now turn to the question of what the outcome of these games will be. Again, we can solve a sequential game by assuming that each player is only interested in maximising his own payoff. Again, it should be noted that the players do not care about each other's payoffs.

Nash equilibrium

Like simultaneous-move games, we can solve sequential games by determining the Nash equilibrium of the game. In order to do this, we will need to represent the game in normal form and identify the best responses of each player, as we did in Section 3.3.2.

As an illustration of this, Figure 3.9 depicts the normal form of the game in Figure 3.8. Solving for the best responses of each player, we can identify two Nash equilibria:

		Incumbent	
		Accommodate	Punish
Entrant	Enter	(10,10)	(−5, 5)
	Not enter	(0,20)	(0,20)

FIGURE 3.9 The normal form of the game depicted in Figure 3.8

- **(Enter, Accommodate)**: If the Entrant chooses to enter, the Incumbent's best response is to accommodate. If the Incumbent chooses to accommodate, the Entrant's best response is to enter.
- **(Not enter, Punish)**: If the Incumbent chooses to punish, the Entrant's best response is to not enter. If the Entrant chooses to not enter, the Incumbent's best response is to punish (the Incumbent cannot do better by choosing an alternative to punish).

The first of these equilibria has some intuitive appeal. Given the payoffs, the best thing the Incumbent can do in response to an entry is to accommodate. The Entrant, predicting this accommodation after entry, should therefore enter the market in the first place. However, the second equilibrium is somewhat less intuitive. In this equilibrium, the Entrant chooses not to enter, because it anticipates that the Incumbent will punish. However, the threat of punishment is not credible; we know that if the Entrant actually does enter the market, the best thing the Incumbent can do in those circumstances is accommodate. In order to address this, we may wish to find a solution concept that only identifies credible equilibria.

Subgame perfect equilibrium

The concept of subgame perfection identifies only credible equilibria. To do this, it breaks down the larger game into smaller mini-games, or 'subgames', each of which begins with a choice by one player. That is, a subgame can be thought of as part of a larger game that looks like a game itself. Thus, in the game depicted in Figure 3.8, the Entrant's choice to enter or not enter begins one subgame and the Incumbent's choice to accommodate or punish is another subgame.

A **subgame perfect equilibrium (SPE)** exists where each player's chosen actions are a Nash equilibrium in every subgame. That is, we would require the Entrant's choice to enter or not enter to be his best response in the circumstances, and we would also require the Incumbent's choice to accommodate or punish to be her best response in the circumstances if she found herself at that node.

Note that the follower's best response depends on what she observes the leader's choice to be. Hence, the leader's best response depends on what he expects the follower will do. That is, the leader will try and anticipate the choice of the follower, before deciding upon his own choice of action. In order to determine the SPE of a game, we solve the game using **backwards induction**. This entails starting at the end of the game, and solving backwards towards the beginning. So, in the game depicted in Figure 3.8, we would first determine what the Incumbent would do if it reached the node marked 'I'. Comparing the payoffs, we can see that the Incumbent would choose to accommodate. Now, we can determine what the Entrant will do at the node 'E', knowing that if it chooses to enter, the Incumbent will choose to accommodate. Again, comparing the payoffs, we can conclude that the Entrant will enter. Hence, the SPE of this game is (Enter, Accommodate).

Solving backwards (and finding the SPE) reflects the fact that the players themselves are rational and forward looking. The Entrant, before making its choice, thinks ahead and tries to anticipate what the Incumbent would do in any given situation. As economists, the way we try to capture and model this forward thinking is to go to the end of the game and work backwards.

Note that the SPE is a Nash equilibrium, but not all Nash equilibria are SPE. This is because some Nash equilibria are sustained by non-credible threats. For example, the equilibrium (Not enter, Punish) is a Nash equilibrium, but not an SPE. This is, in fact, one of the strengths of using backwards induction to determine the equilibrium outcome(s) of a game; an SPE cannot be sustained by non-credible threats that would not actually be employed if the player involved ever had to actually choose.

Also bear in mind that, because subgame perfection requires us to determine the choice of each player at every possible juncture, the specification of the SPE should identify the choice made at each node, regardless of whether or not that node is actually reached.

> **Example.** Jay and Daisy are organising a date. Jay would prefer to go to the opera, whereas Daisy would prefer to go to see a boxing match. However, both would prefer to be together rather than alone. To solve their coordination problem, they have decided that Jay will go to a venue first, and then call Daisy to inform her where he is. Following this, Daisy will then choose where she goes. The extensive form of this game is depicted in Figure 3.10.
>
> Using backwards induction, we first determine what Daisy will do at nodes D_1 and D_2. At D_1, Daisy will choose to go to the opera; at D_1, Daisy will choose to go to the boxing match. Now, Jay knows that if he chooses the opera, Daisy will also choose the opera; if he chooses the boxing match, Daisy will also choose the boxing match. Knowing this, at the node J, Jay will choose the opera as it gives him the higher payoff.
>
> The specification of the SPE must reflect the choices that would be taken at each of the nodes, even though some of the nodes (namely, D_2) are never reached. The SPE is (Opera; Opera (if Opera), Boxing (if Boxing)); this tells us what is chosen at each of the nodes, J, D_1 and D_2 in that order.

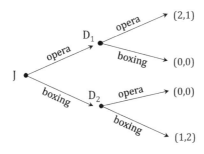

FIGURE 3.10 Extensive form of a game in which Jay and Daisy organise a date

3.6 Concluding comments

The tools outlined in this chapter are particularly useful in thinking about strategic situations in which the interaction between players (be they workers, firms or governments) is critical. One of the advantages of game theory is that it can allow complicated scenarios to be analysed relatively simply. Game theory also has the advantage of making all the assumptions explicit. This makes it possible for others to see what is driving the conclusions of the model.

Notes

1   By convention, the row player's payoff is given first, and the column player's payoff is given second. This is, of course, just a convention; what is crucial, however, is that the payoffs are drawn consistently.
2   There is also a third Nash equilibrium, a 'mixed strategy' equilibrium, in which each player chooses each possible action with a positive probability. This is a more advanced topic, so in this book we will not consider mixed strategy equilibria.
3   Indeed, it is possible that a game has one, but not the other, of these features. For example, the game depicted in Figure 3.2 has a dominant strategy equilibrium, but that equilibrium *is* surplus maximising. Any game that does not satisfy both properties is not a prisoner's dilemma.

PART II

Gains from trade

Trade and the PPF

4.1 Introduction

This chapter provides an introduction to why and how people trade with each other. In particular, we focus on what determines patterns of trade and the underlying sources of the gains from trade. As we will see, trade makes people better off because there are gains from exchange and gains from specialisation.

4.2 Gains from exchange

A basic proposition of economics is that trade makes people better off. One of the reasons that trade makes people better off is because it helps allocate goods and services to those who value them the most.

To understand this, consider a situation in which Baz owns a rarely used bicycle, which he values at $10. Chloe, on the other hand, does not own a bike but would be willing to pay up to $100 to buy a bike. Now, suppose Baz agrees to sell his bicycle to Chloe for $40. In this case, Baz and Chloe are both better off: Baz previously owned a bike that he valued at $10, but now he has $40 instead; Chloe used to have $40, but now owns a bike that she values at $100. Note that both parties to the transaction are better off; trade benefited both the buyer and the seller. This is because the trade is voluntary; neither Baz nor Chloe would agree to the trade if they were worse off. Specifically, Baz would not have agreed to sell the bicycle if the price was less than his valuation of $10 and Chloe would not have agreed to buy the bicycle if the price was greater than her valuation of $100. Similarly, Baz would not have sold the bicycle to Chloe if his valuation was higher than Chloe's (say, $110 instead of $10), as there would be no price that would be acceptable to both of them.

DOI: 10.4324/9781003376644-6

In general terms, trade can only occur if the seller's valuation of the item (v_s) does not exceed the buyer's valuation (v_b). Given that trade is voluntary, the seller will not accept a price (p) lower than his valuation and the buyer will not agree to a price higher than her valuation. Therefore, in order for trade to take place, it must be the case that:

$$v_s \leq p \leq v_b. \tag{4.1}$$

Because no party will consent to a transaction that makes him or her worse off, trade will always make people (weakly) better off.[1]

Two things should be noted here: Firstly, in the above example, the price of $40 was not the only price that allows for mutually beneficial trade; as you can see, a price of $50 or $60 would also be mutually beneficial for both parties. In fact, any price that meets the condition in equation 4.1 will suffice for trade to occur. The price is relevant, however, in determining how the gains from trade are split between two parties. For example, when the price was $40, trade made Baz $30 better off and Chloe $60 better off; however, if the price were instead set at $50, Baz would be $40 better off but Chloe would only be $50 better off.[2] The exact price at which the item is traded depends on bargaining between the parties, which we will discuss later in Chapter 5.

Secondly, the discussion so far has assumed that money is our medium of exchange. However, our results hold true even if the parties barter one good for another. For example, suppose Baz swaps his bicycle for Chloe's skateboard. Baz would only agree to the trade if he preferred the skateboard to the bicycle, and Chloe would only agree if she preferred the bicycle to the skateboard; thus, both parties are made better off. The role of money is simply to help coordinate (or facilitate) trade between parties; that is, it allows Baz and Chloe to trade, even if Chloe does not have anything to trade that Baz wants.

4.3 Gains from specialisation

Trade also allows people to take advantage of gains from specialisation. In order to appreciate why this is so it is first necessary to consider the constraints that individuals face in production. It will then become clear that parties can be made better off by specialising in the production of one good and then trading that good in exchange for other products or services.

4.3.1 The production possibility frontier (PPF)

Sometimes, because resources are limited, we face tradeoffs in terms of what can be produced. If a particular resource is used to make one good, that resource cannot be used to produce another good. To understand this better, we can graph the output that an individual (or a country) can produce for a particular set of resources. This graph is called a **production possibility frontier (PPF)**.[3] The PPF traces out combinations of the quantity of two goods that an individual or a country can produce if it uses all of its resources. An example of a PPF is illustrated in Figure 4.1.

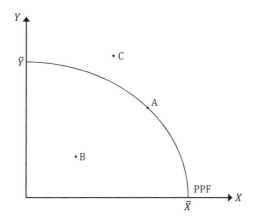

FIGURE 4.1 The production possibility frontier (PPF) traces out combinations of the quantity of two goods (*X* and *Y*) that can be produced if all resources are used

Suppose Australia can use its resources to produce either good X or good Y, or some combination of both. If all of Australia's resources are allocated to making Y, Australia will produce $\bar{Y}$ of Y and zero units of X; similarly, if all of the country's resources go into X production, $\bar{X}$ are made of X but zero units of Y. But combinations of X and Y are also possible – these possible combinations are represented by the line joining $\bar{Y}$ and $\bar{X}$.

There are several points worth noting about the PPF. Firstly, any point inside or on the PPF is obtainable in that it is feasible to produce that quantity of X and Y given the current level of resources and state of technology. Secondly, any point on the PPF (e.g. Point A in Figure 4.1) is efficient in the sense that it makes full use of the available resources, whereas any point inside the PPF (e.g. Point B) is inefficient because it does not make full use of the available resources. Thirdly, any point outside the PPF (e.g. Point C) is not feasible, because production of those levels of X and Y would require more resources (or better technology) than Australia currently has.

As we have discussed, the shape of the PPF depends on the current levels of resources and technology. Therefore, if either the resources available or the state of technology changes, so does the shape of the PPF. If there is an increase in resources or an improvement in technology that boosts the production of both goods, the PPF will shift outwards from origin along both axes, as shown in Figure 4.2. This indicates that more of both X and Y can be produced. This might happen if there is an increase in population (that is, an increase in the available labour) or an improvement in some technology that is used in the production of both goods.

Sometimes, the increase in resources or technology only affects the production of one good. For example, if the two goods were bookshelves and cars, an increase in the availability of high-quality wood would only affect the production of bookshelves; similarly, an improvement in tyre-making technology would only affect the production of cars. In such instances, the PPF will rotate or stretch outwards only along the axis of the affected good, as in Figure 4.3.

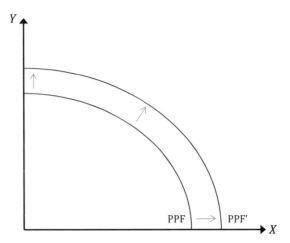

FIGURE 4.2 A production possibility frontier for goods X and Y. If there is a shock that boosts the production of both goods, the PPF will shift outwards from origin along both axes

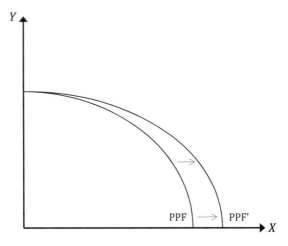

FIGURE 4.3 A production possibility frontier for goods X and Y. If there is a shock that boosts the production of X only, the PPF will shift outwards from origin along the x-axis only

It is, of course, possible that there is a decrease in the level of resources or a decline in the level of technology. In such cases, following the reasoning above, the PPF will shift or rotate inwards towards origin.

Note, however, that while changes in population and in technology can both shift the PPF, an increase in population could increase total output without increasing the quantity of output *per person*. By contrast, increases in technology will increase both total output and output per person. Output per person (or per worker) is really a measure of labour productivity, and it is changes in labour productivity that ultimately drive changes in standards of living (consumption per person or worker). This also helps explain why large countries like China can have significantly higher output than

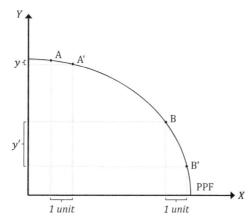

FIGURE 4.4 A production possibility frontier for goods X and Y. A one-unit increase in the production of X is less costly when the output of X is low (e.g. from A to A') than when the output of X is high (e.g. from B to B')

smaller countries, while not necessarily having as high an average standard of living per capita.

Finally, we can use the PPF to measure the opportunity cost of producing a particular unit of a good. Suppose, in Figure 4.4, Australia is currently at a point on the PPF where it is making some of both goods (say, Point A). Note that, because Australia is on the PPF, it is fully utilising its resources. Therefore, in order to increase the production of X, it is necessary to give up some Y. The amount of Y that must be forgone depends on the slope of the PPF. For example, suppose Australia would like to move from A to A', increasing the production of X by one unit. In order to do so, it is necessary to give up y units of Y. However, if Australia were moving from B to B', it would have to give up y' units of Y. As you can see, the slope of the PPF shows the opportunity cost in terms of Y forgone by getting more X.[4]

In general, when the output of X is low, the opportunity cost of an additional unit of X is relatively low. This is because some resources are better suited to making X and others are better suited to making Y, and as we want more X we switch over the resources that are best at producing X first. But as the production of X increases, the resources that are reallocated from Y to X production become increasingly less suited to making X. So, in order to produce an extra unit of X we need to take away increasingly more resources from the production of Y. This is reflected in the shape of the PPF – near the vertical axis the slope is relatively flat, indicating that the opportunity cost of producing some more X (in terms of Y) is relatively small. But as more and more X is produced, the opportunity cost of producing X increases, as indicated by the steeper slope.

4.3.2 Absolute advantage and comparative advantage

Now that we have the means for analysing the production possibilities of one individual or country, we can also compare the production capabilities of different individuals or different countries. In particular, we can examine which individual or country has the

TABLE 4.1 Number of pepper mills and salt shakers that Chris and May can make per day

	Pepper mills	Salt shakers
Chris	8	8
May	2	4

TABLE 4.2 Opportunity costs of producing pepper mills and salt shakers

	Opp cost of 1 pepper mill	Opp cost of 1 salt shaker
Chris	1 salt shaker	1 pepper mill
May	2 salt shakers	$\frac{1}{2}$ pepper mill

advantage in the production of any particular good. In economics, we refer to two types of advantage:

- We say that Party A has an **absolute advantage** over Party B in the production of a good if, for a given amount of resources, A can produce a greater number of that good than B.
- We say that Party A has a **comparative advantage** over Party B in the production of a good if A's opportunity cost of producing that good is lower than B's opportunity cost.

To illustrate the difference between absolute advantage and comparative advantage, consider the following example:

Example. Chris takes one hour to make a pepper mill and one hour to make a salt shaker. May takes four hours to make a pepper mill and two hours to make a salt shaker. Both Chris and May work for eight hours a day. Table 4.1 depicts how much of each good they can make in one working day. As you can see, Chris can produce more pepper mills in a day than May; Chris can also produce more salt shakers in a day than May. Therefore, Chris has the absolute advantage in the production of both pepper mills and salt shakers.

Now consider Chris's and May's opportunity cost of producing pepper mills and salt shakers. If Chris makes one pepper mill, that takes him one hour. In that time, he could have instead made one salt shaker. Therefore, in order to make that pepper mill, he has to give up making one salt shaker, so his opportunity cost of one pepper mill is one salt shaker. Similarly, if Chris makes one salt shaker, he has to give up one pepper mill, so his opportunity cost of one salt shaker is one pepper mill. On the other hand, if May makes one pepper mill, it takes her four hours, in which time she could have made two salt shakers; therefore, her opportunity cost of one pepper mill is two salt shakers. By the same reasoning, her opportunity cost of one salt shaker is half a pepper mill. The opportunity cost of each good for Chris and May is represented in Table 4.2. From this table, we can see that Chris has the comparative advantage in producing pepper mills, as his opportunity cost of producing pepper mills is lower. On the other hand, May has the comparative advantage in producing salt shakers, as her opportunity cost of producing salt shakers is lower than Chris's. Note that May has the comparative advantage in producing salt shakers, even though she does not have the absolute advantage in producing anything.

As illustrated in the above example, it may be possible for one person to have the absolute advantage in the production of both goods. However, as a rule of thumb, it is not possible for one person to have the comparative advantage in more than one good. This is because, for each person, the opportunity costs of the two goods will be the inverse of each other; therefore, if one person has a lower opportunity cost for one good, he must have a higher opportunity cost for the other good.

4.3.3 Specialisation

Now that we have the tools to analyse and compare the production capabilities of two individuals, we can illustrate how those individuals can gain from trading with each other.

Suppose Michelle and Rodney spend ten hours a day making shoes. It takes Michelle two hours to make a left shoe, and half an hour to make a right shoe. Rodney takes half an hour to make a left shoe and two hours to make a right shoe. Table 4.3 shows the maximum number of left shoes and right shoes each person can make in one day: Michelle's and Rodney's PPFs are depicted in Figure 4.5. Let's also suppose that Michelle and Rodney do not like to wear left shoes without right shoes, and vice versa – that is, they like their shoes to be in pairs.

First, let us assume that there is no trade between the parties. If Michelle wants one left shoe for every right shoe, she must produce 4 left shoes and 4 right shoes. Similarly, Rodney will have to produce 4 left shoes and 4 right shoes in order to have pairs. This means that, between them, they can produce 8 pairs of shoes.

Now let us allow the parties to trade with each other. In this case, if Michelle specialises in producing right shoes, she can make 20 right shoes a day; if Rodney specialises in making left shoes, he can make 20 left shoes a day. Between them, Michelle and Rodney can make 20 pairs of shoes. Supposing that they trade between them at a rate of one left shoe for one right shoe, Michelle and Rodney can now each have 10 pairs of shoes. These consumption points are marked in Figure 4.5; note that they lie outside each person's individual PPF. Here, the gains from trade are manifested in the ability of each party to consume more than the amount he or she could produce alone.

TABLE 4.3 Number of left shoes and right shoes that Michelle and Rodney can make per day

	Left shoes	Right shoes
Michelle	5	20
Rodney	20	5

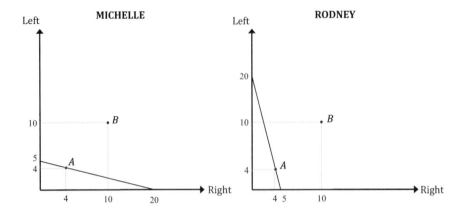

FIGURE 4.5 Michelle and Rodney's PPFs. When Michelle and Rodney cannot trade, their consumption points are given by the point *A*. When Michelle and Rodney can trade with each other, their consumption points are given by the point *B*. Note that point *B* lies outside each person's individual PPF

When the parties specialise in producing the good that they have a comparative advantage in, total production increases (here from a total of 8 pairs of shoes to 20 pairs of shoes between Michelle and Rodney). Total output increases because trade allows parties to specialise in producing the good in which they have the lower opportunity cost. And with more output, both trading parties can potentially be made better off. In other words, trade creates an environment for specialisation to be feasible, increasing the size of the economic pie; this increase in output can potentially be shared so as to make everyone better off than without trade.

Although we have given a specific example to illustrate the gains from specialisation, the idea is a very general one. That is, trade is beneficial to individuals (and indeed countries) because it allows them to specialise in industries where they have the comparative advantage, and trade with others for things that would cost them more to produce personally. Moreover, this principle holds even if one party has the absolute advantage in the production of both goods; what matters are the comparative advantages or opportunity costs of the parties.

4.4 Concluding comments

A basic proposition of economics is that there are gains from trade. Firstly, if trade is voluntary, any party willing to trade must be at least as well off from trading as they were without trading. Secondly, the gains from trade arise due to gains from exchange – reallocating goods to those who value them most – and from specialisation – allowing parties to specialise in producing the good for which they have the lowest opportunity cost. By allowing the parties to specialise in producing the good for which they have a comparative advantage, total output increases, potentially making all trading parties better off.

Notes

1   By the phrase 'weakly better off', we mean that people will either be better off or just as well off as they were before (in other words, no one is worse off). A party will be just as well off after trade as they were before if the price were set exactly at their valuation.
2   Again, if price exactly equals either the buyer's or the seller's valuation, that individual would not gain from trade, but they would not be worse off either.
3   Sometimes it is also called a production possibilities curve (PPC).
4   Of course, the PPF need not be concave. If the PPF is a straight line (that is, its slope is constant), the opportunity cost between X and Y is constant, regardless of how much of either product is made.

CHAPTER 5

Bargaining

5.1 Introduction

Bargaining is an integral part of commerce. For example, a person might bargain over the price of a car with a salesperson, unions bargain with employers over wages and working conditions and in some countries it is usual for bargaining to occur over most goods and services, like haggling at a bazaar.

In the last chapter, we found that when two people trade with each other there are gains from trade. Bargaining helps determine how those gains are split between the parties by determining the price at which a good or service is traded. In this chapter we will build upon the game theory concepts in Chapter 3 to construct a simple model that roughly represents a bargaining process. We do this in order to derive some understanding about what the outcome of bargaining will be. While the material here can be read as a standalone topic, we strongly recommend that you familiarise yourself with Chapter 3 before embarking on this chapter.

5.2 Bargaining and surplus

We will begin by setting up a general framework within which bargaining will take place. Suppose there are two parties to the transaction: the seller (A) and the buyer (B). The parties are bargaining over the price at which a good will be sold. The seller values the good at v_A and the buyer's valuation is v_B. In order for voluntary trade to take place, we know that the seller's valuation of the good must not exceed the buyer's valuation ($v_A \leq v_B$). If the trade takes place, the gains from trade will be the difference between the two valuations – that is, $v_B - v_A$.

DOI: 10.4324/9781003376644-7

The parties bargain with each other in order to determine the price of the good and hence the amount of surplus that each party receives; in other words, bargaining helps determine how the gains from trade are split.

Example. Bill would like to buy a parcel of land from Josie. Josie values the land at $300,000 and Bill values the land at $400,000. If the sale goes ahead the gains from trade will be $100,000, but if the sale does not occur there will be no gains from trade. After extensive bargaining, Bill and Josie come to the agreement that Josie will sell the land to Bill at a price of $328,000. At this price, Bill's net surplus from the transaction is $400,000 − $328,000 = $72,000$. Josie's net surplus from the transaction is $328,000 − $300,000 = $28,000$. The total surplus (that is, Bill's surplus plus Josie's surplus) from the transaction is $100,000 – but it is the price, determined through bargaining, that determines how the surplus of $100,000 is split between the two parties.

5.3 Take-it-or-leave-it negotiations

Let us first suppose that only one take-it-or-leave-it offer will be made (this situation is also called an 'ultimatum game'). Specifically, assume that the bargaining process is as follows: The seller (A) makes an offer to the buyer (B) as to the price of the good. Let us say that A offers a price of p. B can either (a) accept the offer and trade will occur at A's suggested price or (b) reject the offer and no trade occurs.[1] If B accepts the offer, she will receive a surplus of $v_B − p$ and A will receive a surplus of $p − v_A$. If B rejects the offer, the trade does not go ahead, so the surplus of both parties is zero. This sequence of events is depicted in Figure 5.1.

To determine what will happen, we need to solve the game backwards to find the subgame perfect equilibrium – that is, we need to go to the end of the game and work our way to the beginning. This is because A is forward thinking and rational, so he will do his best to anticipate how B will react to any offer he makes. In Figure 5.1, at B, the buyer will accept the offer if her payoff from doing so ($v_B − p$) is at least as good as her payoff from rejecting (zero); otherwise, she will reject the offer. Therefore, at the first stage, the seller can induce the buyer to accept by ensuring that $v_B − p \geq 0$ – that is, $p \leq v_B$. In other words, the highest price that the seller could charge is $p = v_B$.[2] It

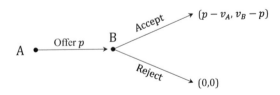

FIGURE 5.1 Negotiation in which A makes a single offer of p

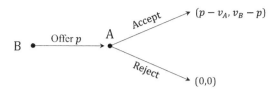

FIGURE 5.2 Negotiation in which *B* makes a single offer of *p*

remains to be determined whether the seller *should* make an offer that the buyer will accept. If the buyer accepts, the seller's surplus will be $p - v_A$; if the buyer rejects, the seller's surplus will be zero. If the seller sets the highest price that will be acceptable to the buyer, his payoff will be $p - v_A = v_B - v_A$. Because we know that the buyer's valuation is at least as great as the seller's ($v_B \geq v_A$), this implies $v_B - v_A \geq 0$. It follows that the seller will prefer to set a price that is acceptable to the buyer.

Therefore, the subgame perfect equilibrium path in this game is as follows: *A* makes an offer of $p = v_B$ and *B* accepts the offer. *A*'s surplus from the transaction is $v_B - v_A$ and *B*'s surplus is zero. As you can see, all the gains from trade in this scenario accrue to *A*.

Let us now suppose that it is the buyer who gets to make the offer. Now, *B* offers a price *p*, which *A* either accepts or rejects. If *A* accepts, the trade goes ahead and the payoffs are $(p - v_A, v_B - p)$ to *A* and *B*, respectively. If *A* rejects the offer, both parties get a payoff of zero. This sequence of events is depicted in Figure 5.2. Solving this game backwards, the seller will only accept the offer at *A* if $p - v_A \geq 0$. Consequently, in order to induce the seller to accept, the buyer must offer at least $p = v_A$. It is in the interest of the buyer to induce the seller to accept because her payoff from acceptance will be $v_B - v_A$, whereas her payoff from rejection will be zero. Therefore, the subgame perfect equilibrium path in this game is as follows: *B* makes an offer of the lowest price that will be accepted – that is $p = v_A$ – and *A* accepts the offer. *A*'s surplus from the transaction is zero and *B*'s surplus is $v_B - v_A$. In this case, all the gains from trade accrue to *B*.

In these single-offer games, the person making the offer receives all the gains from trade. This is because that party is the only party who can make offers and hence has all the bargaining power. The other party only has the power to accept or reject the offer, but rejecting the offer means that they will receive zero surplus.

> **Example.** Andrew wants to sell a bottle of Scotch whisky. Andrew (*A*) values the bottle at $0. Bonnie (*B*) is the only potential buyer and she values the bottle of scotch at $100. Negotiations proceed as follows: Andrew proposes a price *p* that Bonnie can pay for the bottle. Bonnie then accepts or rejects the offer. If she accepts, Andrew gets a payoff of $p - 0$ and Bonnie gets a surplus of $100 - p$. If Bonnie rejects the take-it-or-leave-it offer, bargaining is finished and both parties get a payoff of 0. (This game is the same as illustrated in Figure 5.1.) To determine the outcome of the negotiation, go to the end and solve backwards. The most

Bonnie would be willing to pay for the bottle would be a price of $100. Antici-pating this, Andrew will offer the highest price Bonnie will accept, which is $100 (or $99.99 if he wants to ensure Bonnie is strictly better off accepting the offer). Bonnie accepts this offer – she is no worse off accepting this price than rejecting the offer and getting 0. All the gains from trade go to Andrew – his surplus is $100. Bonnie, while she does end up with the whisky, gets a net surplus of 0 ($100 − $100).

5.4 Multiple-offer bargaining

In some circumstances, it will be more realistic to assume that multiple offers can be made. Thus, one party makes an offer; the other party either accepts it or rejects it and makes a counter-offer, and so on. As an illustration of this, consider the following sequence of events. First, the seller (A) makes an offer of p_1. The buyer (B) can then either accept or reject the offer. If she accepts, trade occurs at the price p_1; if she rejects, she can make a counter-offer of p_2. Finally, the seller can respond by accepting or rejecting the offer of p_2. If he accepts, trade occurs at the price p_2; otherwise, the trade does not go ahead and both parties receive zero surplus. Figure 5.3 depicts the extensive form of this game.

Again, we need to solve the game backwards to determine what happens in the subgame perfect equilibrium.

- At A_2, the seller will only accept an offer if $p_2 - v_A \geq 0$. Therefore, in order to induce the seller to accept, the buyer must offer at least $p_2 = v_A$.
- At B_2, the buyer will offer $p_2 = v_A$ because he wants to get the seller to accept (the buyer's payoff from acceptance will be $v_B - v_A$, whereas her payoff from rejection will be zero).
- At B_1, the buyer will only accept the offer from A if $v_B - p_1 \geq v_B - v_A$, or $p_1 \leq v_A = p_2$. This is because, if the buyer rejects, she can be certain that the seller will later accept an offer of $p_2 = v_A$ (at A_2).

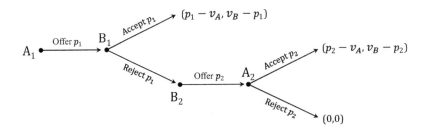

FIGURE 5.3 Negotiation in which *A* makes an offer of p_1 and *B* makes a counter-offer of p_2

- At A_1, the seller might as well make an offer of $p_1 = p_2 = v_A$, because the seller is indifferent between the buyer accepting or rejecting the offer. The seller's payoff from acceptance and rejection will be zero in either case.

In this situation, B receives all the gains from trade. This is because, if it comes to it, she gets to make the last offer; that is, in the last round, she is able to credibly commit that this is the last chance to trade, meaning that A's only possible choices are to accept or reject the offer received.

In general, when multiple offers or counter-offers can be made, the party who can make the final offer holds all the bargaining power. Therefore, under the conditions we have outlined, we would expect the party that makes the final (take-it-or-leave-it) offer to receive all of the surplus.

5.5 Some caveats

It should be remembered that the extreme results derived in the previous sections relied on some very strict assumptions. Where these assumptions do not hold, we might observe different outcomes. Often, in practice, the **gains from trade are shared by the parties**, rather than enjoyed by one party alone. There are several reasons why this may be the case:

1) There may be costs to the bargaining process. These costs may include the cost of time lost by negotiation or the cost of paying someone to negotiate on your behalf. In this case, each party knows that the other will be more reluctant to proceed to the next round of offers and acceptance/rejection, because it will be costly to do so. This implies that parties will be willing to accept slightly lower offers in earlier rounds, if it means they can avoid some negotiation costs.

2) The parties may not know when bargaining is going to end. Negotiating parties typically do not know who will make the last possible offer (that is, the parties are not exactly sure when the negotiations will be terminated if an agreement is not reached). If it is unclear which party will have the 'final say' there will be uncertainty as to the distribution of bargaining power.

3) The parties may not know each other's valuations of the object. In the sections above, the party with the bargaining power offered a price equal to the other party's valuation. However, this will not be possible if the parties do not know each other's valuations, which may mean that the offering party is unable to extract all the surplus.

4) One or both of the parties may have an 'outside option'. An outside option means that if negotiations break down, the parties have the option of trading with someone else. For example, suppose A wants to sell an apple to B. A has an outside option if, in the event that negotiating with B fails, he can sell the apple to C instead. B has an outside option if, in the event that negotiating with A fails, she can buy an apple from D instead. If a party has an outside option and all offers are rejected, that

party will receive a payoff greater than zero. This is because they will receive some surplus from exercising that outside option. Hence, in order to induce acceptance, the other party will need to make an offer at least as good as the outside option.

> **Example.** Suppose Ed wants to buy an apple from Rob. However, Rob also has the option of selling the apple to Hansen for \$5. If Ed proposes a price for the trade, he will need to offer Rob at least \$5 in order for Rob to agree to the trade.

Sometimes, in practice, there is a **breakdown in bargaining**. These situations are also unexplained by the model set out in the previous sections. One reason that this may occur is if there is asymmetric information between the parties. This may occur if the parties do not know each other's valuations of the good. For example, if the seller overestimates the buyer's valuation of the good, he may offer a price that is too high for the buyer to accept. Conversely, if the buyer underestimates the seller's valuation of the good, she may offer a price too low for the seller to accept. In these situations, the two parties may end up not trading, forgoing the potential gains from trade. A similar point can be made when agreement is only reached after a protracted (and potentially costly) delay in negotiations, such as with a strike or a lockout. Even though an agreement is eventually reached, some of the potential gains from trade are lost during negotiations.

5.6 Concluding comments

In Chapter 4, we learned that there are gains from trade. In this chapter, we discussed how those gains are divided between the parties. In general, the party with more bargaining power will receive a greater share of the benefits. In the models we examined we showed that bargaining power can arise if a party has the ability to credibly make the final offer. However, the distribution of surplus can also be affected by bargaining costs, the existence of outside options and beliefs about when negotiations will end. Finally, we found that bargaining may break down in the presence of asymmetric information, meaning that gains from trade may not be realised.

Several implications arise from these sorts of bargaining models. As noted, bargaining power tends to arise from some economic characteristic or the nature of the bargaining process. This means that a party to a negotiation process, such as a business or a union, might want to manipulate how the negotiations occur in order to get more of the gains from trade. For example, a business might explicitly cultivate an outside option in order to strengthen its bargaining position. Similarly, a union might build up a war chest of reserves to help members ensure a long strike (lower their costs of delay, making it more difficult for the other party to outlast them).

Finally, the negotiation process we have considered here involves two parties (and possibly a third party as an outside option). Often there are many potential buyers and sellers who could trade with one another. In such a market, price – and hence the distribution of the gains from trade – is determined by the interaction of these many buyers and sellers in the marketplace. We turn to these sorts of markets now.

Notes

1　Note that this describes many transactions that we are likely to be familiar with; the seller sets a price and the buyer either purchases the good at that price or not.

2　Note that, at a price of $p = v_B$, B gets zero surplus and is indifferent between accepting and rejecting the offer. For convenience, we will assume that if B is indifferent, she accepts the offer. Alternatively, we could assume that an offer slightly less than v_B is made (for example, $v_B - \eta$ where η is a small positive amount, like 1 cent), which makes accepting better than rejecting for B. In this case, our analysis remains the same in substance.

PART III

Market fundamentals

CHAPTER 6

Demand

6.1 Introduction

As noted before, we assume that consumers act in their own best interest. This allows us to examine consumer behaviour under the assumption that a consumer will maximise the benefit (or utility) he or she receives from consuming goods and services, subject to their budget constraint.

In this chapter, we examine the choices of individual consumers in competitive markets. In a competitive market, the actions and choices of individual consumers cannot affect the price in the market, so they make their consumption decisions taking prices as given (that is, consumers are **price takers**). In this setting, we will examine a consumer's decision as to how much of a product to buy, and hence derive demand curves for individual consumers and for the market.

6.2 Benefit and willingness to pay

A consumer derives some **benefit** from consuming a particular good or service. We can measure that benefit by considering the consumer's **willingness to pay (WTP)** for that good or service. For example, to measure the benefit that a consumer receives from consuming a cup of coffee, we could ask, 'What is the highest amount of money that the consumer would be willing to pay for that cup of coffee?' As you can see, this should tell us how much the consumer values the cup of coffee in monetary terms.

When an individual consumes multiple units of a particular good or service, we might like to distinguish between total benefit and marginal benefit. Suppose Candice's willingness to pay for coffee is $4 for the first cup, $3 for the second cup and $2 for the third cup. Her **total benefit (TB)** measures the

DOI: 10.4324/9781003376644-9

benefit that she gets from consuming the total number of cups of coffee; that is, her total benefit for the three cups of coffee is $9 (= 4 + 3 + 2)$. By contrast, her **marginal benefit (MB)** measures how much extra benefit she derives from consuming one extra cup of coffee; thus, her marginal benefit is $4 for the first cup, $3 for the second cup and $2 for the third cup of coffee. Marginal benefit is the change in total benefit derived from consuming one extra unit of the good. If we are given an equation that links total benefit with the number of units consumed (q), we can find marginal benefit by differentiating the total benefit function:

$$MB = \frac{\Delta TB}{\Delta q} = \frac{dTB}{dq} \tag{6.1}$$

In general, we would expect marginal benefit to decline with each additional unit consumed. In the above example, this would mean that Candice would find the first cup of coffee outstanding, the second cup very good, the third cup acceptable, and so on. This decline in MB is referred to as **diminishing marginal benefit**.

It is also typical to draw marginal benefit as a continuous (smooth) function. Due to diminishing marginal benefit, the **marginal benefit curve** would usually be a downward-sloping line, as seen in Figure 6.1.[1]

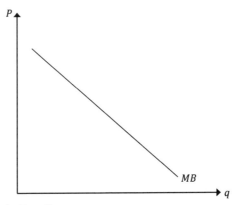

FIGURE 6.1 A typical marginal benefit curve

6.3 Individual demand

We can use a consumer's marginal benefit curve to derive his individual demand curve. **Individual demand** is the quantity of a good or service that a consumer is willing and able to buy at a certain price. Hence, the individual demand curve traces out all combinations of (a) market price and (b) individual quantity demanded at that price, holding everything else constant.

We now need to determine the quantity of a good that an individual demands at a certain price; as we will show, a consumer will purchase units of the good up until the point where $P = MB$. To see this, note that if $P < MB$ for a unit of the good or service, a consumer should buy that unit because his willingness to pay exceeds the price. However, if $P > MB$ for any unit of the good or service, the consumer should not buy that unit because the price of the good exceeds his willingness to pay. We also know that, due to diminishing marginal benefit, the MB of earlier units will be greater than the MB of later units. Because the consumer will buy additional units if $P < MB$ and fewer units if $P > MB$, it follows that a consumer should buy units up until the point where $P = MB$.

Consequently, a consumer's **individual demand curve** is given by his MB curve. Further, because the MB curve is usually downward sloping, so too will be the individual demand curve. A demand curve represents how much a consumer is *willing* and *able* to buy at different prices. Figure 6.2 depicts a typical demand curve. As you can see, the downward slope of the curve means that the higher the market price, the fewer units a consumer buys (q_1, p_1); similarly, the lower the market price, the more units a consumer buys (q_2, p_2). This negative relationship between price and quantity demanded is known as the **law of demand**.

The demand curve is derived by assuming that only price and quantity can change. If there is a change in the price/quantity, there will be a movement along the demand curve itself (as in Figure 6.2), with the change from (q_1, p_1) to (q_2, p_2), which is called a **change in the quantity demanded**. If there is a movement downwards along the demand curve (from (q_1, p_1) to (q_2, p_2) for example), this is called an 'increase in the quantity demanded'; if there is a movement up along the demand curve (that is, from (q_2, p_2) to (q_1, p_1)), this is called a 'decrease in the quantity demanded'.

As noted above, when we derive a demand curve we assume that any other relevant factors (other than the price of the good itself and the resulting quantity demanded) are held constant (*ceteris paribus*). These factors include the income, tastes, expectations about the future and the prices of other related goods. If any of these factors change, the demand curve itself will shift (as in Figure 6.3), with the shift from D_1 to D_2. The shift of the demand curve itself is called a **change in demand**. When the demand

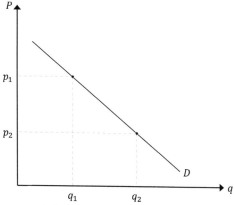

FIGURE 6.2 An individual consumer's demand curve is given by his or her marginal benefit curve. A movement along the demand curve is known as a 'change in the quantity demanded'

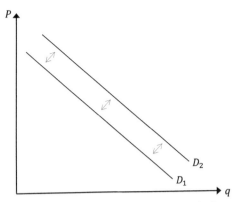

FIGURE 6.3 A movement of the demand curve itself is called a 'change in demand'

curve shifts to the right (from D_1 to D_2), this is called an 'increase in demand'; when there is a shift to the left (from D_2 to D_1), this is called a 'decrease in demand'.

6.4 Market demand

Now that we know that an individual consumer's demand curve is given by his *MB* curve, we can use this to derive the market demand curve. The **market demand** curve traces out combinations of (a) market price and (b) quantities that all consumers in a market are together willing and able to buy at that price. For example, suppose the market price of apples is $4, and that there are just two consumers in the market. At this price, Sonia is willing to buy 6 apples and Elizabeth is willing to buy 3 apples. This means that, at $4, the total quantity demanded in the market is 9 apples.

Hence, the market demand curve can be derived by adding together the quantity demanded by each individual consumer *at each price*. This means that, in our apple example, we would also need to check how much Sonia and Elizabeth would together be willing to buy when the price of apples is $2, $3, $5, $6, etc. This means that, graphically, the market demand curve can be derived by horizontally summing together the individual demand curves (that is, the individual *MB* curves) along the *q*-axis. Figure 6.4 shows two examples of deriving a market demand curve from individual demand curves.[2]

As you can see, the law of demand also holds for the market demand curve. We can also use the term **change in the quantity demanded** to refer to shifts along the market demand curve, and the term **change in demand** to refer to a shift in the demand curve itself.

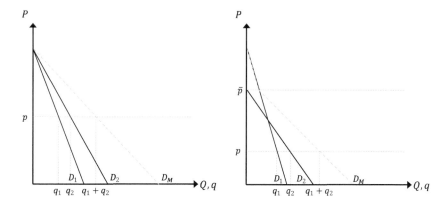

FIGURE 6.4 The market demand curve (D_M) can be derived by summing horizontally the individual demand curves (D_1 and D_2). In the first graph, both individual demand curves have the same P-intercept. If this is the case, then for every price p, the quantity demanded by the market will be the sum of individual consumer demand (that is, $q_1 + q_2$). In the second graph, the individual demand curves have different P-intercepts. Above the price $\bar{p}$, the quantity demanded by individual 2 will be zero; therefore, in this range, the market demand curve follows the individual demand curve for consumer 1. Below the price $\bar{p}$, the quantity demanded by both consumers is positive; in this range, the quantity demanded by the market will be the sum of individual consumer demand (that is, $q_1 + q_2$)

6.5 Concluding comments

We have now derived the individual and market demand curves. A demand curve answers the question 'if the consumer faces a certain price, what quantity would they buy?', for a range of possible prices. It is only possible to answer this question if the consumer is a price taker; the question does not make sense if the consumer can, by his choices, affect the market price. In a competitive market, a demand curve can be drawn because consumers are price takers.

Notes

1   A continuous marginal benefit curve implies that it is possible to consume partial units of a good (e.g. how much petrol to buy). Where the good or service in question is consumable only in whole units (e.g. T-shirts), the continuous marginal benefit curve is usually a close enough approximation. An obvious exception to this is where the consumer would only want to buy one unit (e.g. a house, a car or a holiday), in which case it would not be appropriate to draw a downward-sloping marginal benefit curve.

2   Note that with two or relatively few consumers the market demand curve can have several kinks in it. However, with a large number of consumers (as will be the case in a competitive market), individuals will come into and out of the market at different prices, and changes in the quantity demanded by one consumer will be counterbalanced by other consumers. As a result, the market demand curve can usually be represented fairly accurately using a continuous (smooth) function.

7

Production
and costs

7.1 Introduction

This chapter focuses on how firms operate. We begin by defining what the short and long run are for a firm's production process; in the short run the firm has at least one fixed input of production, whereas in the long run all inputs can be adjusted if the firm wishes to. Second, we analyse the relationship between a firm's inputs and its outputs – that is, its production function – and how this relationship can change over time. We then examine how a firm's output is related to its costs in the short run and in the long run. Finally, we consider how a firm's profit is calculated.

7.2 The short run and long run

A firm, using the available technology, converts inputs – labour, machines (often called capital) and natural resources (typically called land) – into outputs that are sold in the marketplace. Typically, a firm will require more than one input to produce its final output. We define the short run and the long run of a firm in relation to whether or not any of the factors of production are fixed (by 'fixed', we mean that the level of that input used cannot be changed regardless of the output produced).

The **short run** is the period of time during which at least one of the factors of production is fixed. For example, a firm might require both a factory and workers to produce its output. The firm might have a lease on the factory that must be paid, regardless of how much output the firm produces. In that case, the factory is a fixed input until the lease ends. In the **long run**, all factors of

DOI: 10.4324/9781003376644-10

production are variable (that is, not fixed). For example, when the firm's lease of the factory ends, it is free to decide whether or not to renew the lease for that factory.

Note that, in this context, the short run and the long run are not defined in relation to a set period of time, but rather in relation to how long it takes for all of a firm's inputs to become variable. For some industries the short run will be quite short (for example, a relatively simple business like a catering company). For other industries the short run could be many years (for example, pharmaceuticals or the manufacture of aircraft).

7.3 Production

A firm requires inputs or factors of production (labour, capital, land, etc.) in order to produce its final output (i.e. goods or services). A **production function** shows the relationship between the quantity of inputs used and the (maximum) quantity of output produced, given the state of technology. For example, suppose Jonathan owns a factory that makes umbrellas. In the meantime, let us assume that Jonathan cannot increase or decrease the size of his factory – that is, we are in the short run. He can, however, adjust the amount of labour input he uses. If he employs one worker, he can make 60 umbrellas; with two workers, he can make 110 umbrellas; 3 workers, 150 umbrellas; 4 workers, 180 umbrellas. The relationship between inputs (number of workers) and output (number of umbrellas) comprises the production function. Sometimes, a production function can be represented using an equation. For example, suppose the level of output of a good, q, depends on the amount of labour used, L. The production function can be represented by $q = f(L)$. A typical short-run production function looks like the one in Figure 7.1.

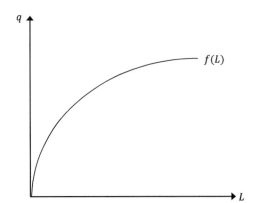

FIGURE 7.1 A typical short-run production function, where L represents the amount of labour employed and $q(L)$ represents the level of output

7.3.1 Marginal product

Once we have a production function, we might be interested in how output changes as we change the quantity of *only one* of the inputs. The **marginal product (MP)** of an input refers to how output responds when there is an increase in the number of that input used. In the example above, hiring one worker (rather than having no workers at all) allows 60 umbrellas to be made rather than 0 – the *MP* of the first worker is 60. If Jonathan has one worker and hires one additional worker, his output will increase from 60 to 110; therefore, the *MP* of the second worker is $110 - 60 = 50$. If Jonathan has three workers and hires one additional worker, his output will increase from 150 to 180; therefore, the *MP* of the fourth worker is 30 umbrellas.

If we are given the production function as an equation, we can use differentiation to find the marginal product of an input. Suppose the production function takes the form $q = f(L)$, where q is the quantity of output and L is the quantity of labour used as an input. In this case, we can find the marginal product of labour by differentiating the production function with respect to L:

$$MP = \frac{\Delta q}{\Delta L} = \frac{dq}{dL}. \tag{7.1}$$

We might also be interested in how the *MP* of an input changes as we increase the use of that input. If the *MP* becomes progressively smaller, this is called **diminishing marginal product**. If the *MP* becomes larger, this is called **increasing marginal product**. In the example above concerning Jonathan's umbrellas, the marginal products of the second, third and fourth workers, respectively are 50, 40 and 30, indicating diminishing marginal product; that is, each additional worker contributes less to output than the worker before.

Again, if we are given the production function as an equation, we can use differentiation to work out how *MP* changes as we increase the quantity of an input. So, if we have the production function $q = f(L)$ and we have found the marginal product, we can differentiate the marginal product with respect to L:

$$MP' = \frac{\Delta MP}{\Delta L} = \frac{dMP}{dL}. \tag{7.2}$$

If MP' is positive (resp. negative), then we have an increasing (resp. diminishing) marginal product.

> **Example.** Shirley owns a hairdressing salon and employs a number of hairdressers. The number of haircuts she can produce in one day is given by the production function $q = 4K^{\frac{1}{2}}L^{\frac{1}{2}}$, where Y is the number of haircuts, L is the quantity of labour and K is the amount of capital employed. Differentiating the production function with respect to L gives
>
> $$MP = \frac{dq}{dL} = 2K^{\frac{1}{2}}L^{-\frac{1}{2}}$$

which is the marginal product of labour. Differentiating the marginal product gives

$$MP' = \frac{dq}{dL}\frac{dMP}{dL} = -K^{\frac{1}{2}}L^{-\frac{3}{2}} < 0$$

which tells us that the marginal product of labour is diminishing – or, in other words, there are diminishing returns to labour.

Diminishing MP is thought to be very common. Firstly, in the short run there is a fixed input of some kind which creates a capacity constraint; this will mean that each additional worker will contribute to output less and less than those first hired. Consider Jonathan's umbrella factory. Because workers have to share factory space and machinery, each additional worker will be able to increase output by less and less. Note that this implies that diminishing MP is a short-run phenomenon; the capacity constraint that drives the phenomenon will only exist if at least one output is fixed. Also note that diminishing MP does not imply or require that the additional workers are worse than those initially hired (in fact, we assume that every worker is identical); rather, diminishing MP arises due to the capacity constraint due to the fixed input. Note here that as at least one factor of production is fixed (the factory), diminishing MP is a short-run concept.

7.3.2 Returns to scale

Now let us allow all inputs into the production process to be variable. In our umbrella manufacturing example, Jonathan can now vary all inputs in the production process; he can choose the factory size as well as the amount of labour utilised. Given that all factors of production are variable, we are in the long run.

With this choice available in the long run, we might also be interested in how the quantity of output responds when we change the quantity of *all* of the factors of production. **Returns to scale** refer to how the quantity of output changes when there is a proportional change in the quantity of all inputs. If output increases by the same proportional change, there are **constant returns to scale** – for example, if we double the quantity of all the inputs and output also doubles in quantity. If output increases by more than proportional increase in all inputs, we have **increasing returns to scale**. If output increases by less than the proportional increase in all inputs, there are **decreasing returns to scale**.

> **Example.** Consider the production function $q = KL$, where q is output, and K and L are capital and labour, respectively. Notice that if we double the quantity of K and L, output increases by a factor of 4. Therefore, we have increasing returns to scale.

Note that when we are examining the returns to scale properties of a firm, all inputs are variable; returns to scale is a long-run concept.[1]

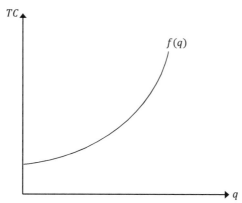

FIGURE 7.2 A typical total cost function, where q represents the level of output and TC represents total cost

7.4 Short-run costs

In order to use the inputs of production and transform them into outputs, a firm will have to incur some costs. These costs include wages paid to workers and the cost of leasing or buying factories and machines. A **cost function** is an equation that links the quantity of output with its associated production cost (i.e. $TC = f(q)$, where TC represents total cost and q represents the quantity of output). Figure 7.2 graphically represents a typical cost function (or 'cost curve'), with output on the x-axis and total cost on the y-axis.

Several things should be noted about the curve in Figure 7.2. First, when output is zero, total cost is positive; this is because, in the short run, some factors of production are fixed and the firm must pay the costs of these factors regardless of the amount of output produced. Second, the total cost curve rises as output increases; this represents the increase in cost as greater quantities of variable inputs are used. Third, the curve rises at an increasing rate; this captures diminishing MP, as a greater quantity of inputs is needed to increase output by the same amount as output goes up.

7.4.1 Fixed and variable costs

In the short run, some inputs will be fixed and some inputs will be variable; as a consequence, a firm will have some fixed costs and some variable costs. **Fixed costs (FC)** are costs that do not vary with the quantity of output produced. So, when a firm's output is zero, all the costs it incurs will be fixed costs:

$FC = TC$ when $q = 0$.

By contrast, **variable costs (VC)** are those costs that vary with or depend on the quantity of output produced. All costs that are not fixed costs will be variable costs.

$VC = TC - FC$.

Example. Consider the cost function $TC = 100 + 20q + q^2$, where q is the level of output produced. In this case, fixed costs are $FC = 100$ (the cost function evaluated at $q = 0$ and variable costs are $VC = 20q + q^2$).

7.4.2 Marginal cost

Sometimes, a firm will be interested in its **marginal cost (MC)** – that is, the increase in total cost that arises from an extra unit of production:

$$MC = \frac{\Delta TC}{\Delta q} = \frac{\Delta VC}{\Delta q}.$$

When we have total cost expressed as a continuous function, the marginal cost can be calculated by taking the first derivative of the total cost function with respect to q:

$$MC = \frac{\Delta TC}{\Delta q} = \frac{dTC}{dq}.$$

Due to diminishing MP, a typical MC curve will eventually be increasing in output; that is, MC has a positive slope. Returning to our umbrella example above, as each worker costs the same to hire but produces progressively less than the previous hire (diminishing MP), the extra cost of producing another unit of output (MC) must go up. Consequently, in the short run diminishing MP implies increasing MC. This is illustrated in Figure 7.3.

7.4.3 Average costs

A firm may also be interested in its average costs – that is, its costs per unit. These costs can be determined as follows, and the typical shape of these curves is illustrated in Figure 7.3.

- **Average fixed cost (AFC)** is the fixed cost per unit of output:

$$AFC = \frac{FC}{q}.$$

  Note that the AFC curve is always downward sloping; the numerator is fixed, but the denominator increases with output.
- **Average variable cost (AVC)** is the variable cost per unit of output:

$$AVC = \frac{VC}{q}.$$

  Because AVC is affected by diminishing MP, the AVC curve will eventually be upward sloping over output.

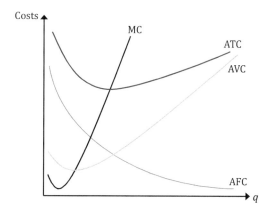

FIGURE 7.3 The typical shape of the average total cost curve, the average fixed cost curve, the average variable cost curve and the marginal cost curve

- **Average total cost (*ATC*)** is the total cost per unit of output:

$$ATC = \frac{TC}{q}.$$

Note that $ATC = AVC + AFC$. Therefore, the shape of the ATC curve is determined by the shape of the AFC curve (which is always declining) and the AVC curve (which can be initially declining, but will eventually be increasing in output). At very low levels of output, it is usually the decline in AFC that dominates, but at higher levels of output, it will be the effect of the upward-sloping AVC that dominates. Together, this will give the ATC curve a U-shape (i.e. initially decreasing, but eventually increasing with output).

The relationship between MC, ATC and AVC is also important. As a rule, the MC curve passes through the minimum of ATC and AVC. To see why this must be the case, consider the following analogy: Suppose a student has an average exam score of 60% and sits for another exam. We can think of the score from the additional exam as the marginal exam score. How will the marginal exam score affect his average exam score? If the student scores above 60%, his average score will increase; if he scores below 60%, his average score will decrease. By the same logic, if the marginal cost of a unit of output is higher (resp. lower) than the average total cost, it will have the effect of increasing (resp. decreasing) the average total cost. Thus, so long as the MC curve lies below the ATC curve, it will drag that curve downwards; so long as MC is above ATC, it will pull that curve upwards. Therefore, as ATC is decreasing when MC is below it, and increasing when MC is above it, ATC must be at its minimum when it is intersected by MC. For the same reasons, MC intersects AVC at its minimum. This is illustrated in Figure 7.3; when drawing cost curves it is important to illustrate this relationship correctly.

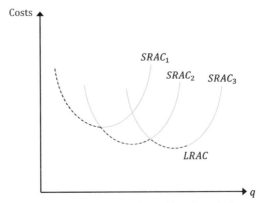

FIGURE 7.4 The long-run average cost curve can be obtained by taking the lower envelope of all short-run average cost curves. In this diagram, the short-run average cost curves are represented by the unbroken short-run average cost (SRAC) curves. The long-run average cost curve is the dashed line that runs beneath them. As more short-run average cost curves are drawn in, the long-run average cost curve will become smoother

7.5 Long-run costs

7.5.1 Long-run marginal cost

In the long run, all inputs are variable. This implies that all costs are variable in the long run. Consequently, the marginal cost of increasing output by one unit must take into account the fact that all inputs can be varied to achieve this increase. Thus, for the same level of output, long-run marginal cost will be less than or equal to short-run marginal cost; the extra flexibility in relation to inputs in the long run means that a firm might be able to increase its output at a lower cost than in the short run. For example, suppose the most cost-effective way for a car manufacturer to increase its output is to buy more machinery, but in the short run only labour is variable. Therefore, if the car manufacturer wishes to increase output in the short run, it must hire more workers; however, in the long run, it can buy more machinery, which gives a lower marginal cost in the long run than in the short run.

7.5.2 Long-run average cost

For the same reason long-run average cost can be no greater than short-run average cost.[2] For example, consider a firm that can choose the size of its factory in the long run. That firm, anticipating a certain output requirement, will choose the factory size that gives it the lowest average cost for that level of output. If the required output was smaller or larger, the firm might choose a different factory size to again minimise average cost. As a result of this, the long-run average cost curve will be the lower envelope of all of the short-run average cost curves. Figure 7.4 illustrates how to derive a long-run average cost curve from several short-run average cost curves.

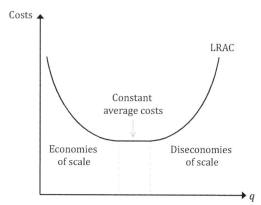

FIGURE 7.5 When the LRAC curve is downward sloping, the firm is experiencing economies of scale; when the long-run average cost (LRAC) curve is upward-sloping, there are diseconomies of scale. When the LRAC curve is flat, there are constant average costs

The term **economies of scale** refers to cost advantages that a firm obtains from increasing its output. Specifically, if long-run average costs are decreasing with output, this is called economies of scale. On the other hand, if long-run average costs are increasing with output, this is known as **diseconomies of scale**. If long-run average costs are constant as output expands, by definition there are **constant average costs**.[3] These three cases are illustrated in Figure 7.5.

7.5.3 A final note

Even though we have allowed all inputs to be variable in the long run, we have also implicitly assumed that several things remain constant. Firstly, we have assumed that input prices are fixed. Secondly, we have assumed that there have been no changes in the state of technology that would affect a firm's ability to produce output. Of course, in the real world these changes are typical and important, but we have abstracted from such changes in order to better understand a firm's costs in both the long run and the short run.

7.6 Total revenue, total cost and economic profit

In order to derive a firm's economic profit, we will need to define its total revenue and total cost. **Total revenue (TR)** is the amount a firm receives for the sale of its output. This will be the price at which the firm sells each unit, multiplied by the quantity of units sold:

$$TR = P \times q \tag{7.3}$$

Total costs (TC) refer to the economic costs that a firm incurs for producing output, as we have discussed in this chapter. When we refer to economic costs, we mean opportunity costs. Recall from Chapter 1 that this includes both the explicit and implicit costs of production. In this context, an example of an explicit cost is the cost of buying the inputs of production; an example of an implicit cost might be forgone earnings.

> **Example.** William uses $300,000 of his savings to invest in a new business venture. If he had kept those savings in his bank account, he would receive interest of 5% per year. Therefore, by investing his savings in the business venture, William forgoes those interest payments and they are part of the implicit cost of investing in the business venture.

Economic Profit (π) is the amount that a firm makes, net of the costs that it incurs. That is:

$$\pi = TR - TC \tag{7.4}$$

One thing to note is that we have used opportunity costs, not just explicit (accounting) costs to calculate profit. An important implication of this is that economic profit may, and typically will, differ from accounting profit – and this affects the way that we interpret economic profit. For example, if a firm earns zero profit, this means that total revenue only just covers total cost (the opportunity cost) – in other words, the firm could earn the same net benefit from undertaking the next best opportunity. It does not mean that the firm has received no accounting profit. Zero economic profit means that a person has no incentive to switch from their first choice to the next best alternative.

> **Example.** Abby makes some cookies at a cost of $20 (including the cost of labour) and sells those cookies for $25. Alternatively, she could have instead put her initial $20 into a savings account, which would have earned $5 in interest. In this case, Abby's accounting profit is $25 − $20 = $5. However, her economic profit must include the implicit cost of $5 in forgone interest payments – that is, her economic profit is $25 − $(20 + 5) = $0. Notice that Abby has no incentive to switch from making cookies to putting her money in the savings account.

7.7 Concluding comments

To have something to sell in the marketplace, a firm converts inputs into outputs. We can represent the relationship between inputs and outputs using a production function. In the short run, at least one input is fixed (like a factory, the size of a restaurant and its decor, the computer system used by a firm). With at least one fixed input, eventually, the additional output generated from using an extra input will decline – that is, there will be diminishing marginal product. This is an important concept as it is the underlying cause as to why the short-run marginal cost curve is upward sloping.

In the long run, a firm is able to vary all of its inputs (there are no fixed inputs or fixed costs). This means that long-run cost associated with a particular level of production should not be more than a firm's short-run cost for the same level of output. For this reason, a firm's long-run average total cost curve is the lower envelope of the short-run average total cost curves. In the long run, if a firm's long-run average cost curve is downward sloping with output, we say the firm is experiencing economies of scale. If long-run total costs are rising with output there are diseconomies of scale. Finally, a horizontal long-run average total cost curve indicates that there are constant average costs.

Notes

1   Moreover, increasing returns to scale is not necessarily incompatible with the short-run notion of diminishing MP.
2   Note that, in the long run, there is only one average cost. We do not need to separate average costs into average fixed cost and average variable cost for the simple reason that there are no fixed costs in the long run.
3   The shape of the long-run average cost curve is determined by returns to scale (discussed earlier in Section 7.3.2). That is, if we have increasing returns to scale (whereby output more than doubles when all inputs are doubled) this will have the effect of creating economies of scale (that is, declining long-run average cost). Similarly, if there are decreasing returns to scale, we will have diseconomies of scale; if there are constant returns to scale, we will have constant average costs. However, it is important not to conflate 'economies of scale' with 'returns to scale'. The former refers to the relationship between output and cost; the latter refers to the relationship between inputs and output.

CHAPTER 8

Supply

8.1 Introduction

In the last chapter we examined a firm's costs and production. We now use those concepts to derive an individual firm's supply function and the market supply function. In this chapter, we will focus on **competitive markets**, in which there are many buyers and sellers, so no individual buyer or seller has the power to materially affect the price in the market. As a consequence, both sellers and buyers in the market are **price takers**.

8.2 Firm supply

Firm supply is defined as the quantity of output a firm is willing and able to supply at a certain price. The supply curve traces out all combinations of (a) market price and (b) quantities that a firm is willing and able to sell at that price.

Given a market price, how much should a firm sell? As we shall see, a firm should sell up until $P = MC$. To see why this is true, first note that the marginal revenue for each unit that the firm sells is the price, P. Now, consider a firm where $P > MC$ for its last unit sold (and this is true for at least one additional unit). If that firm increases its output by one unit, it will increase its profit because the additional revenue from selling that extra unit (P) outweighs the cost of producing that same unit (MC). For example, if the price of a good is $10 but the marginal cost is $4, the firm will receive an extra $6 of profit from selling that unit. Next consider a firm producing where $P < MC$ for the last unit made. If this is the case, the firm should not have produced and sold its last unit. This is because the last unit cost the firm more to produce than the price that the firm received for it; therefore, the firm lowered its profit by

DOI: 10.4324/9781003376644-11

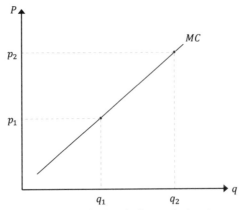

FIGURE 8.1 An individual firm's supply curve is given by its marginal cost curve. A shift along the supply curve is known as a 'change in the quantity supplied'

producing that unit. For example, if the price of a good is $10 but the marginal cost is $14, the firm would receive an extra $4 of profit by not producing and selling that unit of the good.

Generally speaking, this means that a firm should sell an extra unit if $P > MC$, but one fewer unit if $P < MC$; thus, at the end of the day, a firm should sell up until $P = MC$. Figure 8.1 graphically represents this result. Suppose the initial market price is represented by p_1; in this case, profit is maximised if the competitive firm sells up to the quantity where $p_1 = MC$ (that is, q_1). If price, for whatever reason, rises to p_2, the firm will maximise profit by again selling up to the new quantity where $p_2 = MC$ (that is, q_2).

What this means is that a **firm's supply curve** is given by its MC curve. Because the MC curve is upward sloping due to diminishing marginal product, there is a positive relationship between the price of a good and the quantity of that good supplied. This positive relationship is known as the **law of supply**.

The firm's supply curve is derived by assuming that only the price and quantity supplied of the product can change. If there is a change in the price, there will be a movement along the supply curve itself (as in Figure 8.1, with the shift from (q_1, p_1) to (q_2, p_2)), which is called a **change in the quantity supplied**. If there is a movement up along the supply curve (that is, from (q_1, p_1) to (q_2, p_2)), this is called an 'increase in the quantity supplied'. If there is a movement left along the supply curve, (that is, from (q_2, p_2) to (q_1, p_1)), this is called a 'decrease in the quantity supplied'.

As noted, when we derive a supply function we assume that all other relevant factors, other than the price and quantity of the good, are held constant (*ceteris paribus*). These factors include the cost of inputs, technology and expectations about the future. If any of these factors change, the supply curve itself will shift (as in Figure 8.2, with the shift from S_1 to S_2), which is called a **change in supply**. When the supply curve shifts to the right (from S_1 to S_2), this is called an 'increase in supply'; when there is a shift to the left (from S_2 to S_1), this is called a 'decrease in supply'.

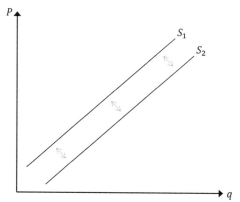

FIGURE 8.2 A movement of a firm's supply curve itself is called a 'change in supply'

One caveat is worth noting. When we discuss short-run and long-run supply we will need to be careful to check whether the firm will want to produce anything at all (that is, $q > 0$). So far, we have simply determined that if a firm chooses to supply a positive quantity, they should supply up until the point where $P = MC$.

8.3 Market supply

Given that an individual firm's supply curve is given by its MC curve, we can use this to derive the market supply curve. The **market supply** curve traces out combinations of (a) market price and (b) quantities that all firms in a market are together willing and able to sell at that price. For example, suppose the market price of carrots is $1. At this price, Jackson is willing to sell 5 carrots and Jared is willing to sell 8 carrots. This means that, at $1, the total quantity supplied in the market is 13 carrots.

Simply put, the market supply curve can be derived by adding together the quantity supplied by each individual firm *at every price*. This means that, in our carrot example, we would also need to check how much Jackson and Jared would together be willing to supply when the price of carrots is $2, $3, $4, etc. This means that, graphically, the market supply curve can be derived by summing together the individual supply curves (that is, the individual MC curves) horizontally along the q-axis. Figure 8.3 shows two examples of deriving a market supply curve from individual supply curves.

The law of supply also holds for the market supply curve. We can also use the term 'change in the quantity supplied' to refer to movements along the market supply curve, and the term 'change in supply' to refer to a shift of the supply curve itself.

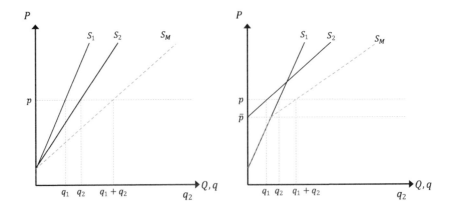

FIGURE 8.3 The market supply curve (S_M) can be derived by summing horizontally the individual supply curves (S_1 and S_2). In the first graph, both individual supply curves have the same P-intercept. If this is the case, then for every price p, the quantity supplied by the market will be the sum of individual firm supply (that is, $q_1 + q_2$). In the second graph, the individual supply curves have different P-intercepts. Below the price $\bar{p}$, the quantity supplied by firm 2 will be zero; therefore, in this range, the market supply curve follows the individual supply curve for firm 1. Above the price $\bar{p}$, the quantity supplied by both firms is positive; in this range, the quantity supplied by the market will be the sum of individual firm supply (that is, $q_1 + q_2$)

8.4 Concluding comments

In this chapter, we derived the individual and market supply curves. A supply curve answers the question 'if the firm faces a certain price, what quantity would they want to supply?', for a range of possible prices. It is only possible to answer this question if the firm is a price taker; the question does not make sense if the firm can choose the market price. We can draw a supply curve in the context of a competitive market, because firms in that environment are price takers.

CHAPTER 9

Equilibrium and welfare

9.1 Introduction

In Chapters 6 and 8, we derived the demand and supply curves. Together, demand and supply determine the price and quantity of a good or service traded in a market. These market outcomes are the focus of this chapter.

9.2 Market equilibrium

A market is in **equilibrium** if, at the market price, the quantity demanded by consumers equals the quantity supplied by firms in the market. The price at which this occurs is called the **market-clearing price** (or 'equilibrium price'). Figure 9.1 depicts a market in equilibrium at point A. At the equilibrium price (P^*), quantity demanded is equal to the quantity supplied ($Q^d = Q^s = Q^*$). This point is called an equilibrium because there is no pressure on the price or quantity traded in the market to change. As we shall see, if a market is not in equilibrium, there will be pressure on price and quantity to move towards the equilibrium price and equilibrium quantity.

First consider the case where the market price (P_1) is above the equilibrium price, as seen in Figure 9.2. As a consequence, the quantity supplied (Q_1^s) exceeds the quantity demanded (Q_1^d). This difference is called **excess supply**, which means that sellers cannot find buyers for all units supplied to the market. In these circumstances, there will be downward pressure on prices, as sellers try to bring more consumers into the market; at the same time, the quantity supplied will fall in response to the decrease in prices. This downward pressure on prices will continue until the excess of supply is eliminated, moving the market towards equilibrium.

Next consider the case where the market price (P_2) is below the equilibrium price, as seen in Figure 9.3. Here, the quantity demanded (Q_2^d) exceeds the

DOI: 10.4324/9781003376644-12

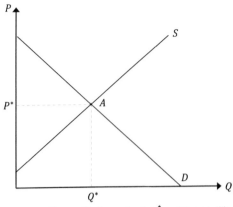

FIGURE 9.1 A market in equilibrium. The equilibrium price is P^* and the equilibrium quantity traded is Q^*

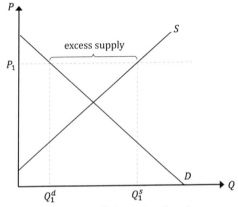

FIGURE 9.2 When market price is above the equilibrium price, there is an excess of supply in the market

quantity supplied (Q_2^s), which is called **excess demand**. This means that sellers do not supply enough units to meet consumer demand. Now, there will be upward pressure on prices, as buyers compete for limited units in the market; this increase in prices will increase the quantity supplied and also decrease the quantity demanded. This upward pressure on prices will continue until the excess demand is eliminated, moving the market towards equilibrium.

How quickly does the market move towards equilibrium? Evidence from experiments and real-world markets suggests that, if there are many buyers and sellers, the adjustment process to the market-clearing price is quite fast.[1]

9.3 Comparative static analysis

Sometimes, markets are affected by a change or event beyond the direct control of buyers or sellers in that market. In such cases, we may want to analyse how that change or event affects the choices of firms and/or consumers in the market, and how those

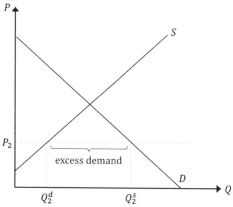

FIGURE 9.3 When market price is below the equilibrium price, there is an excess of demand in the market

choices affect market outcomes. For example, we may want to know what will happen in the market for corn chips if there is a drought, what the impact will be on the market for cars if the cost of steel falls, or how a government campaign promoting healthy living will affect the market for yoga classes. This type of analysis is often called **comparative static analysis**, and essentially involves an examination of how the market equilibrium is affected by the change or event – that is, a comparison of the old and the new market equilibria.

To conduct a comparative static analysis, first assume that the market in question is initially in equilibrium. Next, ascertain whether the change or event will affect the demand curve or the supply curve of the market (or both), and if so, how that curve will shift. Finally, use the demand and supply diagram to analyse the impact of the change or event; that is, compare prices and quantities traded in the market before and after the change.

> **Example.** Consider how the market for corn chips, depicted in Figure 9.4, is affected by an increase in the price of potato chips. The demand for corn chips is denoted by D_1 and the supply of corn chips is denoted by S_1. The market is initially in equilibrium at (Q_1^*, P_1^*). Assuming corn chips and potato chips are substitutes, an increase in the price of potato chips is likely to increase the demand for corn chips, shifting the demand curve to the right, to D_2. This will cause an increase in the quantity supplied, as we move along the supply curve S_1 to the new equilibrium. The new equilibrium price and quantity (Q_2^*, P_2^*) are higher than before the change in demand.

> **Example.** Consider how the market for cars, depicted in Figure 9.5, is affected by an increase in the price of steel. The demand for cars is denoted by D_1 and the supply for cars is denoted by S_1. The market is initially in equilibrium at (Q_1^*, P_1^*). Assuming that steel is an input in the production of cars, the MC of making each car will increase, causing the supply curve to shift upwards (or to the left) to S_2. This will cause a decrease in the quantity demanded, as we move along the demand

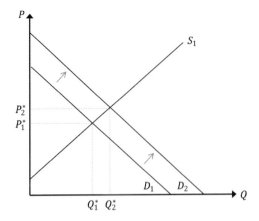

FIGURE 9.4 The market for corn chips when there is an increase in the price of potato chips

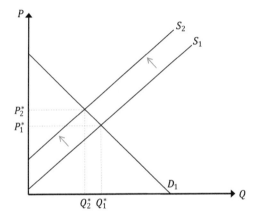

FIGURE 9.5 The market for cars when there is an increase in the price of steel

curve D_1 to the new equilibrium. At the new equilibrium (Q_2^*, P_2^*), price of cars is higher but the quantity traded is lower than before the change in the price of steel.

As you can see, such demand-and-supply analysis is a relatively simple yet extremely powerful tool. This structured method of analysis gives us a formal way of thinking about changes in markets and supporting our intuitive conclusions about how markets work.

9.4 Welfare

Markets are one of the main ways that goods and services are produced and distributed. Of course, consumers and firms will only participate in markets if it is beneficial to them. We can measure and observe changes in these benefits for these participants using **welfare analysis**. In this section, we examine the welfare of consumers and firms.

9.4.1 Consumer surplus

Consumer surplus (CS) is the welfare consumers receive from buying units of a good or service in the market. We can measure consumer surplus by evaluating the net value of a good or service to the consumer, as he or she perceives it. That is, consumer surplus is given by the consumer's willingness to pay, minus the price actually paid, for each unit bought.

To provide some intuition for this, suppose Hamish is considering buying a chocolate bar. His willingness to pay (or marginal benefit) for the chocolate bar is $5.50, but the price of chocolate bars is $2. If he buys the chocolate bar, he will receive $5.50 in benefits, minus the price actually paid of $2. Therefore, his surplus from buying the chocolate bar is $3.50. However, consumer surplus in the market takes into account *every unit* of the good or service purchased. Therefore, if Hamish buys multiple chocolate bars, we would need to add up the surplus from each chocolate bar in order to get his total consumer surplus.

Recalling that the individual demand curve traces out a consumer's marginal benefit or willingness to pay, we can find an individual's *CS* by calculating the area between the individual demand curve and the price line. Similarly, we can find the *CS* of all consumers in the market by calculating the area between the market demand curve and the price line. This area is shown in Figure 9.6.

What happens when the price falls? Consider Figure 9.7, in which the market price falls from P_1 to P_2. As you can see, the area of consumer surplus has now increased, due to two additional benefits: on all the units previously consumed, the difference between *MB* and price is now larger, meaning that the net benefit from consuming

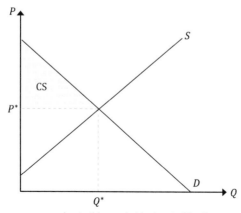

FIGURE 9.6 The area of consumer surplus in this market is denoted by the grey-shaded area

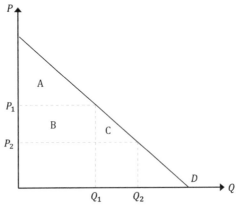

FIGURE 9.7 When the market price falls from P_1 to P_2, the area of consumer surplus increases from A to A+B+C. The area B represents the increase in consumer surplus that arises from an increase in the net benefit of previously consumed units. The area C represents the increase in consumer surplus arising from the consumption of additional units

each of these units has increased; secondly, the lower price now means that more units are purchased, which also generates an additional benefit to consumers.

9.4.2 Producer surplus

On the other side of the market, **producer surplus (PS)** is the welfare producers (that is, firms) receive from selling units of a good or service in the market. Producer surplus can be measured by considering the net benefit of selling a good or service. That is, producer surplus is given by the price the producer receives, minus the cost of production, for each unit of the good or service bought.

Now suppose that Adam is a producer of chocolate bars. As before, the price of chocolate bars is $2, but the marginal cost to Adam of producing the chocolate bar is $0.50. Therefore, if Adam sells the chocolate bar, his net benefit is the $2 received, minus $0.50 in production costs. Therefore, his surplus from selling the chocolate bar is $1.50. However, producer surplus in the market takes into account *every unit* of the good or service sold. Therefore, if Adam sells multiple chocolate bars, we would need to add up the surplus from each chocolate bar in order to get his total producer surplus.

Remembering that a firm's supply curve is given by its *MC* curve, a firm's *PS* can be found by calculating the area between the price line and the firm's supply curve. Similarly, we can find the *PS* of all producers in the market by calculating the area between the price line and the market supply curve. These areas are shown in Figure 9.8.

Let us again consider what happens when there is a change in price. Suppose, as in Figure 9.9, there is an increase in price from P_1 to P_2. *PS* increases for two reasons: on all the units previously sold, the price is now higher, meaning that the net benefit from selling each of these units has increased; secondly, the higher price now means that more units are sold, which also generates some net benefit to producers.

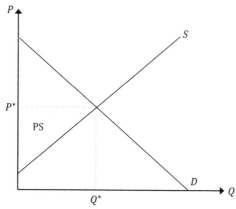

FIGURE 9.8 The area of producer surplus in this market is denoted by the grey-shaded area

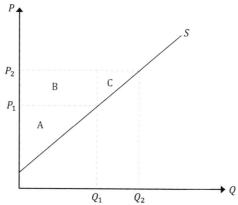

FIGURE 9.9 When the market price increases from P_1 to P_2, the area of producer surplus increases from A to A+B+C. The area B represents the increase in producer surplus that arises from an increase in the net benefit of selling units that would have been sold previously. The area C represents the increase in producer surplus arising from the sale of additional units

9.4.3 Total surplus

We can also measure the total welfare of all participants in the market. Here, there are only two types of participants: consumers and producers. In later chapters, we will allow for other participants in the market (namely, the government). For now, however, **total surplus (TS)** is the sum of consumer surplus and producer surplus in the market equilibrium:

$$TS = CS + PS. \qquad (9.1)$$

As CS is the area below the demand curve and above the price line, and PS is the area below the price line and above the supply curve, it follows that TS is the area between the demand and supply curves, up to the market equilibrium quantity q^*. This is illustrated in Figure 9.10.

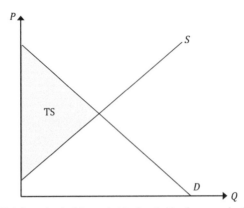

FIGURE 9.10 The area of total surplus in this market is denoted by the grey-shaded area

9.5 Pareto efficiency

To analyse welfare in a competitive market further, we now introduce the concept of Pareto efficiency. An outcome is **Pareto efficient** if it is not possible to make someone better off without making someone else worse off. Conversely, an outcome is *not* Pareto efficient if it is possible to reallocate resources (or do things differently in the market) and make someone better off without making someone else worse off. Another way of thinking about Pareto efficiency in this context is that the Pareto efficient outcome maximises total surplus.

As it turns out, the outcome in a competitive market is Pareto efficient. Consider the market equilibrium in Figure 9.1. For all the trades between 0 and Q^*, the *MB* of the good to the consumer was greater than the *MC* of production. Hence, the consumer was willing to pay more than the minimum amount needed to induce the producer to make and sell the good. Moreover, trading the good yields a net benefit to at least one of the parties and no one is made worse off. For the last unit traded (the Q^*th unit), $MB = MC$, but neither the consumer nor the producer was made worse off.[2]

Suppose, for some reason, fewer than Q^* units are traded in the market. At this quantity, $MB > MC$. This outcome is not Pareto efficient, because it is possible to increase the number of units traded in order to make the consumer and/or the producer better off, without making anyone worse off.

Similarly, suppose more than Q^* units are traded in the market, such that for the last unit $MB < MC$. In this case, all units traded beyond Q^* made someone worse off: either the buyer paid more than his *MB*, the seller received a price less than her *MC*, or both. Therefore, this outcome is not Pareto efficient, because the total surplus would be higher if the trade of units in excess of Q^* did not take place.

Indeed, at the competitive-market equilibrium, all the potential gains from trade are exhausted; there are no consumers left in the market with a willingness to pay more than any seller's cost of providing an additional unit of output. Moreover, the market through the price mechanism ensures that the people with the highest value for the product (those that are willing to pay more than the price) end up with the goods, and that those firms with the lowest cost are the ones who make the goods (the firms that have a *MC* less than the market price). While these actions are completely decentralised, in the sense that there is no one person coordinating the actions of the many parties in the market, a competitive market manages to maximise total surplus (that is, reach a Pareto efficient outcome).

It is important to note that Pareto efficiency has a very strict and specialised definition. In particular, it does not imply either uniqueness or fairness/equity. That is to say, in a given market (or economic situation), there could also be more than one outcome that is Pareto efficient. Further, an outcome that is Pareto efficient is not automatically the fairest or the most equitable, or even the most desirable. In order to determine the 'best' market outcome, it may be necessary to weigh up efficiency against other socially desirable objectives.

9.6 Concluding comments

In this chapter, we defined and calculated consumer surplus, producer surplus and total surplus. We found that the outcome in a competitive market has the following characteristics: (i) via the price mechanism, it allocates goods to consumers who value them most highly; and (ii) via the price mechanism, it allocates demand for goods to sellers who can produce at the least cost. We also found that a competitive market maximises total surplus and, hence, is Pareto efficient. It follows that a person who can dictate the price and quantity of a good traded in the market (a 'social planner') cannot achieve an outcome that is more efficient than the free (competitive) market.

Notes

1   Experimental evidence comes from researchers setting up experiments that simulate economic problems in a laboratory. We discuss this further in Chapter 22.
2   For convenience, although there is no net gain to either party, we just assume that this trade goes ahead; this assumption does not affect our welfare analysis of the market.

CHAPTER 10

Elasticity

10.1 Introduction

In this chapter, we are concerned with measuring how a change in one variable affects another. For example, we might be interested in how the equilibrium quantity traded responds to a change in the market price, or how demand responds to changes in consumer income. One issue with measuring quantitative changes is that different markets use different units of measurement (litres, kilogrammes, ounces and so on), each market has its own price level (a few cents or millions of dollars) and it is even possible that different markets use different currencies. A way we can compare quantitative changes across different situations is to look at proportional (or percentage) changes.[1]

10.2 Measuring elasticity

As discussed in Chapter 2, **elasticity** measures how responsive one variable (y) is to changes in another variable (x). That is, when we increase x by a certain amount, does y change by a small amount or by a large amount? We can calculate elasticity (ε) by dividing the percentage change in y by the percentage change in x:[2]

$$\varepsilon = \frac{\%\Delta y}{\%\Delta x}. \tag{10.1}$$

This tells us that, for a 1% change in x, there will be an $\varepsilon\%$ change in y. As you can see, the larger the absolute value of ε, the more responsive y is to changes in x; conversely, the smaller the absolute value of ε, the less responsive y is to changes in x.

DOI: 10.4324/9781003376644-13

Generally, we can calculate the proportional change in a variable by dividing the change in the variable by the variable itself – that is:

$$\% \Delta x = \frac{\Delta x}{x} \tag{10.2}$$

However, it is not always obvious how to determine what the proportional change in a particular variable is. For this reason, we have two methods of calculating elasticity: the point method and the midpoint (arc) method. It will be appropriate to use the point method for calculating elasticity when we are calculating elasticity *at a single point*. The midpoint (arc) method will be appropriate when we are interested in elasticity *moving from one point to another*. These methods are discussed in more detail below.

10.2.1 Point method

At times we are interested in elasticity at a particular point. For example, suppose the price of a good is P_1, the quantity demanded of that good is Q_1; what is elasticity at the point (Q_1, P_1)? In these cases, we can use the **point method** of calculating elasticity. This simply involves recognising that, for very small changes in the variables, $\frac{\Delta y}{\Delta x} = \frac{dy}{dx}$.

In general terms, the point method can be expressed as follows:

$$\varepsilon = \frac{(\Delta y)/y}{(\Delta x)/x} = \frac{\Delta y}{\Delta x} \cdot \frac{x}{y} = \frac{dy}{dx} \cdot \frac{x}{y} \tag{10.3}$$

Example. Suppose the demand curve for forks is given by $Q = 100 - 2P$, and the price of forks is $P = 30$. What is elasticity at this point? From the demand equation, we know that when $P = 30$, $Q = 40$. The slope of this line is $\Delta Q/\Delta P = -2$. (This can also be derived by the first derivative of the demand equation, which gives us $\frac{dQ}{dP} = -2$.) Substituting these values into the point formula gives:

$$\varepsilon = -2 \cdot \frac{30}{40} = -1.5$$

The interpretation of this is: if the price of forks increases by 1%, the quantity demanded of forks falls by 1.5%.

10.2.2 Midpoint (or arc) method

Sometimes we are interested in elasticity when moving from one point to another. For example, suppose the price of a good changes from P_1 to P_2, which causes the quantity demanded to change from Q_1 to Q_2. Here, we are moving from one point (Q_1, P_1) to another (Q_2, P_2). However, it is unclear in this situation whether we should measure the change in price (resp. quantity) as a percentage of P_1 or of P_2 (resp. Q_1 or Q_2)? To resolve this ambiguity, sometimes we adopt the **midpoint (or arc) method**; that is, when calculating percentage changes, we use the midpoint (or the average) of P_1 and P_2, and the average of Q_1 and Q_2.

In general terms, the midpoint (or arc) method can be expressed as follows:

$$\varepsilon = \frac{(\Delta y)/y^m}{(\Delta x)/x^m} = \frac{\Delta y}{\Delta x} \cdot \frac{x^m}{y^m} \tag{10.4}$$

where $x^m = \frac{x_1 + x_2}{2}$ and $y^m = \frac{y_1 + y_2}{2}$.

> **Example.** When the price of spoons is \$10, the quantity demanded is 50 units. When the price increases to \$20, the quantity demanded falls to 30 units. In order to calculate elasticity, we need to find the average of price and quantity: $P^m = 15$ and $Q^m = 40$. We also need to find the change in price and quantity: $\Delta P = 20 - 10 = 10$ and $\Delta Q = 30 - 50 = -20$. Substituting these values into the midpoint formula gives:
>
> $$\varepsilon = \frac{-20}{10} \cdot \frac{15}{40} = -0.75$$
>
> The interpretation of this is: if the price of spoons increases by 1%, the quantity demanded falls by 0.75%.

10.3 Applications

The concept of elasticity has several important applications in economics. We will discuss some of these now.

10.3.1 Elasticity of demand

One of the most important applications is the **elasticity of demand** (ε_d).[3] It measures how sensitive the quantity demanded of a good (Q_d) is to changes in price (P). Specifically, it tells us the proportional change in quantity demanded of a good, given a 1% change in its price. By substituting Q_d and P into the formulas above, we can write down the midpoint (arc) method and the point method for calculating the elasticity of demand:

Midpoint method	Point method
$\varepsilon_d = \dfrac{\Delta Q_d}{\Delta P} \cdot \dfrac{P^m}{Q_d^m}$	$\varepsilon_d = \dfrac{dQ_d}{dP} \cdot \dfrac{P}{Q_d}$

Given the law of demand, the elasticity of demand will normally be negative (or at least non-positive).[4] For this reason, some authors find it convenient to drop the minus sign when reporting the elasticity of demand, treating the negative sign as implicit. We will not adopt that convention here, but it should be noted that either approach is fine, so long as it is consistently applied.

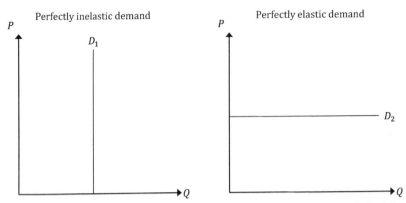

FIGURE 10.1 When demand is perfectly inelastic, the demand curve is vertical (as seen in the left panel). When demand is perfectly elastic, the demand curve is horizontal (as seen in the right panel)

Now that we can calculate the elasticity of demand, let us consider what our results mean:

- If $\varepsilon_d = 0$, demand is **perfectly inelastic**. For a 1% change in price, there is no change in the quantity demanded; in other words, quantity demanded is not at all responsive to changes in price. In this special case, the demand curve is vertical, as shown in Figure 10.1.
- If $-1 < \varepsilon_d < 0$, demand is **inelastic**. For a 1% change in price, the resulting change in quantity demanded is less than 1%; in other words, quantity demanded is not very responsive to changes in price.
- If $\varepsilon_d = -1$, demand is **unit elastic**. For a 1% change in price, there is a 1% change in quantity demanded; in other words, the quantity demanded changes by the same proportion as price.
- If $\varepsilon_d < -1$, demand is **elastic**. For a 1% change in price, the change in quantity demanded is more than 1%; in other words, the quantity demanded is very responsive to changes in price.
- If $\varepsilon_d = -\infty$, demand is **perfectly elastic**. For a small increase in price, the quantity demanded will drop to zero. Intuitively, this means that if a firm raises its price at all, its customers will go elsewhere to buy the product. In this special case, the demand curve is horizontal, as shown in Figure 10.1.

You can see, from the formulas above, that the elasticity of demand depends partly on the slope of the demand curve (that is, $\frac{\Delta Q_d}{\Delta P}$ or $\frac{dQ_d}{dP}$). However, elasticity of demand also depends upon the values of P and Q at the reference point where elasticity is being measured. For this reason, even when the demand curve is a straight line, the elasticity of demand changes as we move along the curve.

> **Example.** Consider the demand curve, $Q_d = 100 - P$. Along the entire demand curve, the slope is constant as $\frac{dQ_d}{dP} = -1$. However, as we move along the curve, elasticity of demand changes. At the point $(Q_d, P) = (90, 10)$, elasticity is given

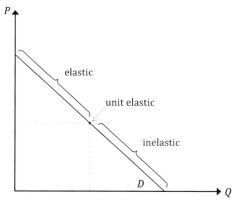

FIGURE 10.2 When the demand curve is linear, elasticity changes as we move along the curve. The curve is most elastic near the *P*-axis and most inelastic near the *Q*-axis

by $\varepsilon = -1 \cdot \frac{10}{90} = -\frac{1}{9}$ and the demand is inelastic. At $(50, 50)$, $\varepsilon = -1 \cdot \frac{50}{50} = -1$, and demand is unit elastic. At $(25, 75)$, $\varepsilon = -1 \cdot \frac{75}{25} = -3$, and demand is elastic.

The reason for this is as follows: Because the slope of the demand curve is constant, the absolute change in quantity demanded is the same for a given change in price as we move along the curve. Elasticity varies because the proportional change in quantity (and price) varies depending on the size of quantity (or price) at a particular point. For instance, when price is low and quantity demanded relatively high, a given change in quantity is a smaller proportional change, whereas the change in price will be a larger proportional change, given that price is relatively low.

Therefore, for every linear demand curve, there is an inelastic section (when quantity is high and price is low); a point that is unit elastic (in the middle of the demand curve); and an elastic section (when quantity is relatively low and price relatively high). In fact, on any linear demand curve, the price elasticity of demand ranges from 0 (when it cuts the *Q*-axis) to $-\infty$ (when it cuts the *P*-axis). This is illustrated in Figure 10.2. This means that care is needed when referring to an 'elastic' or an 'inelastic' demand curve; whether a linear demand curve is elastic or inelastic depends upon where on the demand curve we are.

Elasticity and revenue

Another thing we can determine from the elasticity of demand is how total revenue in the market will change as price changes. As we know from the demand curve, the quantity demanded in the market (Q_d) depends on the market price (P). This means that we can write the quantity demanded as a function of price: $Q(P)$. We also know that the total revenue in the market is the number of units sold multiplied by the price (that is, $P \times Q_d$). Therefore, we can express total revenue as a function of P:

$$TR(P) = P \cdot Q_d(P) \tag{10.5}$$

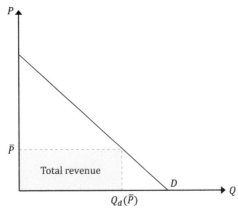

FIGURE 10.3 Total revenue can be calculated by multiplying price and quantity. In this diagram, the size of total revenue is denoted by the grey-shaded area

The size of market revenue can be depicted in a diagram, as shown in Figure 10.3.

We can differentiate this equation with respect to P in order to determine how total revenue changes in response to a small increase in price:

$$\frac{dTR}{dP} = Q_d + P \cdot \frac{dQ_d}{dP} \tag{10.6}$$

By rearranging this equation, we can see how the change in total revenue depends upon the elasticity of demand:

$$\frac{dTR}{dP} = Q_d + P \cdot \frac{dQ_d}{dP} = Q_d \left(1 + \frac{P}{Q_d} \cdot \frac{dQ_d}{dP} \right) = Q_d(1 + \varepsilon_d) \tag{10.7}$$

Equation 10.7 provides a direct link between the price elasticity of demand and the change in total revenue. In order for TR to increase with price, the right-hand side of the equation must be positive. Assuming that $Q_d > 0$, this will be true if and only if $\varepsilon > -1$; that is, if demand is inelastic. On the other hand, if demand is elastic ($\varepsilon < -1$), TR will fall when the market price rises.

Consider this conclusion in light of Figure 10.2. On the elastic part of the demand curve (that is, the upper part) the price needs to be lowered in order to increase TR. On the inelastic part of the demand curve (that is, the lower part) the price needs to be raised in order to increase TR. What this suggests is that TR is maximised when demand is unit elastic, in the middle of the demand curve. Indeed, we can confirm this by noting that when $\varepsilon = -1$, $\frac{dTR}{dP} = 0$.

To provide some intuition for this result, recall that the elasticity of demand measures how responsive the quantity demanded is to changes in price. If demand is elastic, a 1% increase in price will cause a greater than 1% fall in the quantity demanded. This means that the increase in P is more than offset by the decrease in Q_d, causing TR to fall overall. Conversely, if demand is inelastic, a 1% increase in price will cause the quantity demanded to fall but by less than 1%. Thus, the increase in P outweighs the decrease in Q_d, causing TR to increase overall.

10.3.2 Elasticity of supply

The concept of elasticity can also be applied to supply. **Elasticity of supply (ε_s)** measures how sensitive the quantity supplied of a good (Q_s) is to changes in price (P). That is, what is the proportional change in quantity supplied of a good, given a 1% change in its price? The midpoint (arc) method and the point method for calculating elasticity of supply are as follows:

<table>
<tr><td>*Midpoint method*</td><td>*Point method*</td></tr>
<tr><td>$$\varepsilon_s = \frac{\Delta Q_s}{\Delta P} \cdot \frac{P^m}{Q_s^m}$$</td><td>$$\varepsilon_s = \frac{dQ_s}{dP} \cdot \frac{P}{Q_s}$$</td></tr>
</table>

The elasticity of supply is typically positive, due to the law of supply. Again, we can characterise the values of elasticity of supply as follows:

- If $\varepsilon_s = 0$, supply is **perfectly inelastic**. For a 1% change in price, there is no change in the quantity supplied; in other words, quantity supplied is not at all responsive to changes in price. In this special case, the supply curve is vertical, as shown in Figure 10.4.
- If $0 < \varepsilon_s < 1$, supply is **inelastic**. For a 1% change in price, the change in quantity supplied is less than 1%; in other words, quantity supplied is not very responsive to changes in price.
- If $\varepsilon_s = 1$, supply is **unit elastic**. For a 1% change in price, there is a 1% change in quantity supplied; in other words, the quantity supplied changes by the same proportion as the price.
- If $\varepsilon_s > 1$, supply is **elastic**. For a 1% change in price, the change in quantity supplied is more than 1%; in other words, quantity supplied is very responsive to changes in price.

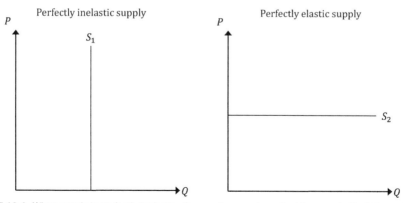

FIGURE 10.4 When supply is perfectly inelastic, the supply curve is vertical (as seen in the left panel). When supply is perfectly elastic, the supply curve is horizontal (as seen in the right panel)

- If $\varepsilon_s = \infty$, supply is **perfectly elastic**. For a small decrease in price, quantity supplied will drop to zero. Intuitively, this means that if the price of a good falls below a certain level, firms will stop supplying the product. In this special case, the supply curve is horizontal, as shown in Figure 10.4.

10.3.3 Cross-price elasticity

Sometimes we are interested in the relationship between the quantity demanded of one good and the price of another related good. This relationship can be examined using **cross-price elasticity**.[5] This measures how sensitive the quantity demanded of a Good A (Q_A) is to changes in price of Good B (P_B).

Midpoint method

$$\varepsilon_{AB} = \frac{\Delta Q_A}{\Delta P_B} \cdot \frac{P_B^m}{Q_A^m}$$

Point method

$$\varepsilon_{AB} = \frac{dQ_A}{dP_B} \cdot \frac{P_B}{Q_A}$$

Example. Suppose that, when the price of teabags is $4 per box, Candice sells 100 litres of milk. If the price of teabags rises to $8 per box, Candice only sells 60 litres of milk. Let us use the midpoint formula to calculate cross-price elasticity. Here, $\Delta Q_A = -40$ and $\Delta P_B = 4$. The average values for price and quantity are $Q_A^m = 80$ and $P_B^m = 6$. Therefore, cross-price elasticity is $\varepsilon_{AB} = \frac{-40}{4} \cdot \frac{6}{80} = -0.75$.

Cross-price elasticity provides some information about the relationship between the two products:

- If $\varepsilon_{AB} > 0$, an increase in the price of Good B is associated with a rise in the quantity demanded of Good A. This means that Good A and Good B are **substitutes**. That is, they are goods that are likely to be consumed in place of each other, for example tea and coffee.
- If $\varepsilon_{AB} < 0$, an increase in the price of Good B is associated with a fall in the quantity demanded of Good A. This means that Good A and Good B are **complements**. That is, they are goods that are likely to be consumed together, for example bacon and eggs.
- If $\varepsilon_{AB} = 0$, an increase in the price of Good B is not associated with any change in the quantity demanded of Good A. This means that Good A and Good B are **independent goods**. That is, the two goods are completely unrelated, for example ice cream and chainsaws.

10.3.4 Income elasticity

The demand for a good may also depend, in part, on a consumer's income. **Income elasticity (η)**[6] measures how sensitive the quantity demanded of a good (Q) is to changes in income (Y). Applying the midpoint and point methods gives us:

Midpoint method   *Point method*

$$\eta = \frac{\Delta Q}{\Delta Y} \cdot \frac{Y^m}{Q^m}$$ $$\eta = \frac{dQ}{dY} \cdot \frac{Y}{Q}$$

We can characterise the good, depending upon its income elasticity:

- If $\eta < 0$, demand for the good decreases when income rises. This type of good is called an **inferior good**. An example of an inferior good might be offal; as income increases, consumers can afford to eat superior cuts of meat.
- If $\eta = 0$, demand for the good does not change when income rises. This type of good is called a **neutral good**.
- If $0 < \eta \leq 1$, when income rises by 1%, demand for the good increases by less than 1%. This type of good is called a **normal good**. An example of a normal good might be food generally; as income increases, consumers will consume more food, but the increase is likely to be proportionally less than the increase in income.
- If $\eta > 1$, when income rises by 1%, demand for the good increases by more than 1%. This type of good is called a **luxury good**. An example of a luxury good might be caviar; if income increases by 1%, the consumption of caviar will likely rise by more than 1%.

10.4 Concluding comments

Elasticity measures the proportional change in one variable, given a proportional change in another variable. The concept can be applied to any two variables of interest. Most commonly, economists will be interested in the elasticity of demand, the elasticity of supply, cross-price elasticity and income elasticity. However, in some cases we might be interested in other relationships. For example, a business might like to know how the quantity demanded for its product changes in response to an advertising campaign; policy makers might want to measure consumers' response to a government subsidy.

The concept of elasticity is unit-free, in the sense that it is measured in proportions and not units (such as pounds, milligrammes, dollars, and so on). This allows comparisons across markets and between countries.

Finally, elasticity will depend on a range of factors, including the time frame considered. In general, we would expect elasticities to be greater in the long run than in the short run, as people have time to adapt to the new change. For example, the elasticity of demand for petrol is likely to be inelastic in the short run, because many machines rely on petrol to run. However, over a longer term, individuals and firms are better able to adopt alternative energy sources, making the demand for petrol more elastic in the long run.

Notes

1   The percentage change is the proportional change in a variable multiplied by 100.
2   Here, %Δ simply means 'percentage change'.
3   Also known as 'price elasticity (of demand)' or 'own-price elasticity (of demand)'.
4   There are exceptional cases in which the law of demand does not hold; that is, the quantity demanded of a good *rises* when there is an increase in that good's price so that the demand curve has a positive slope in that range. These particular goods are called 'Giffen goods'. (A good for which the law of demand holds is called an 'ordinary good'.) However, there is very little evidence to support the existence of Giffen goods in the real world, and we do not focus on them in this text.
5   This is also called 'cross-price elasticity of demand'.
6   Also known as 'income elasticity of demand'.

PART IV

Types of markets

CHAPTER **11**

Introduction to markets

11.1 Introduction to the four types of markets

We have outlined the fundamental tools necessary for a basic understanding of markets. We will see that alternative market structures result in different competitive environments and outcomes. An understanding of how different markets work is essential for both firms competing with each other and for policy makers wishing to influence market outcomes.

In the following chapters, we will look at four different types of markets:

- **Perfectly competitive markets.** In these markets, there are many buyers and sellers. There are low barriers to entry and all producers sell an identical product. Consequently, firms do not have the market power to set prices.
- **Monopoly markets.** Here, there is only one seller and high barriers to entry. As a result, the single producer has the power to choose the price that it charges.
- **Monopolistically competitive markets.** In these markets, there are many firms that differentiate themselves from each other by selling slightly different products. As a result, these firms have some scope to set their own prices. There are, however, low barriers to entry.
- **Oligopoly markets.** In these markets, there is only a handful of sellers and high barriers to entry. Depending on the market, there may or may not be product differentiation. The actions of each firm in the market affect other firms, so firms have some power to set prices but their choices may be dictated by the actions of other firms in the market.

DOI: 10.4324/9781003376644-15

The four types of markets are summarised in the table below:

TABLE 11.1 Four types of markets

	Number of firms	Barriers to entry	Power to set price	Product differentiation
Perfect comp.	Many	Low	No	No
Monopoly	One	High	Yes	N/A
Mono. comp.	Many	Low	Yes	Yes
Oligopoly	Few	High	Yes	Sometimes

CHAPTER **12**

Perfect competition

12.1 Introduction

In previous chapters, we have referred to competition and competitive markets. In this chapter, we examine more formally what is meant by these terms. In particular, we construct a theoretical market, called a perfectly competitive market, that has the most extreme characteristics in terms of competition. We also consider economic outcomes in such a market in both the short and long run, and revisit the profit and welfare implications in each case.

12.2 Characteristics of perfect competition

Perfectly competitive markets have the following characteristics:

1) **Many buyers and sellers.** Any one buyer or seller is only a very small part of the total market in terms of the quantity demanded or supplied.
2) **Homogeneous products.** All goods or services offered in the market are identical so that, for a given price, consumers are indifferent as to who they purchase from. We also assume that all firms have access to the same technology.
3) **Price taker.** Given they are trading a homogeneous product and the number of buyers and sellers, no individual has sufficient market power to influence market prices – that is, every participant is a price taker.
4) **Free entry and exit.** Firms can freely (that is, costlessly) enter and exit the market in the long run. In other words, there are no barriers to entry in the long run.

DOI: 10.4324/9781003376644-16

12.3 Supply in the short run

Recall from Chapter 7 that at least one of a firm's factors of production is fixed in the short run. Consequently, that firm will face a fixed cost of production that will be incurred regardless of its output. In other words, the fixed cost is a sunk cost in the sense that it cannot be recovered no matter what.[1] This means that, in deciding the level of output to produce in the short run, a firm will ignore its fixed costs.

12.3.1 Firm supply in the short run: the shut-down decision

In Chapter 8, we found that if a firm produces output, its supply curve is given by its marginal cost curve. However, we also noted that there may be cases in which a firm will not produce anything at all. If a firm chooses not to produce output in the short run, we say that the firm **shuts down**.

Generally speaking, a firm will shut down if the revenue from selling that output cannot cover the cost of producing it. In the short run, the firm should only take into account its variable costs, as its fixed costs are sunk. That is to say, the firm will have to pay for its fixed inputs regardless of whether or not it produces any output, so it should ignore those costs when deciding whether or not to produce any output. Hence, we can derive the **shut-down condition** that a firm will shut down in the short run if total revenue is less than variable cost:

$$TR < VC. \tag{12.1}$$

We can also divide both sides of Equation 12.1 by the level of output (q) to yield the following condition:

$$\frac{TR}{q} < \frac{VC}{q} \Rightarrow P < AVC. \tag{12.2}$$

This tells us that if the price falls below AVC, a firm will shut down; however, if a firm does produce a positive output, it chooses the level of output in accordance with its supply curve – that is, its MC curve. One final thing to remember is that the MC curve intersects the AVC curve at its minimum.[2]

Therefore, we can rewrite the shut-down rule for a competitive firm given in Equation 12.2 as:

$$P < AVC_{min} \tag{12.3}$$

The flip side of this is, of course, that a firm will produce positive output if $p \geq AVC_{min}$. Therefore, we can say that a firm's short-run supply curve is traced out by the part of its MC curve that lies above AVC_{min}. The short-run supply curve is depicted in Figure 12.1.

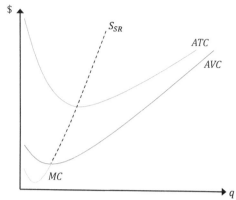

FIGURE 12.1 The short-run supply curve of a firm is traced out by the part of the *MC* curve that lies above *AVC*. In this diagram, it is denoted by the black dashed line

12.3.2 Market supply in the short run

In the short run, there is no entry or exit in the competitive market. A firm is prevented from exiting the market by its fixed costs; if a firm in the market wishes not to produce anything, it shuts down (but does not exit). Additional firms are prevented from entering the market because they do not have the necessary fixed inputs to establish operations. As a consequence, the number of firms in the market is fixed in the short run.

Following the technique outlined in Chapter 8, we can derive the short-run market supply by horizontal summation of the individual supply curves (that is, the *MC* curves above AVC_{min}).

12.3.3 Profits and losses

In a competitive market, it is possible for firms to make profits or incur losses in the short run. Recall from Chapter 7 that profit is simply total revenue minus total cost. Therefore, if a firm is making a positive profit, we know that its total revenue is greater than its total cost:

$$\pi > 0 \Rightarrow TR > TC \tag{12.4}$$

Dividing both sides of this equation by q gives us the equivalent expression:

$$\frac{TR}{q} > \frac{TC}{q} \Rightarrow P > ATC \tag{12.5}$$

In a nutshell, this tells us that if a firm is making profits, it must be the case that the price is greater than the average total cost. Conversely, we can show that if a firm is making losses (i.e. $\pi < 0$), it must be the case that the price is less than the average total cost ($P < ATC$).

Using this information, we can identify in a diagram the area that represents the firm's profit or loss. Figures 12.2 and 12.3 depict a firm making a profit and a loss, respectively. In both figures, the market price is given by P^*. Recall that the firm is a price taker, so this price is determined in the market by the forces of supply and demand (in the left panel), and then the individual firm takes that price as given.

Consequently, the quantity supplied by the firm is q^*, as determined by the firm's supply curve (the MC curve); at that quantity, the firm's average total cost is ATC^*. The difference between P^* and ATC^*, multiplied by the quantity supplied (q^*), represents the firm's profit or loss; in both figures, this is denoted by the grey-shaded areas. In Figure 12.2, price exceeds average total cost, meaning that the grey-shaded area denotes the firm's profits; in Figure 12.3, price is less than average total cost, so the grey-shaded area represents the firm's loss.

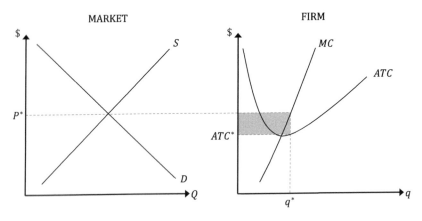

FIGURE 12.2 A firm in a perfectly competitive market, making a profit. The grey-shaded area represents the size of that profit

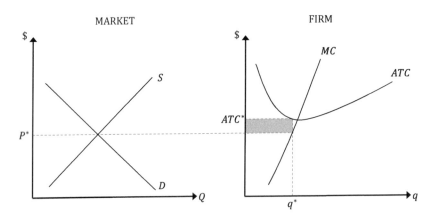

FIGURE 12.3 A firm in a perfectly competitive market, making a loss. The grey-shaded area represents the size of that loss

12.4 Supply in the long run

In the long run, there is free entry and exit in the market. This is because all inputs are variable; a firm wishing to exit the market is not hindered by having to pay fixed costs and a firm wishing to enter the market has the time to acquire all the necessary inputs to start operations. This means that all costs are opportunity costs. Hence, a firm deciding its level of output in the long run will take into account the costs of all inputs.

As we shall see, a firm will enter or exit the market depending on its (anticipated) level profit or loss in the market. The market will reach its long run equilibrium when the number of firms in the market stabilises – that is, there is no longer any entry into or exit from the market. We will argue that this occurs when firms are making zero profits.

In this section, we will discuss how a perfectly competitive market transitions from its short-run equilibrium to its long-run equilibrium.

12.4.1 Firm supply: the exit/entry decision

In the long run, there is free exit from a competitive market. Therefore, if a firm chooses not to produce output in the long run, it can **exit** the market and incur zero production costs. A firm will choose to exit the market if its total revenue is less than its total costs – or, in other words, if its profits are less than zero. From Section 12.3.3, we know that this occurs when $P < ATC$. Because the MC curve intersects the ATC curve at its minimum, we can write the **exit condition** as:

$$P < ATC_{min} \tag{12.6}$$

In the long run, there is also free entry into competitive markets. This captures the fact that firms wishing to enter the market have enough time to obtain the necessary inputs in order to establish operations in the market. A firm will choose to **enter** the market if it can make a profit by doing so ($\pi > 0$). This occurs when $P > ATC$. Noting that the MC curve intersects the ATC curve at its minimum, we can write the **entry condition** as:

$$P > ATC_{min} \tag{12.7}$$

The upshot of this is that a firm's long-run supply curve is traced out by the part of the MC curve that lies above ATC_{min}. The long-run supply curve is depicted in Figure 12.4.

One thing to note, however, is that because all factors are variable in the long run, the firm will choose the most appropriate mix of inputs for its level of output. This may entail a different mix of inputs for various levels of output. What this means is that the firm's long-run marginal cost curve may not be the same as its short-run marginal cost curve – and it is, of course, the long-run marginal cost curve that should be taken into account here. For analytical simplicity, we tend to assume the two curves are identical; however, it is worth bearing in mind that this is not necessarily the case.

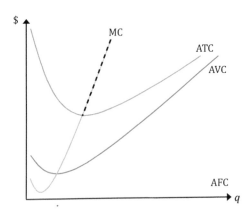

FIGURE 12.4 The long-run supply curve of a firm is traced out by the part of the MC curve that lies above ATC. In this diagram, it is denoted by the black dashed line

12.4.2 Elimination of profits and losses

We have now shown that firms will enter the market if it would be profitable to do so and will exit the market when they are sustaining losses. Together, these decisions will eliminate all profits (and losses) in the market.

- When firms in the market are profitable ($P > ATC$), firm will want to enter the market. The entry of more firms into the market will progressively shift the short-run supply curve to the right, driving the equilibrium price downwards. This shift is illustrated in Figure 12.5 with a shift in the short-run supply curve from S to S'; S' is derived after the entry of new firms into the market, horizontally summing the individual firms' supply curve.
- When firms in the market are sustaining losses ($P < ATC$), they will tend to exit the market. The exit of firms from the market progressively shifts the short-run supply curve left, pushing the equilibrium price upwards. This shift is illustrated in Figure 12.6 with the shift in the short-run supply curve from S to S' after firms have left the industry. (Remember, each short-run supply curve is derived for a fixed number of firms.)

In other words, if the price tends to decrease when it is above ATC and increase when it is below ATC, then it will eventually settle at ATC in the long run. In particular, because the firm supply curve cuts the ATC at its minimum, the price will settle at $P = ATC_{min}$. Thus, because the relationship between price and average total cost determines the level of profits, it follows that there will be **zero profits** in the long run ($\pi = 0$). The long-run equilibrium is depicted in Figure 12.7.

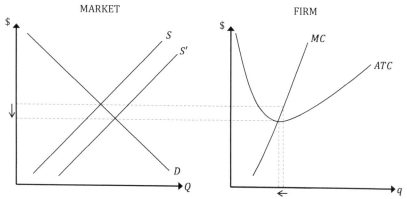

FIGURE 12.5 When the market price is above average total cost, firms in the market are making profits. This will encourage entry into the market, shifting the supply curve right from S to S'. In turn, this will put downward pressure on market prices

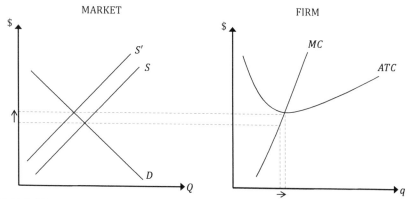

FIGURE 12.6 When the market price is below average total cost, firms in the market are making losses. This will encourage exit from the market, shifting the supply curve left from S to S'. In turn, this will put upward pressure on market prices

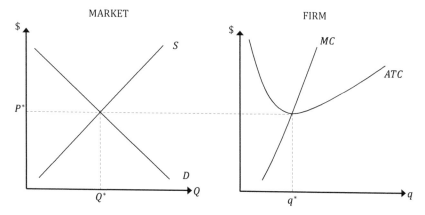

FIGURE 12.7 In the long run, there are zero profits in a perfectly competitive market. This requires $P = ATC_{min}$. Because there are zero profits, there is no incentive for any firm in the market to exit the market and there is no incentive for any additional firms to enter the market. In this diagram, the long-run equilibrium price is P^*, the quantity traded in the market is Q^* and the output of the firm is q^*

12.5 Market supply in the long run

When deriving the long-run market supply curve, we need to account for the fact that the market responds to demand via the entry and exit of firms. In fact, we now know that, in the long run, prices will adjust back to the minimum of the average total cost, no matter what the quantity traded in the market is. This tells us that the long-run supply curve is perfectly elastic at $P = ATC_{min}$, as illustrated in Figure 12.8. An industry with a perfectly elastic long-run industry (or market) supply curve is a **constant-cost industry**. Unless otherwise stated, a competitive industry is assumed to be a constant-cost industry.

This also has another implication. Because a competitive industry minimises ATC in the long run, it also minimises the total cost of production. Moreover, all trade for which $MB > MC$ occur, meaning that all gains from exchange are realised. This means that a perfectly competitive industry maximises the level of total surplus available.

As an example of the dynamics following a change in demand in a constant-cost industry, consider the industry and a representative firm illustrated in Figure 12.9. This Figure shows the short- and long-run changes for both the firm and at the market level following an increase in demand from D_1 to D_2. Note the axes of q and Q for the firm and market. Market price is determined by the intersection of the short-run market supply curve S_1 and demand D_1, as shown in the right-hand panel. Initially the industry is in its long-run equilibrium, as the short-run supply curve S_1 intersects demand D_1 at $P^* = ATC_{min}$. Note that this price $P^* = ATC_{min}$ is the industry's long-run supply curve. In the left-hand panel, the firm has a supply curve of its MC curve above the minimum of its ATC. It takes the market price of P^* as given, and sells the q^* units; this is its profit-maximising output, but it is making zero profits. There is no incentive for entry and exit as all firms in the industry are earning zero economic profits. The equilibrium is also illustrated at the market level.

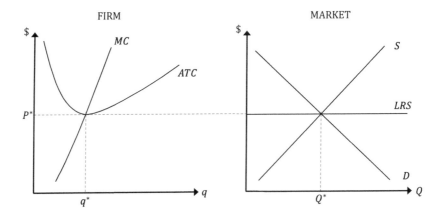

FIGURE 12.8 In the long run, free entry and exit means that the price in a constant-cost industry will always be driven back to ATC_{min}. The long-run market supply curve LRS is perfectly elastic at $P = ATC_{min}$

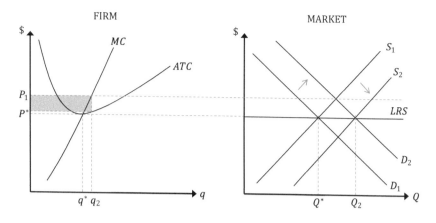

FIGURE 12.9 Following an unanticipated increase in demand, in the short run price rises and firms in the industry make positive economic profits. However, in the long run, entry forces prices back down to the $P^* = ATC_{min}$. Each firm sells q^* units and economic profits are zero

Assume then that there is a shift of demand to D_2. In the short run, there is no entry or exit, so the new market equilibrium is the intersection of S_1 and D_2; price rises to P_2. This is now the price faced by firms (it is their new MR curve). In response they increase their quantity supplied to q_2, and earn positive economic profits, as illustrated by the shaded area.

Finally, consider the new long-run outcome. In the long run, firms are free to enter or exit; given the opportunity for economic profits, new firms will come into the market. With entry, the short-run supply curve will shift to the right. With entry, the market price will be successively determined by the intersection of the short-run market supply curve and D_2. This process of entry and dropping market prices will continue until there is no further incentive for entry (with a short-run supply curve of S_2); this occurs when economic profits are zero, hence when price has dropped to $P^* = ATC_{min}$. In the long-run equilibrium, price equals P^*, which coincides with the long-run supply curve LRS, as well as the intersection of S_2 and D_2. Market output is Q_2.

Note that the price has returned to its original level P^* – again, this is the MR curve for the price-taking firm, and it will supply a quantity of q^*, the same quantity it sold in the original equilibrium outcome with D_1. Thus, although the total quantity supplied in the market has increased (Q_1 to Q_2), each individual firm still sells q^*. The increase in the market output comes about because there are now more firms in the market in the long run.

In a constant-cost industry, this process of entry or exit in the long run following a change in demand ensures that firms earn zero profits and the price is $P^* = ATC_{min}$.

Several caveats are worth noting here. When deriving the long-run industry supply curve in a constant-cost industry, we assume that all firms and potential entrants have the same costs (and access to technology). Consequently, free entry drives price back to the minimum of ATC – this is the only way that there will be no incentive for further entry or exit. However, if potential entrants have higher costs than incumbent firms

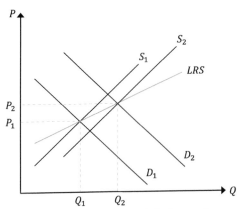

FIGURE 12.10 In an increasing-cost industry, the long-run industry supply curve is upward sloping

(already in the market), the long-run industry supply curve need not be perfectly elastic. One possible example would be the mining industry; existing mines typically have the most accessible mineral deposits (with lower associated costs) than potential entrants, who might have to progressively mine deposits of lower quality or in more difficult and costly locations (deeper under the surface, under the ocean, and so on).

As an illustration, consider Figure 12.10. Following an increase in demand, entry of new firms will continue to occur until the next potential entrant does not anticipate making a positive economic profit (that is, it assumes that following its entry $P <$ ATC_{pe}, where ATC_{pe} is its expected average total costs of production. As the potential entrants have higher costs than the existing market participants, price does not have to fall all the way to the ATC_{min} of firms in the market to prevent further entry; in the long-run equilibrium $P > ATC_{min}$. If we continue to trace out the long-run supply curve (accounting for entry), as demand shifts to the right, with each shift higher-cost firms will enter the market, and the long-run supply curve will be upward sloping. An industry with an upward-sloping long-run supply curve is called an **increasing-cost industry**. Moreover, in an increasing-cost industry, firms (with lower production costs) can earn positive economic profits in the long run.

Finally, consider an alternative scenario, illustrated in Figure 12.11. Suppose that as output in an industry expands, costs for all firms fall. Consider the software industry. As it has expanded (essentially from the 1970s until now), there are increasing numbers of talented programmers and hardware inputs have become cheaper. In this sort of industry, if demand increases, market output will expand and average costs for all firms could actually fall. If this is the case, following an increase in demand, as entry will continue until it is no longer profitable, the new long-run equilibrium price has to be lower than the initial equilibrium price. In this case, the long-run industry supply curve is downward sloping – this is a **decreasing-cost industry**.

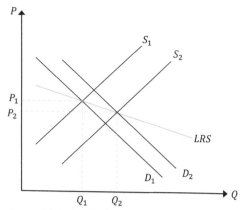

FIGURE 12.11 In a decreasing-cost industry, the long-run industry supply curve is downward sloping

12.6 Concluding comments

In this chapter, we set up a stylised type of competition called a perfectly competitive market. In such a market, we found that firms in the industry can sustain profits or losses in the short run, but that profits and losses will be eliminated in the long run. The driving factor behind this is the assumption of free entry and exit, which allows firms and hence the supply curve to respond to the market price.

In practice, firms in the real world rarely report zero profits, even in markets that are very competitive. There are several reasons why this might be the case. Firstly, it is very unlikely that a real-world market will meet the stringent criteria of perfect competition. For example, firms in the market might have slightly differentiated products or there might not be perfect information about prices. Secondly, it is important to distinguish between accounting profits and economic profits. Real-world firms tend to report accounting profits, whereas this model deals with economic profits. Thirdly, it is possible that real-world markets have not yet 'settled' into their long-run equilibrium. This might occur if there are ongoing demand shocks.

Notes

1   Recall our discussion of opportunity costs versus sunk costs in Chapter 1.
2   See Chapter 7 for why this is the case.

CHAPTER 13

Monopoly

13.1 Introduction

In the last chapter, we looked at a market that exhibited the most extreme characteristics of competition. Now, we turn to the other end of the spectrum: here we examine markets with only one seller. A market with one seller is a **monopoly**, and that seller is a **monopolist**. In this chapter, we will examine how the market power of a monopolist allows it to charge higher prices in order to increase its profits, and we will consider the welfare implications of this market power. We then analyse how the monopolist might use price discrimination to further increase its profits. Finally, we look at the regulation of a natural monopoly, where it is less costly for the whole market to be serviced by one firm rather than two or more.

13.2 Characteristics of a monopoly

Monopolies have the following characteristics:

1) **One seller and many buyers.** There is a single producer of all output in the market.
2) **Price maker.** Because the monopolist is the only firm in the market, it has the market power to determine the price in the market – that is, it is a price maker.
3) **Barriers to entry.** Firms that might like to enter the market are prevented from doing so by barriers to entry. Barriers to entry may exist for a number of reasons: the monopolist may have access to a natural resource or technology that is not available to other firms; the monopolist might hold a patent or a copyright that prevents other firms from selling the same

DOI: 10.4324/9781003376644-17

product; the government might ban entry by other potential sellers; or, the monopolist might simply have a lower cost of production that effectively allows them to prevent other firms from entering the market.

13.3 The single-price monopolist

In this section, we examine the behaviour of a monopolist who charges the same price to all of its consumers (also known as a **single-price monopolist**).

Because the monopolist is the sole producer, it faces all the demand in the market. In other words, the monopolist faces the downward-sloping market demand curve. However, the monopolist does not itself have a supply curve; recall from Chapter 8 that the supply curve applies only to competitive firms, as a supply curve is derived assuming a firm is a price taker.[1] Therefore, we cannot apply our demand–supply framework to determine the price that a monopolist will charge.

Instead, we will determine the monopolist's price by considering its profit-maximising choice. In order to do this, we will first need to understand the monopolist's marginal revenue curve.

13.3.1 Marginal revenue

Marginal revenue is the additional revenue that the firm received from selling one extra unit of a good. Because the monopolist faces a downward-sloping demand curve, if it increases output by one unit the price will fall by some amount. In other words, for a monopolist there are two effects at play: (i) the increase in output increases total revenue, and (ii) the decrease in price decreases total revenue. Either effect could dominate.

To calculate marginal revenue (MR), we differentiate total revenue equation (TR) with respect to output (Q). This tells us how total revenue changes as we increase output by one unit:

$$MR = \frac{dTR}{dQ}.$$

(13.1)

To illustrate how this is done, consider a demand curve given by the equation $P = a - bQ$, where P is price, Q is the quantity demanded, and a and b are positive parameters (for example, the demand curve could be $P = 100 - 2Q$). We can write the total revenue equation as follows:

$$TR = P \times Q = (a - bQ) \times Q = aQ - bQ^2.$$

(13.2)

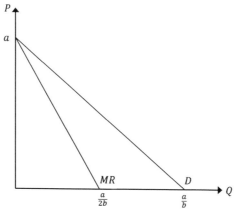

FIGURE 13.1 When the demand curve is linear, the marginal revenue curve has the same vertical intercept and twice the slope of the demand curve

Now, we can differentiate the right-hand side of Equation 13.2 to obtain marginal revenue:

$$MR = \frac{dTR}{dQ} = a - 2bQ. \tag{13.3}$$

Two things should be noted about the MR equation. First, the MR equation has the same vertical intercept as the demand curve; that is, they both cross the P-axis at a. Second, the MR curve has twice the slope of the demand curve; the MR curve has a slope of $-2b$ whereas the demand curve has a slope of $-b$. As a result, the MR curve will intersect the Q-axis at exactly half the quantity of the demand curve intersection; the MR curve cuts the Q-axis at $\frac{a}{2b}$ and the demand curve cuts the Q-axis at $\frac{a}{b}$. This is illustrated in Figure 13.1.

Because we have not specified values for a and b, the equation $P = a - bQ$ could represent any linear demand curve. Hence, our observations about the relationship between the demand and MR equations will hold true for any linear demand curve. What this means is that, for any given linear demand curve, we can obtain the equation of the MR curve by simply doubling the gradient (or slope) of the demand curve equation.[2]

> **Example.** Suppose the demand curve is given by the equation $Q = 100 - 4P$. In order to find the equation of the MR curve, we need to rearrange the demand curve equation so it is expressed with P as the subject: $P = 25 - \frac{1}{4}Q$. Now, to obtain the MR equation, take the slope of the demand curve $(-\frac{1}{4})$ and double it to obtain $MR = 25 - \frac{1}{2}Q$.

13.3.2 Profit maximisation

We can now determine the profit-maximising price (and quality) for a monopolist. Profits will be maximised when a monopolist sets marginal revenue equal to marginal cost. To see why this is the case, recall that profit is the difference between total revenue and total cost:

$$\pi = TR - TC \tag{13.4}$$

Now, to maximise profit, we need to take the first derivative and set it equal to zero:

$$\frac{d\pi}{dQ} = \frac{dTR}{dQ} - \frac{dTC}{dQ} = MR - MC = 0 \tag{13.5}$$

Rearranging gives us the **profit-maximising condition**:

$$MR = MC \tag{13.6}$$

Indeed, if $MR > MC$ the monopolist can increase its profit by selling one extra unit; that is, it should increase production. On the other hand, if $MR < MC$ the monopolist's profit falls from selling the last unit, it would be better off not selling that unit; that is, it should decrease production. Consequently, the profit-maximising level of output for the monopolist is the quantity where $MR = MC$.

> **Example.** Consider a monopolist whose demand curve is given by $P = 100 - Q$ and a total cost curve of $TC = Q^2 + 50$. We can derive the marginal revenue curve by doubling the gradient of the demand curve: $MR = 100 - 2Q$. We can also obtain the marginal cost curve by differentiating the total cost function: $MC = 2Q$. Setting $MR = MC$ yields: $100 - 2Q = 2Q \Rightarrow Q = 25$. We can now substitute $Q = 25$ back into the demand equation to find the monopoly price $P = 100 - 25 = 75$.

The profit-maximising choice for a monopolist is illustrated in Figure 13.2. The monopolist faces a demand curve (D) and a marginal revenue curve (MR). The monopolist also has a total cost curve, from which we can derive marginal cost (MC) and

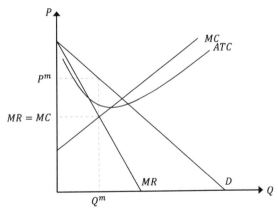

FIGURE 13.2 A profit-maximising monopolist sets $MR = MC$, and thus produces quantity Q^m. At this quantity, the market price will be P^m

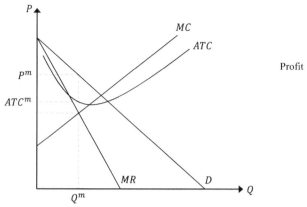

FIGURE 13.3 The monopolist's profit is given by $\pi = Q(P - ATC)$. The area corresponding to the monopolist's profit is shaded grey in this diagram

average total cost (ATC). As can be seen in the diagram, the level of output associated with $MR = MC$ is denoted Q^m. The price associated with this quantity is P^m, which is the profit-maximising price.

We can also use this diagram to show the amount of profit (or loss) made by the monopolist. Recall that profit can be written as follows:

$$\pi = TR - TC = P \times Q - ATC \times Q = (P - ATC)Q \qquad (13.7)$$

Thus, at the profit-maximising outcome (Q^m, P^m), profit is the area between ATC^m and P^m, multiplied by the quantity Q^m. This is represented by the grey-shaded region in Figure 13.3. This also means that the monopolist makes an average profit of $P^m - ATC^m$ on each unit that it sells.

Finally, in the preceding discussion we have framed the monopolist's choice in terms of what price it should charge. That is, the monopolist charges the price P^m, which results in a market quantity of Q^m. However, we might equally look at the problem from the perspective that the monopolist chooses a profit-maximising level of output, Q^m, which determines the price of P^m in the market. Because the demand equation determines the relationship between price and quantity, setting price to maximise profit yields the same outcome if the monopolist chooses the profit-maximising level of output (that is, once either price or quantity is determined, the other variable is determined by the demand curve).

13.4 Welfare under the single-price monopolist

In Chapter 9, we found that welfare is maximised in a competitive market. Recall that, in a competitive market, the market equilibrium is where the demand curve (MB curve) intersects supply (the MC curve) – that is, where $MB = MC$. The quantity traded at this point is called the 'competitive quantity', and is marked Q^* in Figure 13.4. By contrast,

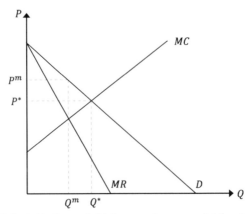

FIGURE 13.4 The quantity traded in the market is lower under monopolist than in a competitive market

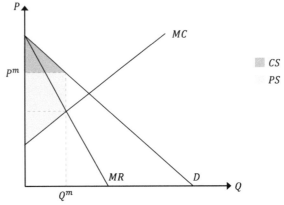

FIGURE 13.5 Consumer surplus and producer surplus under a monopoly

a monopolist trades up to the point where $MR = MC$, selling the 'monopoly quantity', and is marked Q^m in Figure 13.4. Note that as $MB > MR$ for all units $q > 0$, this means that the monopolist sells less than the competitive market quantity Q^*.

13.4.1 Consumer and producer surplus

Let us begin by identifying consumer surplus under a monopoly. Recall from Chapter 9 that the size of consumer surplus is given by the area below the demand curve and above the price line for all units traded. In the case of a monopoly, we will need to use the monopoly price, P^m, rather than the competitive equilibrium price. The area that represents consumer surplus can be seen in Figure 13.5.

Let us now turn to producer surplus. Recall from Chapter 9 that the size of producer surplus is given by the area above the marginal cost curve and below the price line for all units traded. Again, we will need to use the monopoly price, P^m. We will also need to remember that the quantity traded under a monopoly is Q^m, so the untraded units beyond that point to not yield any surplus. Hence, the area of producer surplus will be truncated at Q^m. The area that represents producer surplus can be seen in Figure 13.5.

Compare these areas with the areas of consumer surplus and producer surplus in a competitive market (see Figures 9.6 and 9.8). Notice that the area of consumer surplus under monopoly is smaller than consumer surplus in a competitive market, while the monopolist's producer surplus is larger than that of a competitive market. By charging a higher price, the monopolist is converting some consumer surplus into producer surplus.

13.4.2 Total surplus and deadweight loss

We can now find the total surplus under a monopoly by adding together consumer surplus and producer surplus, as shown in Figure 13.6. Compare this with total surplus in a perfectly competitive market (see Figure 9.10). As you can see, the area of total surplus under a monopoly is smaller than the area of total surplus in a competitive market.

The reason for this is that the quantity traded in the market is lower under a monopoly (Q^m) than under perfect competition (Q^*). As a result, the gains from trade for units between Q^m and Q^* are not realised; that is, there is a loss of welfare resulting from these units not being traded. We refer to this lost welfare as **deadweight loss (DWL)**. The *DWL* of monopoly is also depicted in Figure 13.6.

Thus, a monopoly is inefficient because it does not maximise total surplus. This *DWL* is not caused, per se, by the fact that the monopolist converts consumer surplus into producer surplus. Instead, *DWL is* caused by the fact that this conversion is not perfect; that is, some surplus is lost in the process. By charging a higher price, the monopolist restricts output below the efficient level, and it is this decrease in output that generates the *DWL*. Stated another way, the *DWL* of monopoly is caused because a monopolist restricts its output below the efficient quantity $(Q^m < Q^*)$; as there are consumers in the market with a higher *MB* than the *MC* of producing extra units of the product, total surplus would increase if these extra units were produced (until output reaches Q^*). Rather than total surplus, the monopolist is concerned with maximising

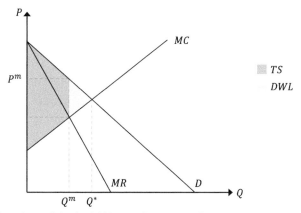

FIGURE 13.6 Total surplus and deadweight loss under a monopoly

its profit; it stops production when $MR = MC$ (at Q^m). As the MR curve lies below MB (the demand curve) for every unit sold except for the very first, it must be the case that $MB > MC$ at the profit-maximising level of output for the monopolist. This ensures that $Q^m < Q^*$ for a monopolist charging a single price to all consumers. As a result, there will be a DWL from monopoly.

13.5 Price discrimination

Let us now turn to the possibility that the monopolist can engage in **price discrimination**. In economics, price discrimination is when a firm charges a different price to different consumers for the same product, or when a firm sells different versions (quality or quantity) of the product when the change in price between the versions does not solely reflect the difference in the cost of production.

Price discrimination allows a monopolist to increase its profit further relative to when it charges the same price to all consumers. Earlier in this chapter, we saw that a monopolist charges a higher price than a competitive firm. But when it does this, the quantity traded in the market falls; in particular, consumers with a lower willingness to pay drop out of the market. The idea behind price discrimination is to bring these consumers back into the market by charging them a lower price, while still charging a higher price to customers with a higher willingness to pay. If a monopolist can charge a high price to those with a high willingness to pay, while also charging a lower price to consumers with a lower willingness to pay, it can increase profits. This is the key intuition behind price discrimination.

In order to engage in price discrimination, a firm will of course need to have the necessary **market power** to determine prices in the market. The firm will also need to be able to **prevent arbitrage**; that is, prevent consumers who are charged a lower price from reselling the product to customers with high willingness to pay. The firm will also need some **information** about different customers and their willingness to pay for the product.

The ability of a monopolist to engage in certain types of price discrimination depends on the information it has and how much it can prevent arbitrage. We now turn to the three different types of price discrimination.

13.5.1 First-degree price discrimination

A monopolist engages in **first-degree price discrimination** (also called 'perfect price discrimination') when it charges each consumer his or her exact willingness to pay (i.e. marginal benefit) for every unit consumed. Consequently, the monopolist extracts all of the consumer's surplus and receives all the gains from trade in every transaction.

> **Example.** Suppose it costs the monopolist $1 to produce an ice cream cone. Bonnie is willing to pay $10 for one ice cream cone, whereas Jen's willingness to pay is

$5. If the monopolist were to charge a single price, it would charge $10 and make a profit of $9. However, a monopolist employing first-degree price discrimination can charge Bonnie $10 for an ice cream cone and charge Jen $5 for an ice cream cone, making a profit of $13.

Of course, in order to engage in first-degree price discrimination, the monopolist will need to have perfect information about each consumer's willingness to pay. It will also need to be able to prevent arbitrage; in the above example, the monopolist would need to be able to prevent Jen from buying two ice cream cones at the lower price and reselling one to Bonnie.

While in the illustration above each consumer purchased at most one unit of the good, first-degree price discrimination can also apply where each consumer buys multiple units of the good (that is, consumers have typical downward-sloping demand curves). In this case, the monopolist can simply price each unit at the relevant consumer's willingness to pay for that unit of the good. The monopolist will continue to sell units to the customer, provided that their $MB \geq MC$. In fact, the MB curve now becomes the MR curve for the first-degree price-discriminating monopolist. Consequently, the monopolist will sell units up to the point where $MB = MC$, meaning that the efficient quantity is traded (i.e. there is no DWL). That is, as the monopolist captures all of the gains from trade, it will want to continue to sell more units, provided $MB \geq MC$. However, as noted above, all surplus in the market is producer surplus. This is illustrated in Figure 13.7.

An alternative way of implementing first-degree price discrimination is by use of a **two-part tariff**. Under a two-part tariff, the monopolist charges the consumer two distinct fees: (i) a fixed fee, F, that does not change with the number of units consumed; and (ii) a per-unit fee, p, that is paid for each unit of the good consumed. In the most obvious cases, the fixed fee could be an entry fee, access fee or membership fee; the per-unit fee would be the price of using the good or service. Examples of this include a joining fee for a gym with a weekly charge, or an access fee for the provision of

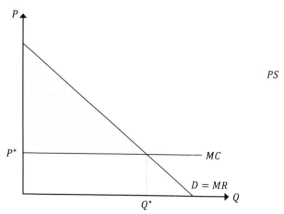

FIGURE 13.7 When the monopolist engages in first-degree price discrimination, the efficient quantity is traded in the market. However, all surplus in the market is producer surplus

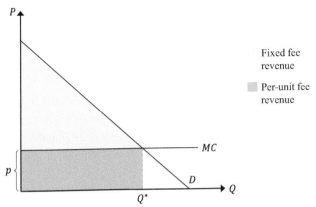

FIGURE 13.8 When the monopolist uses a two-part tariff, it charges a fixed fee (*F*) equal to the size of the lighter grey-shaded triangle. It then charges a per-unit fee (*p*) for each unit consumed equal to *MC*. The total revenue from the per-unit fee is represented by the darker grey-shaded area. The total revenue of the monopolist overall is represented by all of the shaded areas

electricity services and a per-unit fee for the amount of electricity actually consumed. However, there are a number of less obvious cases, where the fixed fee is the price of a core part of the product, and the per-unit price is the price of a non-durable (or less durable) part of the product. Examples of this include a razor handle and razor blades; a printer and ink cartridges; a gaming console and games.

To illustrate how a two-part tariff works, consider Figure 13.8. Suppose D represents the demand curve of a consumer in the market and MC represents the monopolist's marginal cost. In order to induce the consumer to purchase up until the point where $MB = MC$, the monopolist will need to charge a per-unit price of $p = MC$. If the monopolist were not to charge a fixed fee, the consumer would anticipate getting a surplus equal to the area of the light grey triangle; this represents how much more the consumer would have been willing to pay to have access to the product (at a per-unit price of p). Therefore, the monopolist could select a fixed fee that the consumer has to pay before consuming the good, equal to the amount of that consumer surplus ($F = CS$). Thus, the monopolist extracts all of the consumer's surplus, converting it to producer surplus.[3]

Another non-obvious way that a monopolist can engage in first-price discrimination with a pricing mechanism akin to a two-part tariff is to offer every consumer a bundle of their efficient quantity (Q^*, where their $MB = MC$) for a price equal to the area under their demand curve up to Q^*.

13.5.2 Third-degree price discrimination

A monopolist engages in **third-degree price discrimination** when it separates consumers into 'markets' and charges a different price in each market. Some examples of this include adult and student prices for movie tickets; different prices for haircuts for men and women; and different prices for software in different countries.

The information and arbitrage requirements that support third-degree price discrimination are less stringent than for first-degree price discrimination. Firstly, the monopolist needs to have a way of identifying the market that any particular individual belongs to. For example, a monopoly cinema can identify students from non-students as the students have an ID card. Alternatively, a monopolist might be able to identify which type of consumer an individual is from their location (or even the location of their IP address). This information is critical for a monopolist to be able to engage in third-degree price discrimination. Secondly, the monopolist needs to prevent arbitrage between markets; the monopolist, however, does not need to be able to prevent arbitrage within a group. This means that a monopolist can discriminate between groups, but not within groups – this means that they charge a single (different) price to each market. For example, a monopoly cinema charges one price to all students with ID cards and another price to adults without. The monopolist need not prevent one student from on-selling her ticket to another student. Similarly, any adult can buy and resell a ticket to another adult. The cinema does not need to be able to prevent arbitrage (resale) within each market, so they charge one price for a student ticket and a different price for an adult (or non-student) movie ticket. Third, the monopolist does not need to know each individual's demand curve; it only needs to know the demand curve for each market.

Under third-degree price discrimination, the firm essentially acts as a single-price monopolist in each market. This means that it faces a different demand (and hence marginal revenue) curve in each market. Therefore, assuming that the monopolist faces a constant marginal cost, MC, it simply solves for the profit-maximising price/quantity in each market separately. In other words, in Market A, it should set $MR_A = MC$; in Market B it should set $MR_B = MC$; in Market C, $MR_C = MC$; etc.

To illustrate the intuition behind third-degree price discrimination further, consider the case of a monopolist with a constant marginal cost selling to two types of consumers, types A and B, respectively. In each market there is a downward-sloping demand curve and a corresponding marginal revenue curve, labelled here as MR_A and MR_B. To maximise profit, the monopolist will sell at the point where $MR_A = MR_B = MC$. To see why this is the case, first suppose $MR_A > MR_B$; then, the firm could increase profit by selling the last unit of output in market A rather than B. Hence, for profit to be maximised $MR_A = MR_B$. Second, if $MR_A = MR_B > MC$, profit can be increased by increasing output – an extra unit of output generates more revenue than it increases cost. The reverse argument applies if MC exceeds MR. Hence, for profit maximisation MC needs to be equal to MR in both markets.[4]

Finally, note that prices can differ between the two markets. As an example, consider Figure 13.9, which shows a monopolist with a constant MC selling its product to consumers in two markets. As noted above, to maximise profit the monopolist equates $MR_A = MC = MR_B$; however, the price in market A is higher than the price charged in market B. The monopolist charges a higher price in the market with demand that is relatively inelastic, and a lower price in the market with relative elastic demand. For instance, in the example above, often the price for a movie ticket is higher for adults

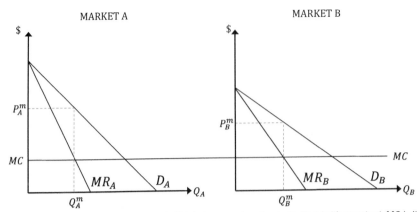

FIGURE 13.9 When a monopolist engages in third-degree price discrimination (with constant MCs), it maximises profit where $MR_A = MR_B = MC$. The price is higher in the market where demand is relatively inelastic; here $P_A > P_B$

than students – this is because adults are in the market with relatively inelastic demand compared with students.

13.5.3 Second-degree price discrimination

A monopolist can engage in **second-degree price discrimination** when it knows that there are different types of consumers in terms of their *WTP*, but it does not know the type of any particular individual consumer. For example, in a market there might be high-value consumers (with a *WTP* for the product of $100) and low-value consumers (with a *WTP* of $50), but the monopolist might not be able to ascertain which group any person falls into. Note the difference between third-degree and second-degree price discrimination; with third-degree, the monopolist needs to know exactly what type of consumer every individual is (a student, a non-student, etc.), but with second-degree the monopolist needs only to know the possible types of consumers.

Because the monopolist cannot identify which type any particular consumer is, it needs to offer different versions of the product (at different prices) so that the consumers 'self-select' through their product choice. The idea here is that the versions of the product will be designed so that the high-value consumer will buy the expensive product, and the low-value consumer will buy the cheaper product. In order to effectively do this, the monopolist must design the different versions so that the high-value consumer is at least as well off buying the expensive product as buying the cheaper option (and the low-value customer must be at least as well off buying the cheaper product as not buying at all). If not, the high-value consumer will opt for the cheaper version, reducing the monopolist's profit.

A classic example of second-degree price discrimination is airline tickets. An airline might know that there are two types of travellers: a business traveller with a high willingness to pay, and a leisure traveller with a relatively low willingness to pay. The problem for the airline is that they do not know whether a potential customer is a business or leisure traveller. So, the airline could offer two types of tickets for sale –

business class (expensive) and economy (cheap). In order to get the business traveller to buy the expensive ticket, she must be better off flying business rather than economy. The airline can 'encourage' this choice by increasing the value of the expensive option (business-class lounge, flexible ticketing arrangements, better food, more comfortable seats) and by making the cheaper option less attractive (lower service quality, inflexible ticketing arrangements, uncomfortable seats, unpalatable food). Reducing the attractiveness of the economy ticket encourages the high-value traveller to opt for the business-class ticket. It also increases the amount that the airline can charge for the expensive option, because the cheaper version of the product gives the high-value consumer less net surplus.

Other examples of second-degree price discrimination abound. The 'versions' of the product sold by the monopolist may be different in quality, quantity or even timing: for example, a soft drink manufacturer may sell cans of soft drink individually or in boxes of 24 with the intention that people who drink more soft drink will opt for the 24 pack; similarly, a toothpaste manufacturer might charge a different per-unit price for a small tube than it does for a larger tube of toothpaste; or, a pub may charge less for drinks during happy hour than otherwise. Fashion labels typically charge higher prices for items in a new collection while offering discounts on last season's stock, discriminating between those consumers who can and cannot wait.

Finally, note that second-degree price discrimination has lower information and arbitrage requirements than the other two types of price discrimination – all that the monopolist needs to know is the different types of consumers there are in the market. Because any individual consumer can purchase any of the versions, there are no advantages to resale and therefore a monopolist need not be able to prevent arbitrage. The monopolist will still need to know the demand curve of individuals who belong to a particular group, but they need not be able to identify which group an individual consumer belongs to. This is because second-degree price discrimination relies on self-selection – that is, the consumer will of their own volition buy the version that is intended for them.

13.5.4 Further comments about price discrimination

Price discrimination is a way that a monopolist can increase its profits. Indeed, the ability to price discriminate will never decrease a firm's profits, because the monopolist always has the option of just charging a single price to all consumers.

As stated above, the ability to employ price discrimination depends upon the firm's ability to prevent arbitrage and the information they have about consumers. Because price discrimination increases profit, it is often beneficial for the monopolist to take steps to prevent resale or to learn more about their consumers. Examples of steps that firms take to prevent resale include terms and conditions that void warranties if the product is resold and the non-transferability of airline tickets. Examples of steps taken to learn more about consumers include online sellers using cookies to track a consumer's previous purchases, location, and so on.

In our discussion above, we discussed the three types of price discrimination. However, it should be noted that it is possible for a monopolist to employ different types of price discrimination in combination. For example, public transport tickets exhibit characteristics of both third- and second-degree price discrimination. Usually, there are different prices for adults and students, who can be differentiated from each other based on whether they hold a student card. There are usually discounted prices at the weekend and consumers are left to decide for themselves when to travel.

13.6 Natural monopoly

A **natural monopoly** is an industry where a single firm can supply an entire market at a lower cost than two or more firms could. Typically, this occurs where the industry has a large fixed cost and relatively low marginal costs. Some examples of natural monopolies are electricity, water and communications networks, where the cost of building the infrastructure is high, but the marginal cost of delivering the service is relatively low.

One example of a natural monopoly is when a firm has declining average total costs for all relevant levels of output required in a market. This might occur if the firm has a high fixed cost and constant marginal costs, as illustrated in Figure 13.10. In this case, a single firm will be able to produce a given level of output at a lower average cost than two or more firms, because a single firm only has to incur the fixed cost once, whereas multiple firms would have to incur the large fixed cost once each.

A natural monopoly arises from the combination of the level of demand and the state of technology (or production costs). It is possible that an industry will cease to be a natural monopoly if the level of demand increases sufficiently such that two firms could meet the required quantity at a lower cost than could one firm. It is also possible that a change in the state of technology will alter the costs of production (and hence the cost function) so that it is cheaper to produce the required output with two or more firms. For example, the telecommunications industry has undergone significant technological changes, meaning that some services that were historically natural monopolies are not anymore.

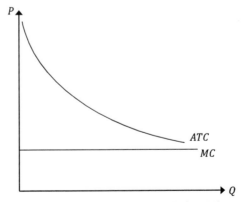

FIGURE 13.10 When a firm has a fixed cost and a constant marginal cost, the average total cost curve will be downward sloping for all values of Q; this industry will be a natural monopoly

13.7 Regulating a natural monopoly

Assuming it is charging a single price (and not engaging in first-degree price discrimination), a natural monopoly will create a DWL. One way the government may wish to address this problem is by intervening in the market. In this section, we discuss three options: government ownership of the monopoly, marginal-cost price regulation and average-cost price regulation.

13.7.1 Government ownership

A privately owned monopoly will maximise profit, disregarding its impact on overall welfare. In principle, the government could take over the ownership and operation of the monopoly and charge the welfare-maximising price (rather than the profit-maximising price).

However, this option can be difficult to implement in practice. The government will need to employ a manager to run the firm; it is unlikely that the government itself will have the skills or knowledge to run such a business. Moreover, the manager will typically have personal objectives that conflict with the goal of welfare-maximisation – a manager may wish to maximise their own perks, empire building, and so on, and without an explicit performance contract, the manager will have little incentive to minimise costs, which itself could lead to a loss in surplus. This could result in *DWL* greater than that of a privately owned monopoly. Of course, this is not to say that government ownership will always be problematic; rather, we should just be mindful that it is not necessarily the best solution in all circumstances, and that care is needed to mitigate the issues that government ownership itself creates.

13.7.2 Marginal-cost price regulation

The government could also regulate the price that the monopolist can charge. In order to maximise surplus, the government may wish to mandate that the monopolist charge the efficient price, $P = MC$. This would ensure that an efficient quantity is traded in the market, thereby eliminating any DWL.

However, at this price, the monopolist only covers its variable costs of production. As seen in Figure 13.11, the monopolist will make a loss equal to the size of its fixed costs and may choose to exit the market in order to avoid incurring that loss. If the government wants the monopolist to stay in the market, it will need to subsidise the monopolist so that the monopolist can cover its fixed costs. Such a subsidy may be problematic. It can be politically unpopular to funnel tax revenue to a monopolist given the many other things a government could do with those funds. Moreover, raising tax revenue generally results in a DWL in another market (as we will see later in Chapter 16), meaning that there may still be a loss of surplus.

13.7.3 Average-cost price regulation

To avoid the need for a subsidy, the government could instead impose a price equal to the average cost, so that the monopolist is able to charge a price that just covers its

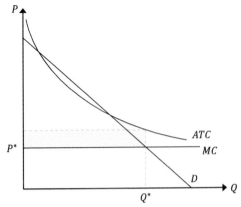

FIGURE 13.11 Under marginal-cost price regulation, the government sets the monopoly price at $P = MC$ (assuming constant MC for simplicity). However, this means that the monopolist makes a loss equal to the grey-shaded area (that is, its fixed costs). The government will need to subsidise the monopolist that amount to prevent them from leaving the market

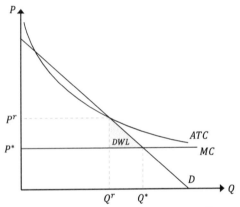

FIGURE 13.12 Under average-cost price regulation, the government sets the monopoly price at $P = ATC$. However, the monopolist will produce less than the efficient quantity, so there is still some dead weight loss equal to the size of the grey-shaded area. However, note that regulation decreases the area of deadweight loss, relative to no regulation at all

cost of production. This type of regulation is illustrated in Figure 13.12. In this case, price is set equal to the point where the ATC curve intersects the demand curve. At this price, the quantity sold in the market is Q^r. Note, however, that this quantity is less than the efficient quantity, Q^*. What this means is that there is still some DWL, albeit at a lower level than without any regulation at all.

13.7.4 Hidden information

As we have seen so far, regulation of a natural monopoly is difficult and the government's ability to improve welfare is not guaranteed. This situation is only worsened when we consider the fact that the government usually has limited information about the market, costs and technologies. Furthermore, the monopolist is more likely to have better information about these factors, but it is not in its interest to reveal this information to the government. For example, if the government is proposing to implement marginal cost pricing, it is in the interest of the monopolist to convince the government that its marginal cost is high, even if its marginal cost is actually low. That way, it gets to charge a higher price and make a profit.

13.8 Concluding comments

In this chapter, we looked at a market in which there were many buyers but only one seller – that is, a monopoly. We first examined what would happen in the market if the monopolist was permitted only to charge a single price to all consumers. In such cases, a profit-maximising monopolist raises prices above marginal costs; consequently, there is a loss in welfare arising from the lower quantity traded in the market. We then considered instances in which a monopolist could increase its profits further by engaging in price discrimination. Finally, we looked at the case of natural monopolies and how they might be regulated or controlled by the government.

Notes

1 The supply curve shows the quantity that a firm will supply, given a certain price – this thought experiment is only valid if a firm assumes that it cannot influence the market price. However, because the monopolist is a price maker, it does not take price as a given.
2 However, to use this shortcut, we will first need to ensure that the equation of the demand curve is expressed with P as the subject.
3 Here, after paying the fixed fee F and the per-unit price p, the consumer has a net $CS = 0$; the consumer is actually indifferent between buying the product and not consuming at all; hence, with first-degree price discrimination, the monopolist captures all of the surplus available from trade. What is critical here is that a fixed fee F cannot be more than the anticipated CS a consumer will accrue once having access to the product. If it is, the consumer will not buy the product at all.
4 If a monopolist has increasing MCs, the same key relationships between MC and MR in both markets hold. However, we need to take into account that an increase in output in one market also increases the marginal cost of production in the other market. We leave this issue aside here to focus on the key intuition of the problem.

CHAPTER 14

Monopolistic competition

14.1 Introduction

Our discussion of markets so far has focused on two extreme cases: first, we looked at competitive markets, where there were many firms each of whom had no market power; second, we looked at a monopoly, where there was just one seller. In reality most markets do not fall at either end of these extremes.

In this chapter, we will look at the case of **monopolistic competition**. In a monopolistically competitive market, there are many firms selling slightly differentiated products. Product differentiation means that there is no perfect alternative to any one product available for sale in the market. Because each firm has a unique product, each seller has some market power in that they can raise their price and not have the quantity demanded for their product fall to zero. This means that firms in monopolistic competition are price makers, not price takers like competitive firms. For example, restaurants sell different types of cuisine and have different menus, meaning that each restaurant has some degree of power to set its own prices. Similarly, convenience stores may be differentiated by their locations; a convenience store one hour away is not quite the same as a convenience store just down the street. As a result, each individual convenience store has some degree of market power and acts like a mini-monopolist in their local market.

14.2 Characteristics of monopolistic competition

A monopolistically competitive market has the following characteristics:

1) **Many buyers and sellers.** This implies that no producer has complete control over the price, because buyers can always switch to other sellers.

DOI: 10.4324/9781003376644-18

2) **Product differentiation.** Each firm sells a slightly differentiated product. This includes differences in the good or service itself, as well as differences in the location of the firm and other factors that may influence the benefit (the convenience, for example) of buying from a particular firm.

3) **Free entry and exit.** Firms can freely (that is, costlessly) enter and exit the market in the long run. In other words, there are no barriers to entry in the long run.

14.3 The short run

In a monopolistically competitive market, each firm sells a slightly differentiated product. Because a firm's product is slightly different from that of its competitors, it has some control over the price it charges. In other words, each firm in a monopolistically competitive market faces a downward-sloping demand curve; that is, if the firm raises its price slightly, there will be some drop off in the quantity demanded, but that quantity demanded does not necessarily fall to zero. This means that a firm in monopolistic competition is a price maker, not a price taker like a firm in a competitive market. Consequently, a monopolistically competitive firm sets a profit-maximising price (or quantity) in the same way that a monopolist does, as described in detail below.

Consider, for example, the case of the restaurant market in an inner-city area. For a particular consumer, there is one Thai restaurant that she likes best – it is her favourite place to eat. If that Thai restaurant raises its prices slightly, this customer might still choose to eat there, even though there are plenty of other options. That is, this Thai restaurant can put its prices up and not have the quantity demanded for its product drop to zero (although it might decrease somewhat). As noted, a competitive firm has no scope to raise price – any increase in price will result in the quantity demanded for its product to falling to zero. This is because consumers can never be induced to pay more than the market price because all goods are identical – all goods are perfect substitutes. This is not the case in monopolistic competition. While different goods might be similar, they are not perfect substitutes, and it is this product differentiation that gives monopolistically competitive firms market power.

Let us now consider the profit-maximising choice of a firm in monopolistic competition. In the short run, the number of firms in the market is fixed. This is because each firm faces a fixed cost of production, which constrains the ability of firms to enter and exit the market in the short run. From the perspective of an individual firm, this means that the number of its rivals is fixed in the short run; hence, its short-run demand curve is derived for a given number of firms currently in the market.

The decisions of a monopolistically competitive firm are depicted in Figure 14.1. The firm faces a downward-sloping demand curve, D. From this, we can determine the marginal revenue curve (MR), which lies below the demand curve.[1] The firm also has a total cost curve, from which we can derive marginal cost (MC) and average total cost (ATC). The firm maximises profit by setting $MR = MC$.[2] The intersection of MR and MC is associated with the quantity q^n and the price P^n.

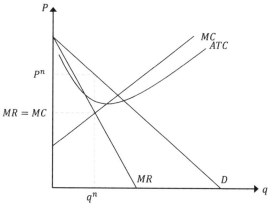

FIGURE 14.1 A firm in a monopolistically competitive market in the short run. The firm maximises its profits by setting $MR = MC$. Thus, the firm sells q^n units of its product, at a price of P^n

Note that this is essentially the same as the problem faced by a monopolist. Indeed, because the firm sells a unique (i.e. differentiated) product, it acts as a mini-monopolist in the market. Hence, in the short run, a firm in a monopolistically competitive market can make an economic profit (or loss), depending on whether the price charged is higher (or lower) than the average total cost.

14.4 The long run

In the long run, there is free entry and exit in the market. Like perfect competition, firms will enter the market if they believe that they can make positive profits by doing so and firms will leave the market if they are sustaining losses.

14.4.1 Effects of entry and exit on demand curves

If a new firm enters the market, this will affect the demand curves of all incumbent firms in the market. There will be two distinct but related effects:

- There will be a decrease in demand for the products of incumbent firms, as the new firm's product offers consumers an alternative. This will shift the demand curve to the left.
- The demand curve for the products of incumbent firms will become more elastic. This represents the fact that if an incumbent firm raises its prices, it is likely to lose more consumers as there are more alternative products for consumers to switch to.

For example, suppose a new laundromat opens up in a suburb neighbouring that of an existing supplier. Some customers may switch from the old laundromat to the new one because it is closer (the first effect). Moreover, customers that stay with the old laundromat will now be more sensitive to changes in its price (the second effect); if the old laundromat were to raise its price by, say, one dollar it would be likely to lose more customers now that there is a nearby alternative.

Conversely, if a firm exits the market, this will affect the demand curves of all firms that remain in the market. Namely, there will be an increase in demand for all remaining firms and the demand curve of those firms will also become less elastic.

14.4.2 Elimination of profits and losses

As in perfect competition, the free entry and exit of firms will eliminate all profits (and losses) in the market. However, under monopolistic competition, this occurs because the entry and exit of firms affect the demand curve of all other firms in the market:

- The entry of firms into the market decreases demand for other firms, thus lowering the price those firms can charge and hence lowering their profits.
- The exit of firms from the market increases demand for other firms, thus increasing the price those firms can charge and hence increasing their profits.

Figure 14.2 illustrates a monopolistically competitive firm in the long run. Notice that the firm still sets $MR = MC$ in order to maximise its profits. This determines the quantity traded by the firm (q^n) and the price that the firm charges (P^n). However, the demand curve (and hence the MR curve) is determined by the entry and exit of firms in the market, such that at the quantity traded (q^n), price is equal to average total cost ($P^n = ATC$) – or, in other words, profit is equal to zero. For both conditions to hold in the long run – that is $MR = MC$ and $P = ATC$ – it must be the case that the ATC is just tangential to the demand curve at q^n (the quantity where $MR = MC$ for the firm). If the ATC cuts the demand curve, there is some quantity of output for which the firm can make a positive profit – this is inconsistent with our assumption of free entry causing zero profits in the long run. Similarly, if ATC always lies above the demand curve, the firm would make a loss at any level of output and would leave the market in

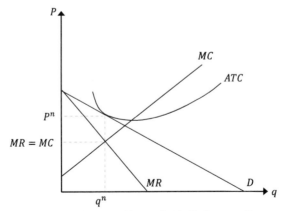

FIGURE 14.2 A firm in a monopolistically competitive market in the long run. Because of the entry and/or exit of other firms in the market, this firm's demand curve (and marginal revenue curve) has shifted such that, at the quantity associated with $MR = MC$, the firm is making zero profits

the long run. The only possibility for profit-maximising by the firm in monopolistic competition ($MR = MC$) and zero profits ($P = ATC$) for $q^n > 0$ is for the ATC curve to just touch the demand curve (and not cross it) at q^n. Furthermore, note here that zero profits means that the firm is making a positive markup on all units it sells ($P > MC$), but these variable profits (that is, revenues minus the variable costs of production) only end up just covering the firm's fixed costs. For example, a convenience store might source a litre bottle of milk for \$2 and sell it for \$5 ($P > MC$), but at the end of the day, all those revenues are exactly equal to all the firm's costs (variable and fixed, assuming the firm is in the market).[3]

14.5 Welfare under monopolistic competition

We have now established that, in the long run, firms in a monopolistically competitive market trade at the point where $P^n = ATC$. Note that, at this point, $ATC > MC$, which means that the average total cost (that is, production costs) is not minimised.[4]

This also implies that $P^n > MC$. Hence, there is a DWL associated with each firm's output, as there are gains from trade that are not realised. This is analogous to the DWL that arises from a monopoly.

However, there are two additional factors that may impact upon welfare that cannot be depicted in the diagram:

- **Business stealing.** A firm entering the market is only concerned with the amount of profit that it can make in the market. It does not account for the fact that its entry takes customers away from incumbent firms. Causing a consumer to switch between firms does not necessarily increase surplus, but it does mean that the economy has to bear another firm's fixed costs of production. This suggests that the number of firms in the market might be too high.
- **Product variety.** On the other hand, a firm entering the market offers additional differentiation in the market. Product differentiation can increase consumer surplus, because a greater variety of products means that the market can better cater to the individual tastes of different consumers. This increase in consumer surplus does not factor into a firm's decision of whether to enter the market, which tends to suggest that the number of firms in the market might not be high enough.

It is unclear which of these two effects will dominate, meaning that there may be too many or too few firms in a monopolistically competitive market.

14.6 Concluding comments

Monopolistic competition sits between the two extremes of perfect competition and monopoly. A firm in monopolistic competition is a price maker – like a monopolist – and can use its market power to set prices greater than marginal cost. However, like in a competitive market, there is free entry and exit in the long run, driving profits to zero over the longer term. The welfare implications of monopolistic competition are somewhat ambiguous. In the long run, because firms set a price greater than marginal cost and earn zero profits, there will be some DWL generated, and each firm will not be producing at a level of output that minimises their costs of production. However, any welfare analysis really should take into account the fact that there is product differentiation. This means that, for a given market, there could be too many firms (if the business stealing effect dominates) or too few (if the product variety effect is more important) relative to the efficient number.

Notes

1   See Chapter 13 for how to calculate the equation of the marginal revenue curve.
2   See Chapter 13 on why this maximises profit.
3   We are, admittedly, being somewhat loose with our use of the term fixed cost here as in the long run there are no fixed costs – we are assuming the firm is producing in the long run, and given it is in the market it will have some variable and some invariant (fixed) costs, like the rent it has to pay for its shop. The intention here is to emphasise that even though a monopolistically competitive firm has a price greater than its marginal cost, it ends up making zero economic profits.
4   Recall from Chapter 7 that the marginal cost curve cuts the average total cost curve at its minimum. If $ATC > MC$, this means that the ATC curve has not yet reached its minimum.

CHAPTER 15

Oligopoly

15.1 Introduction

We now turn to the case of **oligopoly**, a market that contains a small number of firms. Because there are only a handful of key producers in the market, the decisions of each firm have ramifications not only for itself but also for each of its competitors. For example, if Dell adjusts the price of its laptops, this could have an impact on its competitors, like HP. Similarly, if Coles decides to advertise, it might be able to increase its customer base at the expense of Woolworths.

Given the impact oligopolists have on one another, a firm's strategic choice – price, output, product range and so on – will need to take into account what other firms in the market are doing. For instance, if Pepsi introduces a new energy drink, Coca-Cola may choose to respond with its own alternative. In a similar way, if Samsung introduces a new phone handset, Apple may take that into account when designing the new version of its iPhone.

This **strategic interaction** between firms is a key feature of oligopoly, which we can model using game theory. We have previously discussed the core concepts and tools of game theory in Chapter 3. In this chapter, our goal is to illustrate how game theory tools can be applied in the context of an oligopoly. In doing so, we will highlight a few key examples of how firms in an oligopoly strategically interact with each other, but our examples will by no means be an exhaustive demonstration of what game theory can tell us in this context. You should familiarise yourself with the contents of Chapter 3 before embarking on this chapter.

DOI: 10.4324/9781003376644-19

15.2 Characteristics of an oligopoly

Oligopolies have the following characteristics:

1) **Few sellers and many buyers.** Output in the market is produced by a handful of firms.
2) **Price maker.** Because there are only a small number of firms in the market, each firm retains the power to set its own prices.
3) **Barriers to entry.** Entry into the market is difficult, as there are high barriers to entry.
4) **Product differentiation.** Products may be differentiated or not, depending on the market.

15.3 Simultaneous-move games

Often firms will need to make strategic decisions without knowledge of what other firms in the market have decided to do. For example, the board at Pepsi may need to decide how to launch a new energy drink without knowing what its competitors are doing. In such circumstances, firms make decisions as though their choices were made simultaneously, in the sense that they do not have knowledge of other firms' decisions. In such cases, it will be appropriate to analyse the strategic interaction of those firms as a simultaneous-move game.[1]

15.3.1 Price wars: an example of a prisoner's dilemma

In some cases, the 'game' faced by the firms in an oligopoly might resemble a prisoner's dilemma. As an illustration, consider the pricing game outlined in Chapter 3. In that example, two firms faced the choice of setting their prices high (p_H) or low (p_L) without knowledge of what the other firm had chosen. If the firms 'cooperated' and set their prices high, both would receive a profit of $4. However, if one firm chooses p_L undercutting its rival who chose p_H, the payoffs are $5 and $1, respectively. If both firms set their prices low, they would each receive a payoff of $3.[2]

The normal form of this game is represented in Figure 15.1.

		Firm 2	
		p_H	p_L
Firm 1	p_H	(4,4)	(1,5)
	p_L	(5,1)	(3,3)

FIGURE 15.1 Price-setting game in an oligopoly

Firm 2

	NA	A
NA	(0,0)	(−200,100)
A	(100, −200)	(−100, −100)

FIGURE 15.2 Advertising game in an oligopoly. In this figure, 'A' represents the choice to advertise and 'NA' represents the choice to not advertise

This game is a prisoner's dilemma because (a) it has a dominant strategy equilibrium in which both players choose p_L, and (b) this equilibrium does not maximise surplus as both players would receive greater profit if they both chose p_H. Note here that the firms are collectively worse off in the Nash equilibrium than they would be if they could somehow cooperate and both choose p_H. This is not possible, however, as it is individually rational for each firm to opt for the low price. This example is a demonstration that in oligopoly, the competitive interaction between rivals often makes it difficult for firms to not undercut one another, reducing industry profits. Moreover, this suggests that a very competitive outcome (and corresponding level of social welfare) is possible with relatively few firms in the market.

Another example of a prisoner's dilemma in an oligopoly is the decision of two rival firms whether or not to advertise. If neither firm advertises, there will be no effect on customer purchasing behaviour. If one firm advertises and the other does not, the first firm may steal some customers from the second. However, if both firms advertise, the advertising campaigns will cancel each other out and there will be no effect on customer purchasing behaviour. Suppose the cost of advertising is $100, and if only one firm advertises, it can steal $200 worth of business from the other firm, making a $100 net gain. In this case, the normal form of this game is represented in Figure 15.2. Again, the dominant strategy equilibrium is one in which both players advertise, but both players would be better off if neither chose to advertise.

15.3.2 Can firms avoid the prisoners' dilemma?

As discussed earlier, one defining characteristic of a prisoner's dilemma is that its equilibrium does not maximise profits. Indeed, in the examples above, both firms would prefer that they both charged a high price or did not advertise, but given the incentive structure they face, neither firm can credibly commit to doing so.

What if the firms are allowed to talk to each other before they set prices (ignoring the fact that this sort of communication is illegal in most jurisdictions)? This is often called **pre-game communication**. In the prisoners' dilemma scenario, pre-game communication is of little use. To see this, suppose the firms could meet before they set their prices. Each might agree to choose p_H, but consider their incentives after they leave the meeting. If Firm 1 assumes that Firm 2 will stick to the agreement, Firm 1 is better off reneging on the agreement ('cheating') and choosing p_H. If, on the other hand, Firm 1 thinks Firm 2 will cheat, then it is also better off cheating too. Pre-game communication has not altered the incentives for each firm (both firms have a dominant strategy to choose p_L), so the firms cannot credibly agree to choose p_H.

The key reason pre-game communication does not help is that it has no commitment value. To overcome this, firms need to find a way to make a **binding commitment** that they cannot break. For example, the firms could lobby the government to institute laws that stipulate minimum prices or restrict advertising, which would provide a binding commitment that helps them avoid the prisoner's dilemma. A binding commitment works by restricting the choices of the firms – here, they can no longer choose to price low or advertise.

Another way firms might be able to get out of their prisoners' dilemma trap is if there is a **repeated game** – that is, the firms compete in the marketplace not just once, but many times. Pepsi and Coke, for instance, do not just play a price-setting game once; rather, they set prices this week, then the next week, then the following week, and so on. Importantly, this means a firm can choose its actions based on what its rivals did in the past – that is, a firm can punish (or threaten to punish) a rival that does not cooperate.

However, repeated interaction does not automatically guarantee that the firms will cooperate. Let us first consider a **finite game**, where a game is repeated a known number of times. To illustrate, suppose the pricing game described above is played twice. In the first round, the firms will try to anticipate what will happen in the second round. In the second round, the firms are playing the game for the last time, with no further rounds to play. Hence, in the second round, the incentives of the firms are the same as when they are playing the game only once; regardless of what happened in the first round, the dominant strategy of both firms is to set the price at p_L. Thus, in the first round, both firms know that the outcome in the second round is a fait accompli; no matter what they choose in the first round, they cannot induce cooperation in the second round. Therefore, in the first round, the incentives are as though they were playing a single round of the game, so both parties have a dominant strategy of pricing at p_L. This analysis can be extended to include any game that is repeated a limited number of times: firms have no incentive to cooperate in the last round; therefore, firms have no incentive to cooperate in the second-to-last round; therefore, firms have no incentive to cooperate in the round before that, and so on.

As you may have noticed, the reason the firms cannot cooperate is because there is a definite end to the game. In the last round, the actions of each firm have no effect on future rounds (as there are none), and this sets off the chain reaction of non-cooperation backwards through every period. This suggests that it may be possible for firms to cooperate in an **infinite game** – where the game is repeated infinitely or there is no definite end to the game.[3]

To see what might happen, suppose the pricing game is played an infinite number of times. There are two classic strategies that firms could adopt (these are by no means the only possibilities). The first is a **trigger strategy**. With a trigger strategy, a firm starts the first period by setting a high price. Then, in the second period, if their rival sets a high price in the first period, the firm again sets a high price again. If not – that is, if their rival sets a low price in the first period – the trigger is pulled and the firm now sets a low price in the second and all subsequent periods. In other words, once its rival cheats, the firm punishes it by setting a low price in *every* future period. If the anticipated cost of punishment is large enough, a firm might not be tempted to cheat; in other words, the threat of punishment allows the firms to stick to high prices (or to 'tacitly collude'). A trigger strategy is one of the most severe punishments a firm can (credibly) impose on their rivals – once someone cheats at any point, they are punished forever.

The other classic strategy is known as a **tit-for-tat strategy**. With a tit-for-tat strategy, a firm starts by setting a high price in the first period, then in every subsequent period it sets a price equal to their rival's price in the previous period. That is, if its rival priced low in the previous period, the firm will price low in the current period; if its rival set a high price in the previous period, the firm will set a high price in the current period. This works as a deterrent because any undercutting to a low price will be followed by a period of punishment. Moreover, to escape the punishment, a firm will have to unilaterally raise its price above its rival (which will cause a loss in profits). Again, a tit-for-tat strategy can help firms maintain higher prices if the firms think the cost of being punished outweighs the larger short-term gains.

15.4 Product choice: an application of a coordination game

Oligopolists often need to make a decision about what type of product they should sell – should a car manufacturer concentrate on high-end luxury vehicles or should it produce family cars? Should a firm develop a new breakfast cereal aimed at health-conscious consumers, or make a sugary cereal for kids? At other times location is important – for example, two fast-food restaurants might need to decide on the location of their respective outlets. We can model these choices using a coordination game.

Consider, for example, two firms deciding where to set up a restaurant. Suppose there are two possible locations, A and B. If the firms set up restaurants in different locations, each will get all the customers at that location; however, if the firms set up business in the same location, they will have to share the customers at that location. The normal form of this game is represented in Figure 15.3.

In this game, there are two Nash equilibria: (A,B) and (B,A). That is, the parties would like to coordinate their actions to set up their restaurants in different places. We

		Firm 2	
		A	B
Firm 1	A	$(\frac{1}{2},\frac{1}{2})$	(1,1)
	B	(1,1)	$(\frac{1}{2},\frac{1}{2})$

FIGURE 15.3 Location-choice game in an oligopoly

Firm 2

		X	Y
Firm 1	X	(30,50)	(0,0)
	Y	(0,0)	(60,20)

FIGURE 15.4 Platform choice for game developers

could also set up an analogous model where the firms would like to develop differentiated products, so they can corner a segment of a market – that is, they would like to accentuate **product differentiation**. Note that because there are multiple equilibria, we do not know which Nash equilibrium will be realised in practice.[4] Moreover, firms that find themselves in a coordination game like this will be very keen to avoid coordination failures (either both choosing *A* or both choosing *B*) – meaning that they both locate in the same place or develop identical products.

Of course, there may be some scenarios where the firms would want to choose the same thing. For example, suppose firms 1 and 2 are each developing a new computer game. Each firm simultaneously chooses to use platform *X* or platform *Y*. If both firms choose *X*, Firm 1 receives a payoff of 30 and Firm 2 a payoff of 50. If both firms choose platform *Y*, Firm 1 receives a payoff of 60 and Firm 2 receives 20. If Firm 1 chooses *Y* and Firm 2 opts for *X*, both firms earn 0. Similarly, if Firm 1 opts for *X* and Firm 2 for *Y*, both firms earn 0. This coordination game is illustrated in Figure 15.4.

There are two Nash equilibria in this game: (X, X) and (Y, Y). In this game, the two developers want **minimal product differentiation**. If one firm is choosing *X*, the best response for the other firm to also choose *X*. Similarly, *Y* is the best response to a rival's choice of *Y*. There could be many reasons for this. For example, having games use the same platform might increase the size of the market by making the products of both firms compatible or easier for the consumer to use. There are many other examples of this scenario: sometimes restaurants are all located together; technology companies often want to use the same platform or technology; new phone handsets from different companies tend to be very similar in look and functionality; and political parties often seem to offer voters very similar policies.

Overall, this suggests that sometimes firms in an oligopoly prefer to offer products that are different from their rivals (product differentiation) but in other cases they may prefer to offer products that are similar (minimal product differentiation). Which case applies depends on the specifics of the market of interest.

15.4.1 Can firms avoid coordination failure?

As noted above, in a coordination game there is the possibility of a coordination failure, but there are several ways firms can try to avoid this. First, the parties could engage in **pre-game communication**, as discussed above. Take the game illustrated in Figure 15.3. In this case each player might communicate before choosing their actions and come to an agreement as to what they will do. Note that, once an agreement is reached, no party has an incentive to deviate from that agreement, because the agreement is a Nash equilibrium. Unlike the prisoners' dilemma above, in which both players have an incentive to renege on any deal, with a coordination game, as the parties are communicating that they will play a strategy that is a Nash equilibrium, the pre-game communication is credible.

Another way that firms may coordinate with each other might be through customs or social norms. This is where there is no explicit agreement between the parties, but an implicit understanding has been reached over time. To understand how this might help, imagine that the firms are ice cream trucks that decide where to set up business at the beginning of each day. Over time, a custom or norm that Truck 1 goes to location A and Truck 2 goes to location B might develop. In this case, there is a well-established pattern of behaviour between the parties.

15.5 Sequential games

So far we have considered simultaneous games in which firms take their actions without observing what their rivals have chosen. But in many economic and business situations, one player (or firm) takes their action and their choice is observed by others before they themselves choose what to do. For example, one firm, Firm A, might choose to build a small or a large factory. This choice is observed by Firm B, which then decides on its own factory size. This sequencing of actions has important implications; it means that the second-movers make their choices knowing exactly what the leader did. Moreover, the leader knows that when they make their choice, the followers will observe what they have done and react accordingly. This can have important economic implications. We model these situations now using sequential games.[5] This allows us to focus on several key game theoretic insights for business strategy, including first- and second-mover advantages and the value of commitment.

15.5.1 Credible threats

As we saw in Chapter 3, some Nash equilibria are sustained by non-credible threats that a player would not actually implement if they were ever actually called upon to do so. Given that players are forward-looking and rational, they will do their best to anticipate what the other players will do in the future given the situation they find themselves in. We expect rational profit-maximising players will not react to non-credible threats, so we are really interested in thinking about equilibria in oligopoly markets that are credible. To eliminate Nash equilibria that rely on non-credible threats, we solve backwards, looking for the subgame perfect equilibria. In a subgame perfect equilibrium, every player's strategy is a Nash equilibrium in every subgame. What this means is that we are only interested in equilibria in which all players would choose their best response in every part of the game, even if that part of the game tree is not reached.

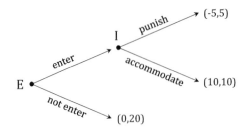

FIGURE 15.5 Entry game in an oligopoly

As noted in Chapter 3, solving backwards is how we capture the fact that players can look into the future and anticipate what the other players will do.

In the oligopoly context, focusing on credible Nash equilibria is important. As an example, let us revisit the entry game first outlined in Chapter 3. In that example, there was an incumbent firm and a potential entrant. The Entrant first chooses whether or not to enter the market. After observing this decision, the Incumbent decides whether to accommodate or punish the entrant. If the Entrant does not enter, the Entrant receives a profit of $0 and the Incumbent receives $20. If the Entrant enters and the Incumbent accommodates, each firm makes a profit of $10. Finally, if the Entrant enters and the Incumbent punishes, the profits are −$5 and $5 to the Entrant and the Incumbent, respectively. The extensive form of this game is represented in Figure 15.5.

As we have previously found, this game has two Nash equilibria: (Enter, Accommodate) and (Not enter, Punish). However, only the subgame perfect equilibrium (Enter, Accommodate) is credible. In the equilibrium (Not enter, Punish), the potential entrant chooses not to enter because the incumbent has threatened punishment; however, this threat of punishment is not credible because if the potential entrant actually entered, it would not be in the best interest of the incumbent to choose Punish – rather, the Incumbent is better off choosing Accommodate. In other words, the threat of punishment is not credible.

We can see this solving backwards for the subgame perfect equilibrium. Considering what the Incumbent would do first, if the game ever reached that point, the Incumbent prefers to accommodate; $10 beats $5. Given this, the Entrant expects the Incumbent to Accommodate if ever they have a choice, so the Entrant's choice is to not enter the market and receive a payoff of $0, or enter and receive a payoff of $10. Thus, we predict that entry will occur because the Incumbent will Accommodate once the Entrant has entered the market.

This entry game is, of course, just one example. But it makes a general point: using subgame perfect equilibria is a powerful tool in oligopoly markets when actions are taken sequentially by firms – it allows us to focus on credible outcomes, which is appropriate for forward-looking and rational profit-maximising firms, who will try their best to anticipate the actions of the other players in the future.

15.5.2 First-mover advantage

Sometimes in sequential games, it is better to be the leader – that is, there is a **first-mover advantage**. As noted above, if the first mover (the leader) can commit to its action, the follower firms must then adapt their actions to what the leader has done. For example, it might be advantageous to be the first developer to build a hotel in a new resort area; alternatively, the leader gets to choose the technological standard that it prefers. In this section we consider several examples where there is a first-mover advantage.

Consider another coordination game outlined in Figure 15.6. In this simultaneous game there are two firms, 1 and 2, who can choose between two types of technologies, B and N. The payoffs are as outlined in the figure. In this game there are two Nash equilibria, (B, B) and (N, N). But note that the preferences of the two firms are asymmetric; Firm 1 prefers the (B, B) equilibrium while Firm 2 gets a higher payoff in the (N, N) equilibrium.

Now modify this game so that Firm 1 gets to make its choice first. Firm 2 observes the action of Firm 1 before making its own choice. The payoffs are the same as in the simultaneous-move game above. This sequential version of the game is illustrated in Figure 15.7.

Solving backwards, let us solve for the subgame perfect equilibrium of this game. First, assume that Firm 1 chose B. In this case Firm 2 can opt for B and get 30, or N and get 0. So if Firm 1 chooses B, Firm 2 will also choose B. Second, consider what Firm 2 will do if Firm 1 opts for N. Now Firm 2 can get 50 from N but 0 if it chooses B; following Firm 1's choice of N, Firm 2 will also choose N. Working backwards, when

		Firm 2	
		B	N
Firm 1	B	(50,30)	(0,0)
	N	(0,0)	(30,50)

FIGURE 15.6 Simultaneous technological choice

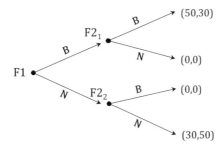

FIGURE 15.7 Technological choice game with a first-mover advantage

		Firm 2	
		E	*NE*
Firm 1	*E*	(−100, −100)	(500,0)
	NE	(0,500)	(0,0)

FIGURE 15.8 Natural monopoly entry game

Firm 1 makes its choice of action it will take into account how Firm 2 will respond. Given Firm 2's responses, Firm 1 will get a payoff of 50 from opting for *B* (as Firm 2 also chooses *B*) or 30 if it opts for *N* (as Firm 2 will respond by also opting for *N*). Firm 1's best option is *B*. As a consequence, the SPE outcome of the game will involve Firm 1 choosing *B*, then Firm 2 choosing *B*.

In the simultaneous version of game there were two Nash equilibria. In the sequential version, Firm 1 being the first mover essentially chooses the equilibrium that it prefers; in a coordination game with asymmetric payoffs, there is a first-mover advantage.

Consider now another market-entry game illustrated in Figure 15.8. In the game two Firms, 1 and 2, simultaneously choose whether to enter a new market (*E*) or to not entry (*NE*). If both firms enter, each gets a payoff of −100. If both firms choose *NE*, each firm receives a payoff of 0. If Firm 1 chooses *E* and Firm 2 opts for *NE*, the payoffs are 500 and 0 to Firms 1 and 2, respectively. Finally, if Firm 2 enters and Firm 1 does not, Firm 1 gets 0 and Firm 2 get a payoff of 500.

In this game – another coordination game – there are two Nash equilibria, (E, NE) and (NE, E). Essentially, this market is a natural monopoly, which only has room for one firm. If both enter, each firm suffers losses. An outcome when both firms do not enter cannot be an equilibrium – each firm would prefer to deviate to be the sole entrant. This means that we would expect one of the Nash equilibria to ensue – either Firm 1 or 2 will enter, and the other firm will stay out of the market.

Now modify this game to allow Firm 1 to make its choice first; Firm 2 then observes this choice before taking its action. In a similar manner to above, let us solve for the subgame perfect equilibrium by solving backwards. Here, if Firm 1 enters (*E*), Firm 2 will choose not enter (*NE*). On the other hand, if Firm 1 opted for *NE*, Firm 2 would choose *E*. Working backwards, Firm 1 will opt for *E*, and the SPE outcome will have Firm 1 entering the market and Firm 2 choosing *NE*. Once again, being the first mover is advantageous; it allows Firm 1 to enter the market knowing Firm 2 will stay out and *NE*.

The two previous examples show that there can be a first-mover advantage. This suggests that in situations like this, if possible, a firm should try to manipulate the environment they are in to ensure that they are the firm that gets to be the leader.

15.5.3 A second-mover advantage

While the benefits of being a leader in a market are often emphasised, it is sometimes the firms that are followers that do better. For example, Microsoft did not develop the

Firm 2

		I	*W*
Firm 1	*I*	(4,4)	(2,6)
	W	(6,2)	(1,1)

FIGURE 15.9 Free-riding game

first computer operating system, and the iPhone was not the first smart phone. In these games there is a **second-mover advantage**.

As an example, consider the following game shown in Figure 15.9. In this game, a new product needs to be developed, which requires some investment. If both firms invest they share the development costs. But if only one firm invests, it incurs all the development costs, while the firm that waited can take advantage of the other firm's investment in product development. So, the two firms can simultaneously choose to invest (*I*) or to wait (*W*). If both invest each firm receives a payoff of $4. If they both choose *W* the payoff to each firm is $1. If one firm chooses *I* and the other firm *W*, the payoff to the investor is $2 while the firm that waited gets $6.

There are two Nash equilibria in the game: (I, W) and (W, I). In either equilibrium one firm enters and the other waits. It is evident that it is better to be the second firm in the market and waiting allows a firm to free ride on the leader's investment. In a market like this, there is a second-mover advantage; if it is possible, a firm would like to commit to being the second mover.

Another game in which there can be a second-mover advantage is a zero-sum game, such as the classic 'matching pennies game' illustrated in Figure 15.10. In this game, the two firms simultaneously choose their possible actions of either *H* or *T*. If both firms choose the same action (both *H* or both *T*), Firm 1 gains $1 and Firm 2 loses $1. If the actions do not match (one firm chose *H* and the other *T*), Firm 2 gains $1 and Firm 1 loses $1. This game is called a zero-sum game because, in each possible outcome, the total sum of the payoffs is zero – that is, whatever amount one player gains, the other loses.

If this game is played simultaneously, there is no Nash equilibrium; in any of the possible outcomes there is always a firm that has a profitable unilateral deviation.[6] However, suppose instead that the game is played sequentially, with Firm 1 moving first. Now being the second mover is very advantageous: whatever Firm 1 does, Firm 2 can react optimally to ensure that it gets the dollar.

In a strategic situation like this, the second mover is better off. Consider two television stations, each with a new blockbuster show. It could be that the station that holds off announcing when it will screen its big show can trump the station that locked in its schedule first. (Of course, in situations like this, both firms will try to finalise their schedules as long as they can.)

FIGURE 15.10 A 'matching pennies' game

15.6 Concluding comments

In this chapter, we discussed how game theory might be used to analyse strategic inter-actions in an oligopolistic market. Importantly, the examples we have given are by no means an exhaustive demonstration of how game theory might be applied in these situations.

Several key implications for oligopolistic markets were discussed. First, oligopolists might find it difficult to not strongly compete with one another (by pricing low, adver-tising and so on). While individually rational, competing hard can potentially lower total industry profits, subsequently making each firm worse off. If they can, firms would like to find ways not to compete so hard; one way this can occur is if firms interact with each other, not once, but many times. With repeated interaction, it is possible that the threat for future punishment can help firms to (tacitly) cooperate.

Second, when firms take their actions in sequence, profit-maximising firms will try to anticipate what their rivals will credible do in the future. Focusing on credible outcomes requires that we solve the game backwards (looking for the SPE of the game). In sequential games, there can be either first- or second-mover advantages, depending on the economic environment firms find themselves in.

Notes

1 See Chapter 3 for more details.
2 A similar game can be devised when firms choose output levels.
3 It could also include cases where each firm knows the game will end, but they are never exactly sure when that will happen. So, in any given period, firms know that there is a possibility that the game could continue.
4 We discuss this issue further below in the section on sequential games.
5 See Chapter 3 for more details.
6 There is actually a mixed strategy equilibrium in this game, when players put a positive probability on playing more than one action. However, as mentioned in Chapter 3 we do not focus on mixed strategy equilibria in this book.

PART V

Market failures

CHAPTER 16

Price regulation, taxes and subsidies

16.1 Introduction

In previous chapters, we analysed various types of market structures and the different outcomes they produce. For the most part, we assumed that there was no intervention in the market by the government. In this chapter, we consider two common types of government intervention: (a) price regulation and (b) taxes and subsidies. For the purpose of this chapter, we will assume that the market is efficient in the absence of government intervention (that is, the market is a competitive market). In this framework, we examine how government intervention affects market prices, the quantity traded and welfare in the market.

16.2 Price regulation

One way that a government can intervene in the market is by regulating the price of a good or service. Price regulation typically takes the form of a **price floor**, where the government sets a minimum price at which a good or service can be traded, or a **price ceiling**, where the government sets a maximum price.

16.2.1 Price floor

When a government puts in place a price floor, it sets a minimum price at which a good or service may be sold. For example, the Australian government historically maintained a price floor in the market for wool. Currently, there are laws that guarantee minimum wages for certain jobs, which is essentially a price floor in the labour market.

DOI: 10.4324/9781003376644-21

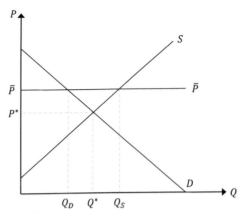

FIGURE 16.1 A price floor set at $\bar{P}$

Figure 16.1 illustrates the effect of a price floor on market outcomes. In the absence of any government intervention, the equilibrium price and quantity will prevail in the market – that is, (Q^*, P^*). In order for a price floor to affect the market outcome, the price floor must be set above the equilibrium price, P^*. A price floor set below P^* is **non-binding**, because the equilibrium price is already above the minimum price (the price floor). By contrast, a price floor set above P^* (say, at $\bar{P}$) is **binding** because the market equilibrium price is less than the minimum price at which the good or service may be sold; hence, the price in the market will need to rise from P^* to $\bar{P}$ in order to meet the requirements of the price floor.

Raising the price above P^* affects the quantity demanded and the quantity supplied in the market. At $\bar{P}$, the quantity demanded by consumers is Q_D, whereas the quantity supplied by producers is denoted Q_S. This results in an **excess supply** of $Q_S - Q_D$. For example, suppose the government implements a price floor in the labour market by setting minimum wage laws. This will result in excess supply of labour (that is, the amount of labour supplied by workers exceeds the quantity of labour demanded by firms). There will be unemployment; at the going wage rate, there are workers who are willing to work who are not being employed by firms. Sometimes, a government deals with the excess supply by purchasing the excess, $Q_S - Q_D$. In fact, this occurred in the market for wool in Australia; over time the Australian government accumulated a large stockpile of wool as a result.

Of course, the change in the market price has welfare implications, as depicted in Figure 16.2. Consumer surplus decreases for two reasons: firstly, the price has increased, meaning that consumers receive less surplus on each unit purchased; secondly, consumers buy fewer units overall, meaning that surplus is lost through the decrease in the quantity traded. On the other hand, producer surplus is affected by two countervailing effects: firstly, producers sell fewer units overall, which decreases surplus; however, producers receive more surplus on each unit sold, as a result of the increase in price. Overall, there is deadweight loss in the market. Note here, also, that this is the best possible outcome in terms of welfare resulting from the price floor (that is, it is the smallest possible DWL) as it is assumed that it is the lowest-cost firms that

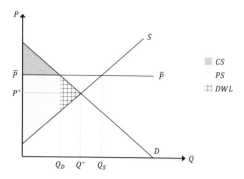

FIGURE 16.2 The welfare effects of a price floor set at $\bar{P}$

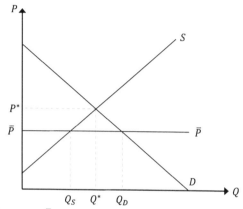

FIGURE 16.3 A price ceiling set at $\bar{P}$

are supplying the product. If this is not the case, the loss of welfare from the price floor will be even larger.

16.2.2 Price ceiling

When a government puts in place a price ceiling, it sets a maximum price at which a good or service may be traded.

Figure 16.3 illustrates the effect of a price ceiling on market outcomes. In the absence of any government intervention, the equilibrium price and quantity will prevail in the market – that is, (Q^*, P^*). In order for a price ceiling to affect the market outcome, the price ceiling must be set below the equilibrium price, P^*. A price ceiling set above P^* is **non-binding**, because the equilibrium price is already below that price ceiling. By contrast, a price ceiling set below P^* (say, at $\bar{P}$) is **binding** because the equilibrium price is greater than the maximum price at which the good or service may be sold; hence, the price in the market will need to fall from P^* to $\bar{P}$ in order to meet the requirements of the price floor.

Again, pushing the price below P^* affects the quantity demanded and the quantity supplied in the market. At $\bar{P}$, the quantity demanded by consumers is denoted by Q_D, whereas the quantity supplied by producers is denoted by Q_S. This results in an **excess**

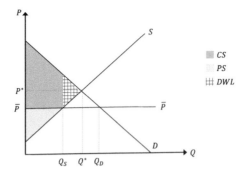

FIGURE 16.4 The welfare effects of a price ceiling set at $\bar{P}$

of demand of $Q_D - Q_S$; in other words, at that price there are not enough units supplied to meet the quantity demanded.

This raises the question of how the existing units of the good should be allocated to consumers. There are several ways this issue of allocation might be addressed.

- **Queuing.** One way of rationing a limited number of goods amongst consumers is on a first-come, first-served basis, which often results in queues. This way, only consumers who are willing to wait receive the good.
- **Discrimination between consumers.** Another way of distributing the good is for a government official to pick and choose which consumers should receive the good. However, this may be problematic if the official distributes the goods on the basis of nepotism rather than who values the good the most.
- **Side payments.** In either case, there is a possibility that consumers will make side payments (that is, payments in addition to the price) to the firm or the government official to guarantee access to the product. This is generally viewed as underhand or corrupt behaviour, and may be illegal.

Again, the change in the market price has welfare implications, as depicted in Figure 16.4. Consumer surplus is affected by two countervailing effects: firstly, consumers receive more surplus on each unit purchased, as a result of the decrease in price; however, consumers purchase fewer units overall, meaning that surplus is lost through the decrease in the quantity traded. Producer surplus decreases for two reasons: firstly, producers receive less surplus on each unit sold due to the lower price; secondly, producers sell fewer units overall, meaning that surplus is lost through the decrease in the quantity traded. Overall, there is deadweight loss in the market. Note again that we have assumed that the consumers with the highest MB of the good are the ones who actually get to buy it (that is, the consumers with MBs at the very top left of the demand curve). If other consumers who do not value the product as highly (but still have a $MB > \bar{P}$) receive the product instead, the resulting DWL will be even larger.

16.2.3 Price controls in the long run

Supply and demand change over time, which may affect the equilibrium price and quantity. This means that a price ceiling or price floor that was non-binding may become binding, or vice versa.

Typically, supply and demand will be more elastic in the long run, as participants in the market adjust to market conditions. This can mean that shortages or excesses of a product may worsen in the long run. For example, consider rent-control laws that set a price ceiling on residential leases. In the short term, this may only generate a small excess of demand. However, in the long run, participants in the market will respond to the price control. Landlords know that earnings from their rental properties are capped by the price ceiling and may prefer to invest elsewhere. Moreover, the price control makes renting cheap relative to, say, making mortgage payments on a house, so more people will prefer to rent rather than buy a house. The combination of the increase in demand and decrease in supply of rental properties will worsen the issue of excess demand over the longer term.

16.3 Taxes and subsidies

We now turn to the effect of taxes and subsidies on market outcomes. We will restrict our analysis to taxes and subsidies on consumption and production, but it is important to be aware that other types of taxes (such as property and income taxes) and other types of subsidies (such as export or employment subsidies) also exist.

16.3.1 Taxes

A **tax** is a compulsory payment made to the government. In this section, we will consider **per-unit taxes** (or 'specific taxes'), where the tax for each unit is a fixed amount – that is, for every unit, a tax of t must be paid to the government. This can be distinguished from an *ad valorem* **tax**, where the amount of the tax is a fixed percentage of the price.

Tax on consumption

Let us first examine the case where the tax must be paid by consumers. For every unit purchased, consumers must pay the market price P to the producer as well as a tax of t to the government. Hence, the total amount paid by consumers is $P + t$.

The effect of a tax upon demand is illustrated in Figure 16.5. Before the tax is introduced, the demand curve and the supply curve (D_0 and S_0) yield the equilibrium (Q^*, P^*). Once a tax of t is introduced, consumers must factor the tax into their purchasing decisions. Now, consumers will only buy an additional unit of the good if the total amount paid ($P + t$) does not exceed their marginal benefit (MB); that is to say, the maximum price P that consumers would be willing to pay for any unit is $P = MB - t$, as $P + t = MB$. The maximum price that consumers are willing to pay

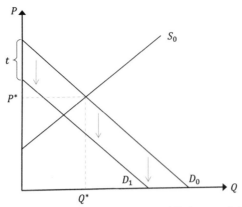

FIGURE 16.5 A tax on consumers causes the demand curve to shift downwards by the size of the tax

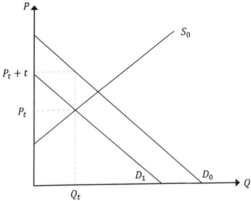

FIGURE 16.6 A tax on consumers creates a new market price and quantity at (Q_t, P_t). However, the total amount paid by consumers is $P_t + t$

is reduced by the size of the tax; in other words, the demand curve shifts vertically *downwards* by the size of the tax, to D_1.

This creates a new equilibrium at the intersection of S_0 and D_1, as seen in Figure 16.6. At this new equilibrium, the quantity traded in the market is Q_t, and the price in the market (received by producers) is P_t. However, the total amount paid by consumers is $P_t + t$, as they must pay the market price, plus the tax of t to the government.

Tax on production

Let us now turn to taxes paid by producers. For every unit sold, producers must pay a tax of t to the government. Hence, the total amount that a producer receives for selling a unit of the good is $P - t$, which represents the price received minus the payment of the tax.

The effect of a tax upon demand is illustrated in Figure 16.7. Before the tax is introduced, the demand curve and the supply curve (D_0 and S_0) yield the equilibrium (Q^*, P^*). Once a tax of t is introduced, producers must factor that tax into their

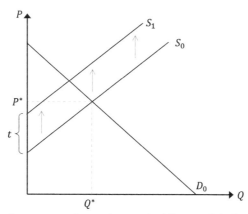

FIGURE 16.7 A tax on producers causes the supply curve to shift upwards by the size of the tax

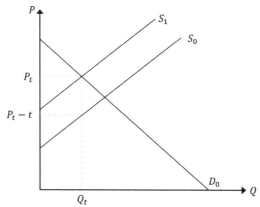

FIGURE 16.8 A tax on producers creates a new market price and quantity at (Q_t, P_t). However, the net amount received by producers is $P_t - t$

production choices. Now, producers should only sell an additional unit of the good if the amount they receive covers their marginal cost; that is to say, the minimum price that producers should be willing to accept is $P = MC + t$. Hence, the minimum price that producers are willing to accept is increased by the size of the tax; in other words, the supply curve shifts vertically *upwards* by the size of the tax, to S_1.

This creates a new equilibrium at the intersection of S_1 and D_0, as seen in Figure 16.8. At this new equilibrium, the quantity traded in the market is Q_t, and the price in the market (paid by consumers) is P_t. However, the net amount received by producers is the market price minus the tax of – that is, $P_t - t$.

Effects of tax on welfare

The effect of a tax is to drive a wedge between the price paid by consumers (P_C) and the amount received by producers (P_P). This will have implications for welfare, as illustrated in Figure 16.9. Both consumer surplus and producer surplus will decrease as a result of the tax, for two reasons: firstly, fewer units are traded in the market;

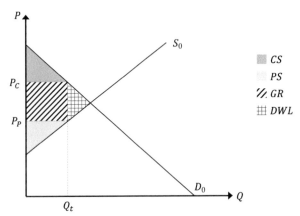

FIGURE 16.9 The welfare effects of a tax

secondly, on each unit, consumers pay a higher price and producers receive a lower price relative to a market without a tax.

However, as a result of the tax, the government now receives some surplus in the form of tax revenue. The total revenue received by the government is denoted by the size of the tax (t), multiplied by the number of units taxed (Q_t). This is represented by the area GR in Figure 16.9. The surplus to the government must also be factored into total surplus; hence, total surplus is given by the sum of consumer surplus, producer surplus and government revenue ($TS = CS + PS + GR$).

As a result, the deadweight loss from taxation (DWL) is given by the criss-crossed region in Figure 16.9. This DWL is caused by a reduction in the quantity traded in the market (from Q^* to Q_t). The larger this reduction, the greater the DWL. Hence, the size of the DWL depends on how elastic the demand and supply curves are. The more elastic the demand and/or supply curves, the greater the effect of the tax on the quantity traded in the market, which will result in a greater DWL.

Incidence of tax

The concept of tax incidence analyses how the burden of the tax is distributed between consumers and producers. The **legal incidence of the tax** refers to who is legally responsible for paying the tax. It answers the question: is this tax levied on consumers or on producers? By contrast, the **economic incidence of the tax** refers to who, as a matter of fact, actually bears the burden of the tax.

As a general rule, the legal incidence of the tax has no bearing on the economic incidence of the tax. Rather, the economic incidence of the tax is determined solely by the relative elasticities of demand and supply curves. A corollary of this is that taxes on consumers and taxes on producers will have identical welfare effects. Thus, if the demand curve is elastic relative to the supply curve, producers will bear a greater share of the tax burden; conversely, if the supply curve is elastic relative to the demand curve, consumers will bear a greater share of the tax burden. Usually, the economic incidence

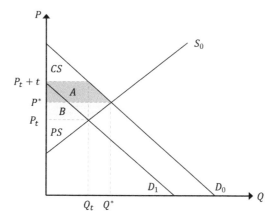

FIGURE 16.10 A tax on consumers in the market for tomatoes. The legal incidence of the tax is borne by consumers, but the economic incidence of the tax is shared. The price that consumers pay increases from P^* to $P_t + t$, whereas producers receive P_t following the introduction of the tax, rather than P^*

of the tax is shared between both parties, but there may be exceptional cases if either curve is perfectly elastic or perfectly inelastic.

Example. Consider the market for tomatoes depicted in Figure 16.10, where the market price is P^*. Suppose a per-unit tax of t is levied on consumers, shifting the demand curve downwards. Now, the total price paid by consumers is $(P_t + t)$ and the price received by producers is (P_t). In this case, the legal incidence of the tax is on consumers, because it is they who are legally responsible for paying the tax. However, the economic incidence of the tax is split between consumers and producers, as consumers pay a higher price than they did without the tax and producers receive less than they did per unit sold than they did without the tax. The loss of consumer surplus is denoted by the area A, and the loss of producer surplus is denoted by the area B.

Example. Consider the market for jumpers. Demand in the market is given by $P = 24 - Q_d$, where P is market price and Q_d is quantity demanded. Supply is given by $P = 2Q_s$, where Q_s is the quantity supplied. The market equilibrium price and quantity traded are $P^* = 16$ and $Q^* = 8$. Now assume that a per-unit tax of \$3 is imposed on consumers (the legal incidence is on consumers in the market). If producers receive a price of P_t following the introduction of the tax, consumers will pay $P_t + 3$ in total for each unit they buy. Consequently, consumers will adjust their willingness to pay such that $P_t + 3 = 24 - Q_d$, or that $P_t = 21 - Q_d$. The supply curve is unchanged: $P_t = 2Q$. To find the new equilibrium after the imposition of the tax, we equate the new demand curve (with the tax) with the supply curve, so that $21 - Q = 2Q$; the new quantity traded is $Q_t = 7$. From this, the suppliers will receive a price of $P_t = 14$, and consumers will pay a total price (to the producers and to the government) of $P_c = 14 + 3 = 17$. In this example, consumers pay an extra \$1 per unit and suppliers receive \$2 less per unit.

Now suppose the tax is imposed instead on suppliers. After the tax, the demand curve will be unchanged; $P_c = 24 - Q$, where P_c is the price consumers pay in the market after the tax has been imposed. Suppliers, however, will take into account that they have to pay \$3 to the government for each unit they sell; the supply curve will now be $P_c - 3 = 2Q_s$, or $-P_c = 2Q_s + 3$. Again, to find the market equilibrium, equate demand with the new supply curve; the new equilibrium with the tax has a quantity traded of $Q_t = 7$, with a consumer price $P_c = 17$ and a supplier price of $P_s = P_c - 3 = 14$. This outcome is the same as when the tax was imposed on consumers – that is, the economic incidence of the tax is the same regardless of whether consumers or producers are legally required to pay the tax.

16.3.2 Further analysis

Let us now explore a little further some of the issues highlighted in the sections above.

First, we know that the incidence of the tax is invariant to which side of the market legally pays for the tax. Rather, it is the relative elasticities of supply and demand that determine how much of a tax is paid for by consumers and producers; if demand is relatively inelastic (the curve is relatively steep), consumers will pay more of the tax ($P_c - P^*$ will be larger than $P^* - P_s$, where P_c is the full price consumers pay and P_s is the net price received by suppliers). Conversely, if supply is relatively inelastic (relatively steep), suppliers will bear relatively more of the incidence of the tax ($P^* - P_s$ will be larger than $P_c - P^*$).

If one side of the market is perfectly inelastic, that side will pay for all of the tax. Consider Figure 16.11. Here, demand is perfectly inelastic, so consumers end up paying for all of the tax, and suppliers continue to receive P^* per unit. The same idea

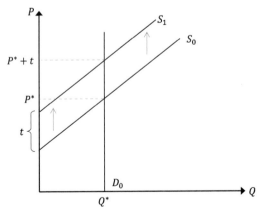

FIGURE 16.11 If demand is perfectly inelastic, when a tax of t per unit is instituted, consumers pay for all of the tax; following the introduction of the tax consumers pay $P^* + t$ whereas suppliers continue to receive P^*

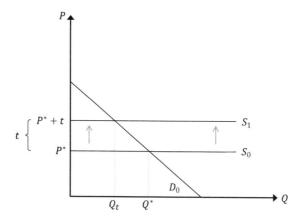

FIGURE 16.12 When a tax of t per unit is implemented and supply is perfectly elastic, consumers pay for all of the tax; following the introduction of the tax, consumers pay $P^* + t$ whereas suppliers continue to receive P^*

applies if supply were perfectly inelastic and demand was downward sloping – suppliers would bear all of the incidence of the tax. A similar idea applies if one side of the market is perfectly elastic – the other side of the market bears all of the incidence of the tax. Consider Figure 16.12, the market with a perfectly elastic supply curve and a downward-sloping demand curve. The tax on suppliers shifts the supply curve up by the size of the tax to S_t. Consumers now pay $P_c = P^* + t$ and suppliers continue to receive a price of $P_s = P^*$, after passing the tax t onto the government.

When both demand and supply are downward and upward sloping, respectively, then both sides pay for some of the tax, the precise incidence depending on the relative elasticity of supply and demand.

Second, the DWL generated by a tax depends on the elasticity of supply and demand. A DWL is caused by a reduction in the quantity traded (from q^* to q_t). The larger this reduction, the bigger the DWL. For a given tax t, the reduction in quantity is going to be larger the more responsive market participants are, because the wedge between the D and S curves must be equal to the size of the tax. The flatter the curves, the greater the reduction in quantity required to achieve the necessary gap between the two curves. For example, consider two markets with the same demand curve that both experience the implementation of a per-unit tax t. As in Figure 16.13, the two markets have different supply curves, the first being relatively elastic and the second relatively inelastic. The more elastic the supply curve, the greater the reduction in quantity caused by the tax and the larger the DWL generated. (The same logic applies to the elasticity of demand.) This means that, other things being equal, a greater DWL is caused by a tax in a market with relatively responsive (elastic) supply and demand curves.

Third, consider the impact on tax revenue and DWL as a tax is increased. With zero tax there is no DWL or tax revenue. If a small tax is levied, it causes a wedge between the demand and supply curves, reducing the quantity traded. This creates a DWL. As the tax is increased, the wedge becomes larger and the DWL increases. This is true up

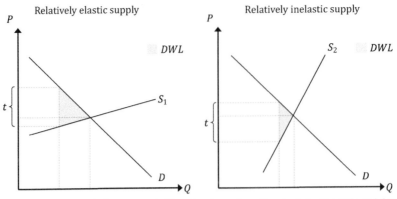

FIGURE 16.13   The deadweight loss generated by a tax depends on the elasticity of supply and demand. In each panel the demand curve and the tax implemented are the same. There is a larger DWL generated in the market with relative elastic supply (the left-hand panel) as compared with the DWL in the market in which supply is relatively inelastic (the right-hand panel)

to when the tax is equal to the difference between the *MB* of the first unit consumed and the *MC* of the first unit made – that is, the difference between the height of the demand and supply curves at $Q = 0$. Once a tax is this large, there is no trade and all the potential gains from trade are lost (the DWL is equal to the area between the demand and supply curves between 0 and Q^*).

Now consider the relationship between the size of the per-unit tax and tax revenue. As the tax increases, tax revenue first rises, then falls. The logic is very similar to why total expenditure in a market can rise or fall with a price increase. To see this, start with a tax of $t = 0$. With no tax, tax revenue is zero. If a small tax is implemented, tax revenue is the area of the rectangle equal to the size of the tax t times the quantity traded q_t. Implementing a small tax from a base of $t = 0$ generates some tax revenue, so tax revenue increases with a tax increase. This is true for further small tax increases; the tax revenue rectangle increases as the proportional increase in the height of the rectangle outweighs the reduction in the length (given by q_t). But as the tax gets larger, the proportional decrease in quantity begins to outweigh the proportional increase in the tax, and total tax revenue starts to fall. This continues up until the tax totally crowds out the market (with a tax equal to the difference between *MB* and *MC* at $q = 0$). At this level of taxation, the quantity traded is zero and there will be no tax revenue.

This observation that tax increases and subsequently falls is often referred as the Laffer curve, named after Arthur Laffer, who in the early 1980s persuaded President Reagan to decrease income tax rates in the USA. This contention was that income rates were so high that if the government reduced them, people would respond by working more, decreasing the DWL from taxation and increasing government revenue. Income tax rates were decreased in the USA, but tax revenues fell. This suggests that previous levels of income tax were not so high that they were causing tax revenue to decrease.

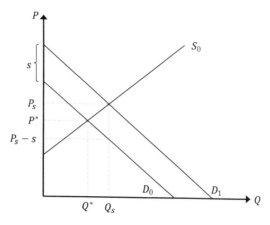

FIGURE 16.14 A subsidy for consumption creates a new market price and quantity at (Q_s, P_s). The total amount paid by consumers is $P_s - s$

16.3.3 Subsidies

A **subsidy** is a payment made by the government to an individual or firm, and can be thought of as a negative tax. For this reason, much of the analysis concerning taxes can be modified to describe the effects of a subsidy.

Subsidies for consumption

In the case of a subsidy for consumption, the government makes a payment of s to consumers for every unit of the good purchased. That is, for every unit consumed, consumers must pay the market price P to the producer, but will receive a subsidy of s from the government. Hence, the total amount paid by consumers is $P - s$.

The effect of this subsidy will be to shift the demand curve *upwards* by the size of the subsidy, s. This is depicted in Figure 16.14 with the movement of the demand curve from D_0 to D_1. As a result, the new quantity traded in the market is Q_s and the price in the market (received by producers) is P_s. However, the net amount paid by consumers is $P_s - s$, as after they pay the market price to producers, they also receive the subsidy of s from the government.

Subsidies for production

Alternatively, the government may subsidise production, by making a payment of s to producers for every unit of the good sold. As a result, the producer will receive the price P from consumers, as well as a subsidy of s from the government. Thus, the total amount received by producers is $P + s$.

As a result of this subsidy, the supply curve will shift *downwards* by the size of the subsidy, s. This is depicted in Figure 16.15 by a movement of the supply curve from S_0 to S_1. As a consequence, the new quantity traded in the market is Q_s and the price in the market (paid by consumers) is P_s. However, the total amount received by producers is $P_s + s$, which includes the subsidy.

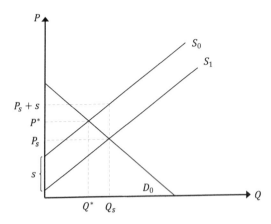

FIGURE 16.15 A subsidy for production creates a new market price and quantity at (Q_s, P_s). The total amount received by producers is $P_s + s$

Economic incidence of a subsidy

Like a tax, the economic incidence of a subsidy does not depend on the legal incidence of the subsidy (that is, whether the government technically pays the subsidy to consumers or producers). As before, the economic incidence depends on the relative elasticities of demand and supply. With a subsidy, it is the relatively inelastic side of the market that enjoys more of the benefits in terms of the price they pay or receive. For example, if demand is perfectly inelastic and the supply curve is upward sloping, the resulting consumer price falls by the size of the subsidy, and the final price (including the subsidy received) by producers remains unchanged.

Effects of subsidies on welfare

The effect of a subsidy is to increase the quantity of a good traded in the market, as depicted in Figure 16.16. Moreover, the price paid by consumers (P_C) is now less than the price received by producers (P_P), as the government subsidy makes up the difference. As a result, both consumer surplus and producer surplus increase for two reasons: firstly, more units are traded in the market; secondly, on each unit, consumers pay a lower price and producers receive a higher price relative to a market without a subsidy. The areas of consumer and producer surplus are depicted in Figure 16.15.

However, as a result of the subsidy, the government must now make payments to consumers and/or producers, which represents *negative* government revenue – or in other words, negative surplus. The size of this negative surplus is denoted by the size of the subsidy (s), multiplied by the number of units subsidised (Q_s). This is represented by the area GR in Figure 16.17. This negative surplus must also be factored into the total surplus; hence, total surplus is given by $TS = CS + PS - GR$. As a result, there is DWL arising from the subsidy, as depicted in Figure 16.17. This DWL is caused by an increase in the quantity traded in the market, beyond the efficient level (from Q^* to Q_s).

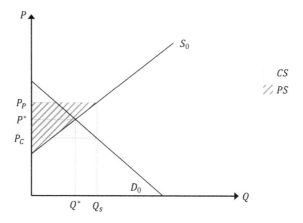

FIGURE 16.16 Consumer surplus and producer surplus as a result of a subsidy

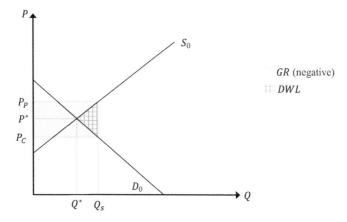

FIGURE 16.17 Government revenue and deadweight loss as a result of a subsidy

An alternative intuition for this DWL is as follows: Each extra unit produced between Q^* and Q_s has an MB indicated by the demand curve (D_0), whereas the MC of production is given by the supply curve (S_0). Consequently, as $MB < MC$ for each of these units, the total surplus must fall because the subsidy encourages too much production of the good (beyond the efficient quantity Q^*).

16.4 Concluding comments

Government intervention can affect the price and quantity of goods traded in the market. In this chapter, we found that if a market is initially efficient, the introduction of a price control, tax or subsidy makes the market less efficient (that is, it results in deadweight loss). This is because the intervention moves the quantity traded in the market away from the efficient quantity. In the coming chapters, however, we will explore the possibility that, if the market is not efficient to begin with, government intervention can make the market more efficient.

Externalities

17.1 Introduction

As we have seen in previous chapters, competitive markets are usually Pareto efficient. This is because all mutually beneficial trades[1] occur, maximising the gains from trade and hence total surplus. However, there are some situations where the market outcome will not be efficient; these are called **market failures**.

This chapter examines one type of market failure: externalities. An externality is a cost or benefit that accrues to a person who is not directly involved in an economic activity or transaction. The presence of an externality means that the market outcome may not be efficient, because the market does not take into account the external costs and benefits of producing or consuming a product. This means that a competitive market can end up producing too much of a product (when there are external costs) or too little (when there are external benefits).

We begin with a discussion of the nature of externalities and the market failure associated with them and then turn to several possible solutions to this market failure.

17.2 External costs and benefits

An **externality** is a cost or benefit of an economic activity that accrues to a person not directly involved in that activity.[2] These costs or benefits are also known as 'external costs' or 'external benefits'.

- A **positive externality** occurs when economic activity results in external benefits for a third party. For example, if a student decides to pursue further education, there may be benefits to society as a whole from having

DOI: 10.4324/9781003376644-22

better-educated citizens, in addition to the individual benefits that are enjoyed by the student themselves.

- A **negative externality** occurs when economic activity results in external costs for a third party. For example, if a factory manufacturing spanners pollutes a river in the course of production, this is a cost borne by people wishing to use the river downstream rather than by the manufacturer or the end consumers of the spanners.

The following subsections examine the effects of positive externalities and negative externalities in turn. To illustrate a positive and a negative externality we first consider a positive consumption externality and a negative production externality.

17.2.1 Positive consumption externalities

Consumers derive benefits from consuming goods. However, in the presence of a positive externality, the consumption or production of the good also has external benefits for a third party. Hence, the benefit to society as a whole (the 'social benefit') must include both the consumer's benefit and the external benefit.

Formally, the marginal benefit to society of an additional unit of the good is known as the **marginal social benefit** (*MSB*). It is made up of two components: the **marginal private benefit** (*MPB*) that is enjoyed by the consumer and the **marginal external benefit** (*MEB*) that accrues to a third party:

$$MSB = MPB + MEB \tag{17.1}$$

Figure 17.1 represents the relationship between the *MPB* and the *MSB*. Note that, in the presence of a positive consumption externality, the marginal social benefit is higher than the marginal private benefit – the difference between the *MSB* and the *MPB* is the size of the externality, for any given unit. In Figure 17.1, the increasing gap between the *MPB* and the *MSB* indicates that the positive externality is increasing with output. This need not be the case – there could be a constant positive externality per unit of the good consumed, in which case *MPB* and *MSB* would be parallel. Alternatively, a diminishing

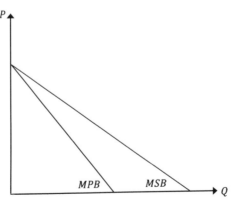

FIGURE 17.1 The relationship between *MPB* and *MSB* in the presence of a positive externality

gap between *MSB* and *MPB* would represent a declining positive externality as more of the good is consumed. Finally, if there is no positive consumption externality, $MEB = 0$ and $MSB = MPB$.

17.2.2 Negative production externalities

Similarly, producers incur costs from producing goods. When a negative production externality is present, the consumption or production of the good also has external costs for a third party. Hence, the cost to society as a whole (the 'social cost') must include both the producer's cost and the external cost.

Formally, the marginal cost to society of an additional unit of the good is known as the **marginal social cost** (*MSC*). It is made up of two components: the **marginal private cost** (*MPC*) that is incurred by the producer and the **marginal external cost** (*MEC*) that is incurred by a third party:

$$MSC = MPC + MEC \tag{17.2}$$

Figure 17.2 represents the relationship between the *MPC* and the *MSC*. Note that the presence of the negative externality means that the marginal social cost is higher than the marginal private cost. The size of the negative externality is the difference between the *MSB* and the *MPB* for a given level of output. Note in Figure 17.2, the increasing gap between the *MSC* and the *MPC* indicates the negative externality is increasing with the level of output produced in the market. Of course, the size of the externality need not be increasing with output – for example, there might be a constant negative externality incurred for every unit of output in which case the *MSC* and the *MPC* would be parallel. Finally, if there is no negative externality, then $MEC = 0$ and $MSC = MPC$.

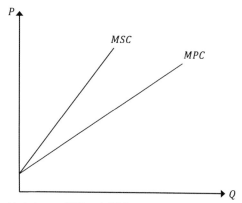

FIGURE 17.2 The relationship between *MPC* and *MSC* in the presence of a negative externality

17.3 The problem with externalities

When there are no externalities, all the benefits of consumption are enjoyed by consumers, as depicted by the demand curve. Conversely, all the costs of production are incurred by producers, as depicted by the supply curve. As a result, the market equilibrium accounts for all costs and benefits from production and consumption.

Externalities are a source of market failure because they represent external costs or benefits that are not accounted for by the market. Because consumers only account for their own private benefits and producers only account for their own private costs, the market equilibrium is determined by the demand (MPB) and supply (MPC) curves:

$$MPB = MPC \tag{17.3}$$

However, from the perspective of society as a whole, any external costs and benefits associated with the consumption or production of the good should also be taken into account when determining what is 'optimal' or efficient. Hence the socially optimal equilibrium is determined by the intersection of the marginal social benefit and marginal social cost curves:

$$MSB = MSC \tag{17.4}$$

17.3.1 Positive consumption externalities

In this way, the external benefits or costs resulting from the externality mean that the market equilibrium is not the same as the socially optimal equilibrium. Figure 17.3 compares the equilibrium quantity Q^M and the socially optimal quantity Q^* in the presence of a positive consumption externality. In this case, the MSB curve is higher than the MPB curve due to the external benefit. However, the MSC curve and the MPC curve are the same because there is no negative externality.

At market equilibrium, there is under-production relative to the socially optimal level of output, Q^*. In particular, note that the units between Q^M and Q^* are not traded in the market because consumers and producers have no private incentive to do so; for these units, the MPC exceeds the MPB. However, from the viewpoint of society as a whole, it would be desirable for these units to be traded, because their MSC is less than their MSB.

Because these socially beneficial trades do not go ahead, there is deadweight loss associated with the market equilibrium. The area of deadweight loss is shaded grey in Figure 17.3.

17.3.2 Negative production externalities

Similarly, a negative externality can also mean that the market equilibrium is not the same as the socially optimal equilibrium. Figure 17.4 compares the market equilibrium quantity Q^M and the socially optimal quantity Q^* in the presence of a negative production externality. In this case, the *MSC* curve is higher than the *MPC* curve due to the external cost. However, the *MSB* curve and the *MPB* curve are the same because there is no positive externality.

Now, at the market equilibrium, there is over-production relative to the socially optimal level of output, Q^*. The units between Q^* and Q^M are traded in the market because, for these units, the *MPB* of consumers exceeds the *MPC* of producers. However, from the viewpoint of society as a whole, it would be desirable for these trades not to go ahead, because their *MSC* is greater than their *MSB*.

Because the amount traded in the market is greater than the socially optimal amount, there is a deadweight loss associated with the market equilibrium. The area of deadweight loss is shaded grey in Figure 17.4.

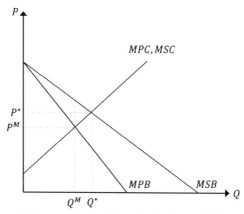

FIGURE 17.3 The market equilibrium and the socially optimal outcome in the presence of a positive externality. The area representing deadweight loss is shaded in grey

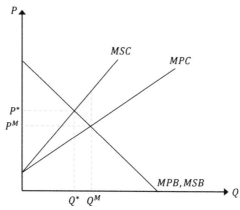

FIGURE 17.4 The market equilibrium and the socially optimal outcome in the presence of a negative externality. The area representing deadweight loss is shaded in grey

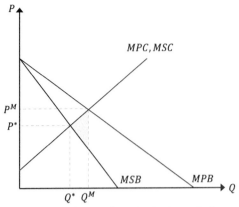

FIGURE 17.5 The market equilibrium and the socially optimal outcome in the presence of a negative consumption externality. The area representing deadweight loss is shaded in grey

17.3.3 Positive production and negative consumption externalities

Thus far we have concentrated on two types of externalities: positive consumption and negative production externalities. In many ways, it does not really matter which side of the market the externality can be attributed to – what is more important is that the external cost or benefit drives a wedge between private and social marginal benefits or costs. As a result, the market outcome will not necessarily coincide with the socially efficient outcome. For completeness, however, we briefly outline the two other types of externality – a negative consumption externality and a positive production externality.

Figure 17.5 illustrates a negative consumption externality, which could represent the consumption of a product like cigarettes where bystanders incur the cost of passive smoke. In this case, the MSB is less than the MPB by the size of the externality; this is represented by the vertical downwards shift of the MSB from the MPB by the size of the negative consumption externality at every level of output ($MSB = MPB - MEC$, where MEC is the size of the external cost). In this case market output is too high ($Q^M > Q^*$), and a DWL results, as illustrated by the shaded area on the figure; for every unit between Q^* and Q^M the cost to society for each unit (MPC) exceeds the extra benefits generated (MSB).

A positive production externality is illustrated in Figure 17.6; an example of this is research and development. While the investing firm could get a private return from their efforts, other firms (not necessarily in the same industry) might also enjoy some benefits from this R&D. These 'spillovers' are externalities because the investing firm only considers its private benefits (and costs) when making its R&D choice. With the positive production externality shown in Figure 17.6, the MSC is lower than the MPC by the size of the positive externality. Consequently, the market output, where $MPB = MPC$, results in an equilibrium quantity Q^M less than the surplus-maximising outcome Q^*. The DWL is the shaded area – for every unit between Q^M and Q^* the $MPB > MSC$; the DWL indicates the surplus forgone in the market equilibrium relative to the efficient outcome.

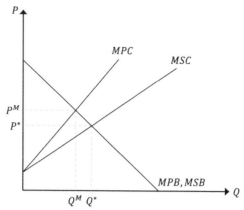

FIGURE 17.6 The market equilibrium and the socially optimal outcome in the presence of a positive production externality. The area representing deadweight loss is shaded in grey

17.4 Solutions to externalities

A number of solutions exist to correct the deadweight loss arising from an externality. In this section, we consider three solutions: (a) the Coase Theorem, (b) taxes and subsidies, and (c) standards and regulations.

17.4.1 Private-market solutions: the Coase Theorem

One way that an externality may be corrected is via private bargaining between the involved parties. In this way, the market participants and the third parties affected by the externality can 'renegotiate' the market outcome, such that the socially optimal outcome is implemented and the deadweight loss is eliminated. To understand how this works, consider the following example:

> **Example.** A beekeeper and an almond grower have farms next to each other. The beekeeper's bees provide a positive externality for the almond grower by pollinating his almond flowers, which increases almond production. If the beekeeper increases her number of hives, even more flowers will be pollinated. This suggests that if the beekeeper decides how many hives to keep based on her interests alone, this number may be fewer than is socially efficient because the almond grower also benefits from each additional hive. However, this can be addressed via private negotiation between the parties. The parties may come to an agreement that the almond grower will pay the beekeeper to increase her number of hives. Note that this agreement is viable so long as the MSB (that is, the beekeeper's MPB plus the almond grower's MEB) exceeds the beekeeper's marginal cost of maintaining the additional hive, which is the same condition necessary for the extra hive to increase total surplus.

The idea that private bargaining can implement a socially efficient outcome is articulated in the Coase Theorem. This theorem is formally stated below.

Coase Theorem. Provided property rights have been clearly assigned and there are no transaction costs, bargaining will lead to an efficient (i.e. socially optimal) outcome, regardless of the initial allocation of property rights.

The Coase Theorem depends crucially on property rights. In this context, the 'property right' referred to is the right to decide whether and to what extent the economic activity causing the externality goes ahead. Thus, the Coase Theorem is essentially an application of the gains from trade principle, where the parties are simply trading property rights rather than goods or services. In the example above, the property right being traded is the right to determine whether or not the beekeeper maintains an additional hive. This right was initially held by the beekeeper, but could be sold to the almond grower.

Importantly, the attainment of the socially optimal outcome does not depend on *how* property rights are allocated, but merely on the fact that they *have* been allocated. Nevertheless, the allocation of property rights will have implications for how the gains from trade are distributed between the parties.

> **Example.** Alex owns a factory that generates some black smoke as a byproduct of its production. The smoke drifts over to Bob's laundromat; however, Bob requires clean air in order to properly wash clothes. At present, Alex makes $300 from operating the factory, whereas Bob could make $500 profit from washing clothes. In this situation, the socially efficient outcome is that the factory ceases production, so that the laundromat can operate (because 500 > 300). Provided that there are no transaction costs and that property rights are clearly defined, the parties can negotiate to achieve this outcome, regardless of who initially holds the property right.

> - Suppose that Alex initially holds the right to decide whether the factory operates. Alex values this right at $300, because that is the profit that she can make from deciding that the factory will operate. Bob, on the other hand, values the right at $500 because that is the profit he can make from deciding that the factory will not operate. Consequently, Alex will sell Bob the right to decide for a price between $300 and $500, and the factory will cease to operate.
> - Suppose that Bob initially holds the right to decide whether the factory operates. Bob values the right at $500 because that is the profit he can make from stopping factory operations and running his laundromat. On the other hand, Alex values the right at $300, because that is the profit that she can make from operating the factory. Because Bob values the right more highly than Alex does, he will not sell the right to her. Hence, Bob will decide that the factory should cease to operate.

Note that the factory ceases to operate, whether the property right is allocated to Alex or to Bob. Nevertheless, the allocation of property rights affects how surplus is distributed between the parties.

- When Alex initially holds the property right, Bob must buy the right from her at a price of $p (300 $\leq p \leq$ 500). Thus, Alex's surplus after the trade is $p and Bob's surplus is $500−$p.
- When Bob initially holds the property right, the property right is not traded. As a result, Alex's surplus is $0 and Bob's surplus is $500.

While the Coase Theorem offers an important insight into how externalities can be addressed by private negotiations, it relies on certain conditions. Thus, the Coase Theorem may fail in the real world if these conditions are not met, for example:

- **Property rights not defined.** The importance of property rights was discussed above. If initial property rights are not properly defined, the parties will not have a 'starting position' from which to begin their negotiations. That is, if it is not clear who initially owns the property right, it will not be possible for parties to trade that right.
- **Transaction costs.** The Coase Theorem assumes that there are no transaction or bargaining costs. However, in the real world, there are often both implicit and explicit costs to negotiating, executing and enforcing an agreement. If these costs are too high, it can prevent the parties from negotiating or trading at all, because the gains to be made do not outweigh the costs. This is more likely to be a problem if the effect of the externality is dispersed amongst many parties, such that the relative benefit to any one individual from negotiating for a better outcome is small relative to the costs.
- **Identity of parties unknown.** If the parties are unable to identify each other, it will not be possible for them to engage in negotiations. For example, if a factory owner is unable to identify who is affected by its pollution or the affected parties are unable to discover the source of the pollution, the parties will not be able to negotiate with each other. Again, this is more likely to be a problem if there is a large number of parties.

17.5 Government solutions to externalities

Governments may intervene where private markets are unable to correct market failures on their own. Two typical government interventions are: (i) taxes or subsidies; and (ii) a regulation (or standard).

17.5.1 Taxes and subsidies

As discussed earlier in the chapter, the presence of an externality causes a divergence between the market equilibrium quantity (Q^M) and the socially optimal quantity (Q^*).

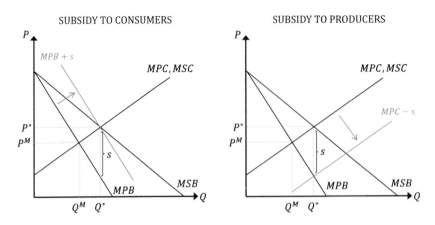

FIGURE 17.7 A subsidy granted to the consumer and to the producer, used to address a positive externality

From Chapter 16, we also know that a tax or a subsidy can influence the quantity traded in the market. Thus, a tax or subsidy can be used to 'correct' the market failure caused by an externality, by reducing or increasing the quantity traded in the market to the socially optimal level.[3]

Positive externality

In the presence of a positive externality, the quantity traded in the market (Q^M) is less than the socially optimal quantity (Q^*). To raise the quantity traded in the market to Q^*, governments can grant a subsidy to either consumers or producers, creating an incentive for the market participants to increase the quantity traded.

Figure 17.7 depicts the effect of subsidising consumers or producers. When the subsidy is given to consumers, the demand curve (the *MPB* curve) shifts up by the size of the subsidy per unit, increasing the quantity traded in the market. Similarly, when the subsidy is given to producers, the supply curve (the *MPC* curve) shifts down by the size of the per-unit subsidy, increasing the quantity traded in the market.

The trick, of course, is to set the size of the subsidy just right so that the socially optimal quantity is achieved. As you can see from Figure 17.7, this means that the size of the subsidy (*s*) should be equal to the size of the externality (that is, the difference between *MPB* and *MSB*) at the socially optimal quantity. Because the size of the subsidy is equal to the size of the externality, the subsidy causes market participants to 'internalise' the externality. This implements the socially optimal outcome and hence eliminates any deadweight loss.

Negative externality

When there is a negative externality, the quantity traded in the market (Q^M) is greater than the socially optimal quantity (Q^*). To lower the quantity traded in the market to Q^*, governments can impose a tax on either consumers or producers, creating an incentive for the market participants to decrease the quantity traded.

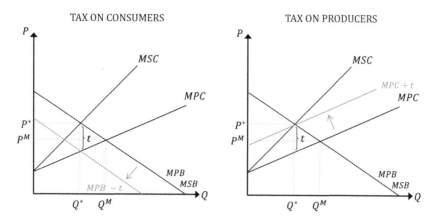

FIGURE 17.8 A tax imposed on the consumer and on the producer, used to address a negative externality

Figure 17.8 depicts the effect of taxing consumers or producers in the presence of a negative production externality. When the tax is imposed on consumers, the demand curve (the *MPB* curve) shifts down by the size of the tax, decreasing the quantity traded in the market. Similarly, when the tax is imposed on producers, the supply curve (the *MPC* curve) shifts up by the size of the tax, decreasing the quantity traded in the market.

Again, the size of the tax needs to be calibrated so as to achieve the socially efficient quantity. As depicted in Figure 17.8, this means that the size of the tax (t) should be equal to the size of the externality (that is, the difference between *MPC* and *MSC*) at the socially optimal quantity. Because the size of the subsidy is equal to the size of the externality at the efficient level, the subsidy causes market participants to 'internalise' the externality – they act as if they take the externality into account, even though they are actually considering only their private benefits and costs, which now include the Pigovian tax. This implements the socially optimal outcome and hence eliminates any deadweight loss.[4]

17.5.2 Quantity regulation

In the previous section, we discussed how a government could use taxes and subsidies to indirectly implement the socially optimal outcome. However, as an alternative, the government could simply regulate the quantity traded in the market directly by mandating that a certain quantity (specifically, the efficient quantity) be produced.

Example. Suppose that, in equilibrium, the quantity of vuvuzelas traded is 500. However, because the use of vuvuzelas produces a negative externality (noise pollution), the socially optimal quantity of vuvuzelas is actually 100. The government could implement the socially optimal outcome by mandating that no more than 100 vuvuzelas be produced.

One way of implementing quantity restrictions is by requiring a licence to produce (or consume) a unit of output and by limiting the number of licences issued. If the licence must be obtained by the party creating the externality, the licence can also be thought of as a licence to create the externality. For example, suppose that the manufacturing of cars is associated with some level of pollution. Because the two go hand in hand, a licence to manufacture a certain number of cars can equally be thought of as a licence to emit a certain level of pollution. Similarly, in the vuvuzelas example above, the government could regulate the quantity in the market by issuing licences to either producers or consumers (even though the externality is generated by consumption, the government can regulate output on the other side of the market with the same economic effects).

17.5.3 Taxes and subsidies versus quantity regulation

From our discussion above, we can see that taxes and subsidies are aimed at implementing the socially optimal outcome by influencing the price in the market, whereas regulations and tradeable permits aim to do so by influencing the quantity traded. But which of these two approaches is better? As it happens, this will depend on the circumstances of the case, but there are some factors worth considering. One advantage of quantity regulation is that it creates certainty about the level of output – such as certainty about the pollution. This is particularly valuable when the government is unsure about how market participants will react to a tax or subsidy.

On the other hand, a tax has several advantages. First, because the tax is a price to pollute, firms will have an incentive to avoid the tax if they can. If a new pollution-reducing technology becomes available, for example, a tax gives firms an incentive to adopt the technology so as to avoid paying the tax. A regulation does not necessarily give the firms an incentive to continue to reduce emissions beyond what is required by the regulation.

Second, some firms can reduce emissions more cheaply than other firms. For example, more modern factories might be able to reduce emissions relatively more easily than older establishments. Similarly, the technology in some industries might lend itself more to reducing pollution emissions than in other industries. A tax, by setting a price for polluting, allows for unequal reductions of emissions across firms and industries. This, in turn, reduces the cost of achieving the required reduction in emissions, as a greater share is undertaken by the firms that can do so at a lower cost. A regulation, on the other hand, might require all firms to make the same reductions in emissions. This means that reducing emissions is not done in the least-cost way; low-cost firms do too little and firms for which reducing emissions is costly do too much.[5]

17.5.4 Tradeable permits

As noted, a regulation has the advantage that it gives certainty about the level of pollution that will be emitted. A tax on emissions has the advantage of providing incentives for firms to reduce output in order to reduce pollution, as they face a cost when they do so. A tradeable market is an attempt to capture both of these advantages while addressing an externality. **Tradeable permits** are a special type of licence that may be transferred between parties; thus, consumers (resp. producers) may trade with each other for the right to consume (resp. produce) units of output. Essentially, this system creates a market for, say, pollution. If a firm holds a permit, the opportunity cost of using it is that it cannot sell it; if it sells it, the opportunity cost is that it cannot use it. This creates an incentive for a firm with a relatively low value for the permit to trade it with another firm that values it more. Remember, a permit is essentially a licence to pollute – so that means that firms that do not highly value the right to pollute (such as a firm making a low-value product) will sell their permits to those who value the right to pollute more highly (such as a firm that makes a high-value product). Similarly, a firm that can reduce its emissions relatively cheaply will be willing to sell its permit to a firm that has a higher cost of reducing emissions. This market for permits means that, regardless of the initial distribution of permits, the firms will trade the permits so that the efficient outcome is achieved.

> **Example.** Suppose the government issues 100 permits to produce a vuvuzela: 50 permits are given to Firm A and 50 permits are given to Firm B. Due to their different production costs, Firm A can make $1 profit per vuvuzela, Firm B can make $5 profit per vuvuzela. Therefore, Firm A values each permit at $1 and Firm B values each permit at $5. As a result, Firm A will sell all its permits to Firm B at a price between $1 and $5. At the conclusion of trade, Firm B will hold 100 permits, and surplus will be maximised.

> **Example.** Consider the case when the government wishes to allocate 600 permits to pollute between two firms, A and B. Firm A can make $5 profit from each permit. Firm B can make $10 profit from the first 400 permits, then $2 profit from every subsequent permit used thereafter. The government initially allocated 300 permits to each firm, but they are both free to trade the permits between each other. Firm B can make $10 for each permit for the first 400 permits, but it only has 300. B will negotiate and offer to buy an additional 100 permits from A, for a price between $5 and $10. Firm A will be willing to sell too, as it can make at least $5 per permit from the trade. But this is where trading stops. After B has 400 permits, any subsequent permits are only worth $2 to it, and this is not going to be enough to induce Firm A to sell. So, even though we started with an allocation of 300 for each firm, Firms A and B end up with 200 and 400 permits, respectively. This outcome, moreover, is the outcome that maximises total surplus. This final allocation produces the highest level of profit given that there are 600 permits available in total. A similar process would occur if Firm A was initially allocated all of the permits and B got none; B would buy 400 permits from A for a price between $5 and $10 and surplus would be maximised.

While theoretically the government can achieve the same outcome regarding an externality with either a tax or tradeable permits, this assumes that there are no transaction costs. With all government interventions in the market, it is important to consider how much it costs for them to be implemented. Specifically, it is likely that there will be different costs (setup costs, enforcement costs, corruption, and so on) with a Pigovian tax than there are with a tradeable permit system. If these costs are lower with a tax than with a tradeable permit system, it could well be that the Pigovian tax is a lower-cost way of addressing a negative externality.

17.6 Concluding comments

Externalities are a source of market failure because they represent costs and benefits that are not accounted for by the market. As a result, the market equilibrium that results from the private decisions of consumers and firms will not necessarily be the socially optimal outcome. There are a number of solutions to this problem. The Coase Theorem postulates that, if property rights are defined and there are no transaction costs, parties will privately negotiate to implement the socially optimal outcome. Failing this, there are also a number of government policies that can be used to correct externalities; these include taxes, subsidies, quantity regulation and tradeable permits.

Notes

1 By 'mutually beneficial trades', we mean trades that can benefit both the buyer and the seller.
2 Put another way, externalities can be thought of as 'spill-over effects' from economic activity.
3 These taxes or subsidies are also called 'Pigovian taxes' or 'Pigovian subsidies', after Arthur Pigou, who developed the concept of externalities.
4 Note that this is an example of a tax that does not cause a DWL.
5 As an example, say the government wants to reduce total emissions by 500 units due to a negative externality, and there are two firms in the market. It costs the first firm $5 to reduce emissions by one unit; on the other hand, it costs the second firm $12 per unit of emissions reduction. Hence, it costs society $7 more for each unit reduction in emissions undertaken by the second firm than the first firm. If the government's regulation stipulated that both firms must reduce emissions by 250 units, the target of a total reduction of 500 units will not be achieved at a lowest cost.

CHAPTER 18

Public goods and common resources

18.1 Introduction

So far in this book, we have examined goods or services that can be considered private goods. In this chapter, we examine different types of goods: public goods and common resources. Because of their nature, public goods and common resources can also be a source of market failure.

18.2 Public goods

A **public good** is a good or service that is non-excludable and non-rivalrous.

1) **Non-excludable.** A good is non-excludable if the owner or provider of the good cannot stop people from consuming it (and receiving the benefit from doing so). For example, a person living in a country with a national defence service cannot be excluded from enjoying the benefit of that service. Similarly, a person living in a region that maintains a clean environment or good biodiversity cannot be excluded from enjoying the benefit of those goods.
2) **Non-rivalrous.** A good is non-rivalrous if one person's consumption of a good does not interfere with another person's ability to consume the same unit of the good. For example, one person using a street light to find their way home does not prevent another person from using that same street light.

By contrast, a **private good** is one that is excludable (the owner or provider of the good can prevent others from enjoying it) and rivalrous (one person's consumption of the good prevents another person's consumption of the good).

DOI: 10.4324/9781003376644-23

For example, a donut is a private good because it is possible to refuse to sell or give someone a donut (excludable) and because the same donut can only be consumed once (rivalrous).

18.2.1 The marginal benefit curve for a public good

With a private good, the market demand curve is obtained by the horizontal summation of all the individual marginal benefit (*MB*) curves along the *Q*-axis (recall our discussion in Chapter 6). This is because private goods are rivalrous, so if several individuals wish to consume the good, they will each need to separately buy their own units. Thus, the total quantity consumed in the market is the sum of each individual's consumption.

However, society's total *MB* curve for a public good is obtained by the vertical summation of all the individual *MB* curves along the *P*-axis.[1] This is because public goods are non-rivalrous, so if several individuals wish to consume a good, they can share units of that good. For example, suppose Aliya values the construction of a lighthouse at $30 and Victoria values the construction of a lighthouse at $50. Because the lighthouse can guide both of their ships, Aliya and Victoria can 'share' the same lighthouse; that is, they do not need one each. Together, Aliya and Victoria would be willing to pay $80 for the lighthouse. Therefore, the market's total willingness to pay is given by the sum of each individual's valuation of the good.

> **Example.** The local council is thinking about setting aside more space for parks. Erin's marginal benefit for additional parks is $MB_E = 10 - q$ and Jess's marginal benefit for additional parks is $MB_J = 20 - 2q$, where q is the number of additional parks. The *MB* curves are depicted in Figure 18.1. For simplicity, let us assume that Erin and Jess are the only two residents who will make use of the additional parks. To obtain the total *MB* curve (that is, the market demand curve), we need to vertically sum Erin's *MB* curve with Jess's *MB* curve. The total *MB* curve is also depicted in Figure 18.1 and is given by the equation $MB_T = 30 - 3q$.

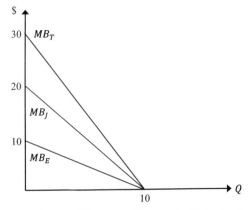

FIGURE 18.1 The market demand curve (MB_T) for a public good is obtained by the vertical summation of each individual's marginal benefit curve

18.2.2 The problem with public goods

As we have previously established, the efficient quantity of a good is the quantity at which $MC = MB$. In the case of a public good, this means the quantity where the marginal cost of providing the good is equal to society's total MB for the good.

> **Example.** The local council is thinking about setting aside more space for parks. Erin's marginal benefit from additional parks is $MB_E = 10 - q$ and Jess's marginal benefit for additional parks is $MB_J = 20 - 2q$, where q is the number of additional parks. The total willingness to pay for an additional park is given by the equation $MB_T = 30 - 3q$. Suppose the council's cost of building a new park is $21 per park. To find the efficient or socially optimal number of parks, we need to solve $MC = MB_T$. This gives $21 = 30 - 3q$ or $q = 3$.

The market failure associated with public goods arises from two sources:

- Because the good is non-rivalrous, each individual consumer undervalues the good relative to its total MB to society. As a result, it might be the case that no individual consumer would purchase any units of the good, even though the collective willingness to pay exceeds MC. In the example above, when the marginal cost of parks is $21, neither Erin nor Jess would consume parks if they had to bear the cost individually. However, because they can share the parks (and also the burden of paying for the parks), it is socially optimal that they consume three parks together.
- Because the good is non-excludable, consumers cannot be excluded from enjoying the public good even if they have not paid for it (this is called 'the free-rider effect'). This makes it difficult for private firms to enforce payment and hence make profits from the sale of a public good; as a result, there is little to no provision of public goods by the private sector.

The upshot of this is that there tends to be an under-provision of public goods in the free market relative to the efficient quantity. As a result, public goods are often provided by the government, which can enforce payment for the public good through the taxation system. Indeed, governments in the real world tend to be responsible for providing national defence services, street lighting, parks, environmental quality and so on.

18.3 Common resources and the Tragedy of the Commons

Common resources are often thought of as 'partial' public goods because they are non-excludable, but rivalrous. Examples of common resource goods might be: fishing stocks on the high seas; mineral deposits where there is no effective government oversight; or the use of a road or a bridge that the government cannot, or chooses not to, restrict the use of.

The market failure arising from common resources is over-exploitation. This problem is frequently referred to as the **Tragedy of the Commons** and is often described as follows: Suppose the residents of a village share a field where each may graze cattle. The field is non-excludable because no villager can be prevented from using the field to graze cattle, but rivalrous because grazing by one villager depletes the amount of grass available for the next villager's cattle. Consequently, when a villager uses the field for grazing, she reaps all of the benefits of doing so (her cattle are fed) but the cost is shared amongst all the villagers (the stock of grass is depleted). As a result, each individual villager uses the field for grazing more than she would if she alone bore the entire cost of doing so, leading to overgrazing.

One way to address the over-exploitation of common resources is to create enforceable property rights over the good. In the case of the communal grazing field, this could take the form of land ownership or a permit to graze. By doing so, the good ceases to be non-excludable, making it much easier to prevent overuse of the resource. Similarly, driving on a congested bridge increases the cost for other users. If property rights are allocated, the owner of the bridge could introduce a toll that effectively makes drivers 'internalise' the congestion cost their road use imposes on others.

18.4 Concluding comments

Because of their non-rivalrous nature, the 'market demand' curve for public goods is given by the vertical sum of each individual's *MB* curve. As a result, each individual consumer undervalues the public good relative to the willingness to pay of society as a whole. Moreover, their non-excludable nature means that there tends to be an under-provision of public goods by private firms.

Consequently, public goods tend to be provided by the government. Notwithstanding this, it is important not to conflate the economic concept of a 'public good' with the more common 'publicly owned good'. Indeed, many publicly owned goods are not public goods. For example, it is not unusual for services such as water supply, health care and telecommunications to be provided by the government. However, individuals can easily be excluded from accessing these goods, so they are not public goods.

Common resource goods are those that are non-excludable, but rivalrous. They often suffer from over-exploitation, which may be mitigated by the allocation of property rights.

Notes

1   Note that sometimes society's total *MB* for a public good is referred to as the 'market demand' curve for the public good; at times we use this terminology too. However, as discussed below, the *MB* curve for a public good is not really a demand curve in the traditional sense because it is non-excludable.

PART VI

International trade

CHAPTER 19

International trade

19.1 Introduction

In Chapter 4, we showed that trade between individuals can be mutually beneficial for all parties involved. This is also true at an international level: there can be gains from trade if countries produce goods in which they have a comparative advantage, and then trade those goods with other countries.

In this chapter, we extend our analysis of international trade further, to examine what determines whether a country is an exporter or importer of a particular product. We also examine the welfare effects of international trade, as well as the effects of government policies with respect to trade, including tariffs and quotas on imports.

19.2 The welfare effects of international trade

In our analysis, we will focus on the effects of international trade on a single country. This requires us to distinguish between the country's market for a good ('the domestic market') and the international market for the same good ('the world market'). We will assume that the country is a **small country**, such that market outcomes in the domestic market have no effect on the world market's outcomes – that is, changes in prices and the quantity traded in the domestic market do not affect world prices.[1]

19.2.1 Welfare under autarky

Let us first suppose that the country does not trade with the world market (often called **autarky**). In Chapters 6–9, we derived the demand and supply

DOI: 10.4324/9781003376644-25

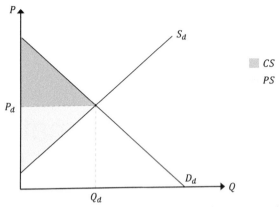

FIGURE 19.1 The market equilibrium for a country in autarky is given by the intersection of the domestic demand curve and the domestic supply curve. In this figure, this is denoted by (Q_d, P_d)

curves and hence determined the market equilibrium. Now, we will assume that these curves refer to domestic demand (that is, the demand of consumers within a country) and domestic supply (that is, the supply of producers within a country). Thus, the intersection of the domestic demand (D_d) and supply (S_d) curves denotes the market equilibrium (Q_d, P_d) for the country in autarky. Figure 19.1 depicts the market outcomes of a country in autarky, as well as consumer and producer surplus.

19.2.2 Welfare with international trade

Now, suppose the country opens up to international trade; that is, domestic consumers and producers can now trade with consumers and producers in the world market. Because of the small country assumption, the price at which the good is traded in the world market (P_w) is determined independently of the domestic market equilibrium. This means that, from the perspective of the single country, world demand and world supply are perfectly elastic at P_w – a domestic consumer can buy a unit of the good from foreign producers at the price P_w, and a domestic producer can sell a unit of the good to international consumers at the price P_w.

The relationship between the domestic equilibrium price (P_d) and the world price (P_w) will determine whether the country is an exporter or an importer of the good. Indeed, the relationship between P_d and P_w is an indicator of comparative advantage: if the $P_d < P_w$, the country has a comparative advantage in producing that good; if $P_d > P_w$, the country has a comparative disadvantage.

An exporting country

Suppose $P_d < P_w$, as depicted in Figure 19.2. If the country opens up to international trade, the effective demand curve faced by domestic producers will change from D_d (the domestic demand curve under autarky) to the kinked demand curve depicted in Figure 19.2. The construction of the effective demand curve can be explained as follows: If a producer wishes to sell a unit of the good, she will try to do so for the

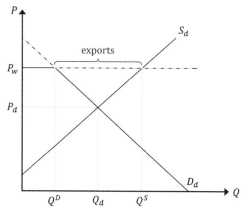

FIGURE 19.2 A country that is open to international trade is an exporter if the domestic equilibrium price (P_d) is lower than the world price (P_w). The effective demand curve for an exporting country is traced out by the dashed line

highest price possible. For the first Q^D units, the highest price is offered by domestic consumers. However, if more than Q^D units are required, foreign consumers now offer the highest price, P_w.

The equilibrium price in the presence of international trade is given by the intersection of the domestic supply curve and the effective demand curve; that is, the price in the domestic market, with international trade, will be P_w.[2] As the price moves from the domestic equilibrium price (P_d) to the world price (P_w), illustrated in Figure 19.2, the domestic quantity supplied will increase to Q^S and the domestic quantity demanded will decrease to Q^D; the quantity supplied by domestic producers now exceeds the quantity demanded by domestic consumers. The difference in these quantities is sold to the world market; thus the country is an exporter of the good.

The welfare effects of international trade for an exporting country are depicted in Figure 19.3. Because the price rises to P_w, domestic consumers are made worse off for two reasons: Firstly, the increase in price means that less surplus is received on each unit purchased; secondly, consumers buy fewer units overall, meaning that surplus is lost through the decrease in the quantity purchased. On the other hand, domestic producers are made better off for two reasons: firstly, the increase in price means more surplus is received on each unit sold; secondly, as they are now able to sell to the world market, producers sell more units overall.

On the whole, total welfare increases. The loss of consumer surplus (A) is more than offset by the increase in producer surplus ($A + B$). Comparing Figures 19.1 and 19.3, there is an additional surplus (B) with international trade that was not previously available under autarky. As total surplus is higher with international trade, autarky cannot be pareto efficient. To see this, note that a change from autarky to international trade generates sufficient extra surplus for producers such that they can (at least theoretically) compensate consumers fully for their loss in surplus (A) and still be better off by B.

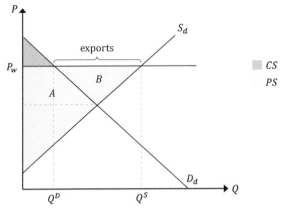

FIGURE 19.3 Consumer surplus and producer surplus for an exporting country

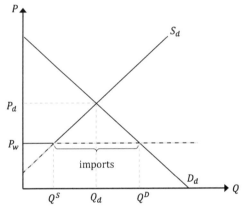

FIGURE 19.4 A country that is open to international trade is an importer if the domestic equilibrium price (P_d) is higher than the world price (P_w). The effective supply curve for an importing country is traced out by the dashed grey line

An importing country

Now suppose $P_d > P_w$, as depicted in Figure 19.4. If the country opens up to international trade, the effective supply curve faced by domestic consumers will change from S_d (the supply curve under autarky) to the kinked supply curve depicted in Figure 19.4. The construction of the effective supply curve can be explained as follows: If a consumer wishes to buy a unit of the good, he will try to do so for the lowest price possible. For the first Q^S units, the lowest price is offered by the domestic producers. However, if more than Q^S units are required, foreign producers now offer the lowest price, P_w.

The equilibrium price in the presence of international trade is given by the intersection of the domestic demand curve and the effective supply curve; that is, the price in the domestic market, with international trade, will be P_w.[3] As the price moves from the domestic equilibrium price (P_d) to the world price (P_w), there will be changes in the domestic quantity demanded and the domestic quantity supplied. As seen in

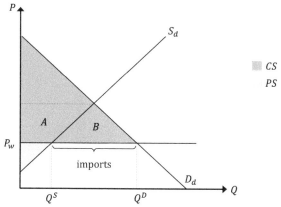

FIGURE 19.5 Consumer surplus and producer surplus for an importing country

Figure 19.4, the domestic quantity supplied will decrease to Q^S and the domestic quantity demanded will increase to Q^D. The quantity demanded by domestic consumers now exceeds the quantity supplied by domestic producers. The difference in these quantities will be supplied by the world market; thus the country is an importer of the good.

The welfare effects of international trade on an importing country are depicted in Figure 19.5. Because the price falls to P_w, domestic producers are made worse off for two reasons: Firstly, the decrease in price means that less surplus is received on each unit sold; secondly, producers sell fewer units overall, meaning that surplus is lost through the decrease in the quantity sold. On the other hand, domestic consumers are made better off for two reasons: Firstly, the decrease in price means that more surplus is received on each unit purchased; secondly, as they are now able to buy from the world market, consumers buy more units overall.

On the whole, total welfare increases. The loss of producer surplus (A) is more than offset by the increase in consumer surplus ($A + B$). Comparing Figures 19.1 and 19.5, we can see that there is additional surplus from international trade (B in the Figure) that was not previously available under autarky. Given that total surplus is larger with international trade, autarky cannot be a Pareto efficient outcome. Indeed, it is (theoretically) possible for consumers to compensate producers for all of their losses of surplus (A) given a move from autarky to international trade, and still be better off by B.

19.3 Barriers to trade

As discussed above, local producers may be negatively affected by international trade if the price of imports (that is, the world price) is lower than the autarky equilibrium price. Governments sometimes try to protect local industries by setting up trade barriers that make it more difficult to import goods into the country. In this section, we discuss two governmental policies designed to act as barriers to trade: tariffs and quotas.

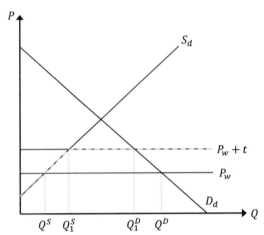

FIGURE 19.6 The effect of a tariff on domestic market outcomes for an importing country. The effective supply curve is traced out by the dashed grey line

19.3.1 Tariffs

A **tariff** is a tax on importing a good into a country, which increases the cost of importing the good. For example, a tariff might require a foreign firm to pay $10 to the government for every guitar it brings into the country to sell. In this section, we examine the welfare effects of a tariff on domestic consumers, domestic producers and the economy as a whole.

To begin, suppose that the world price of a good is below the autarky equilibrium price, so the country is an importer of the good.[4] Now, suppose the government implements a tariff that requires foreign firms to pay t to the government for every unit imported. As depicted in Figure 19.6, the effect of this tariff is to raise the price of imports in the domestic market by the size of the tariff (t) from P_w to $P_w + t$.[5] The change in the price of imports will affect the shape of the effective supply curve, because domestic producers are now 'competing' with the higher price. There will be an increase in the domestic quantity supplied from Q^S to Q_1^S. There will also be a decrease in the domestic quantity demanded from Q^D to Q_1^D. Intuitively, this is because the tariff makes foreign producers less competitive in the domestic market, giving domestic firms a greater share of sales. The quantity of imports decreases from $Q^D - Q^S$ to $Q_1^D - Q_1^S$.

The welfare effects of the tariff are depicted in Figure 19.7. As a result of the tariff and hence the increase in price, domestic consumers are made worse off for two reasons: Firstly, the increase in price means that less surplus is received on each unit purchased; secondly, consumers buy fewer units overall, meaning that surplus is lost through the decrease in the quantity purchased. Specifically, CS falls by the area $C+A+G+B$ in the figure. On the other hand, domestic producers are made better off for two reasons: Firstly, the increase in price means more surplus is received on each unit sold; secondly, producers sell more units overall. Specifically, PS increases by area C. Moreover, the tariff creates government surplus as the government now receives

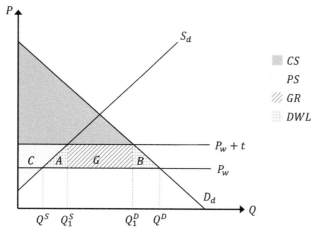

FIGURE 19.7 The welfare effects of a tariff

revenue from foreign producers who import the good. Government tariff revenue is $t.[Q_1^D - Q_1^S]$ or area G in the figure.

Importantly, the increase in producer surplus and government surplus (tariff revenue) does not fully offset the decrease in consumer surplus. The resulting deadweight loss of the tariff is depicted in Figure 19.7 as areas $A + B$. The triangle of deadweight loss next to the demand curve (B) arises from the decrease in the quantity demanded from Q^D to Q_1^D, and thus is often referred to as the deadweight loss from underconsumption. The DWL arises because for each unit between Q_1^D and Q^D there is a consumer with a higher MB than the MC of acquiring the good (which is P_w), but the tariff puts a wedge between this price and the price consumers have to pay, which is $P_w + t$. As a consequence, the total surplus would increase if consumption was increased to Q^D.

The triangle of deadweight loss next to the supply curve (A) arises from the increase in the domestic quantity supplied from Q^S to Q_1^S, and thus is often referred to as the deadweight loss from overproduction. This DWL from overproduction arises because, between Q^S and Q_1^S, the economy could have imported the good at a marginal cost of P_w – the country can have as much of the good as it wants at the going world price. But instead of doing this, the tariff raises the price enjoyed by domestic producers, increasing domestic output from Q^S to Q_1^S, even though the MC of production is higher for domestic firms than P_w over this range of output. This means that the economy is not minimising the cost of obtaining the good, reducing the total surplus by the additional costs incurred over and above P_w between Q^S and Q_1^S.

Together, the DWLs from underconsumption and overproduction make up the total deadweight loss from the tariff. The total DWL from the tariff is $A + B$.

19.3.2 Quotas

A **quota** is a legally enforced limit on the number of goods that may be imported into a country. For example, a government might stipulate that no more than 100 cars may

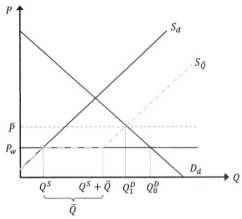

FIGURE 19.8 The effect of a quota on domestic market outcomes for an importing country. The effective supply curve is traced out by the dashed grey line

be imported into the country. In this section, we examine the welfare effects of a quota on domestic consumers, domestic producers and the economy as a whole.

To begin, suppose that the world price of a good is below the autarky equilibrium price, so the country is an importer of the good.[6] Now, suppose the government imposes a quota of $\bar{Q}$. As depicted in Figure 19.8, the introduction of a quota will create an additional kink in the effective supply curve, for the following reasons: As discussed above, for the first Q^S units, the lowest price is offered by domestic producers; for units beyond Q^S, the lowest price is offered by foreign producers. However, the imposition of the quota means that no more than $\bar{Q}$ units of the good may be imported, so after $Q^S + \bar{Q}$ units, consumers must return to domestic producers to buy the good. In other words, the next segment of the effective supply curve is the portion of the domestic supply curve above P_w. Therefore, beyond $Q^S + \bar{Q}$ units, the effective supply curve is made up of the remainder of the domestic supply curve, shifted right by the size of the quota.

Hence, the domestic market outcome will be determined by the intersection of the domestic demand curve and the new effective supply curve ($S_{\bar{Q}}$). The price of the good will increase from P_w to $\bar{P}$. The domestic quantity demanded will be Q_1^D; to meet this demand, $\bar{Q}$ units will be imported, with domestic producers supplying the balance.

Let us now consider the welfare implications of a quota. As it happens, the effect of a quota on the welfare of domestic consumers and domestic producers echoes the effects of a tariff, as depicted in Figure 19.9. Domestic consumers are made worse off for two reasons: Firstly, the increase in price means that less surplus is received on each unit purchased; secondly, consumers buy fewer units overall, meaning that surplus is lost through the decrease in the quantity purchased. Domestic producers are made better off for two reasons: Firstly, the increase in price means more surplus is received on each unit sold; secondly, producers sell more units overall. As with a tariff, the import quota creates a DWL because it puts a wedge between P_w and the price the good is traded for in the domestic market. Because domestic price is higher, there is a DWL

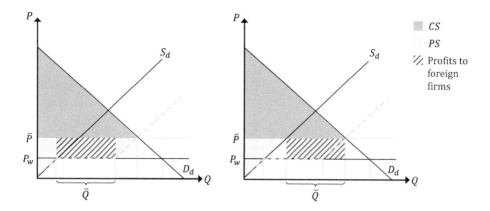

FIGURE 19.9 The left panel depicts the welfare effects of a quota. Domestic producer surplus is accrued on those units sold by domestic producers (the first few and last few units). The intermediate units are imported and hence foreign firms make profits on these units. The right panel depicts an equivalent way of showing the welfare effects of a quota. The relevant areas are equivalent because the domestic supply curve is parallel to the last section of the effective supply curve

from underconsumption and overproduction. The intuition is the same as with a tariff, as discussed in Section 19.3.1.

However, under a quota system, the government does not receive any revenue because foreign firms do not make any payments to the government for importing the good. Instead, foreign firms make additional profits from units imported and sold in the country because they can now sell those goods at a higher price. The size of these additional profits is shown in Figure 19.9.

19.3.3 Tariffs vs. quotas

As we now know, a tariff acts as a barrier to international trade by increasing the price of imports, whereas a quota places a limit on the quantity of imports. However, for a given tariff, there is an equivalent quota that will yield the same price, quantities and level of imports traded in the domestic market. Conversely, for every given quota, there is an equivalent tariff that gives rise to the outcomes in the domestic market.

The key difference between tariffs and quotas is who receives the benefit from the increase in the price of imports. As discussed above, when a tariff is in place this benefit accrues to the government in the form of tariff revenue. By contrast, when a quota is in place, the benefit is enjoyed by the importer, who can buy a good on the international market for P_w and sell it on the domestic market for $\bar{P}$. In this case, however, the government can capture this extra surplus by requiring foreign firms to purchase an import licence at a price of $\bar{P} - P_w$ per unit imported. There would be a similar result if the government allocated the licences through a competitive auction process; the price for a licence to import a good would be (approximately) $\bar{P} - P_w$ per unit. As a consequence, the government would capture the whole of the foreign firms' surplus, making the quota scheme equivalent to a tariff. Importantly, however, the two deadweight loss triangles remain.

19.4 Arguments against free trade

In our analysis above, we found that international trade increased the total surplus overall and that the imposition of governmental barriers to trade resulted in a deadweight loss. Despite this, several arguments are often made against free trade.

- **Infant industries.** It is sometimes argued that protection is necessary in the short term to help a domestic industry develop. Once the industry has had a chance to establish itself, the barriers to trade can be removed allowing the industry to successfully compete on the world market. However, evidence from real markets suggests that this strategy has not been successful; for example, tariffs on manufactured goods like cars remained in place for decades, often with limited success in generating an internationally competitive industry.
- **Strategic trade policy.** Another argument is that trade protection can allow a country to manipulate the international trading environment in its own interest. Realistically, however, most countries will not be large enough to unilaterally affect the world market. Secondly, in order to implement this strategy, governments would need to perfectly understand the behaviour of private market firms and other governments around the world, which is near impossible.
- **Anti-dumping measures.** Dumping occurs when foreign firms sell their goods in a country at a price below cost, with the intent of forcing local producers out of business. This is done so that the foreign producer can capture the entire domestic market. In principle, certain types of trade protection may be effective at preventing foreign firms from dumping goods into a country, either by restricting the quantity of imports or by setting a minimum price at which those goods can be sold. An issue arises, however, in that anti-dumping measures are often used to protect inefficient domestic industries when there is no evidence that international competitors are pricing below costs. These actions hurt domestic consumers, who face higher prices and less product variety.
- **Environmental and social standards.** Sometimes, it is contended that domestic firms face higher costs of production because they have to comply with higher standards – such as environmental standards, labour laws or product standards – than do foreign firms. While this may be true, it is not clear that imposing trade barriers is the best way to deal with this issue, particularly when it is possible to address those issues more directly.
- **Employment protection.** Another argument made for trade protection is that barriers are needed to promote employment in the protected industries. While trade barriers do have this effect, they also divert employment away from other sectors in the economy, particularly those where the country might genuinely have a comparative advantage.

19.5 Concluding comments

In this chapter, we analysed the effect of international trade and barriers to trade on market outcomes and welfare. We found that free trade increases welfare, while restrictions on free trade tend to decrease total surplus. We also examined the strength of some arguments in favour of trade protection.

Notes

1   In many markets, this is a reasonable assumption for a country like Australia. Given its size, Australia's contribution to world trade is often dwarfed by the USA, Europe and Asia.
2   Alternatively, the P_w line becomes the perfectly elastic demand and supply curves faced by domestic producers and consumers. This means that any market participant can buy and sell as much as they want at P_w. Consequently, domestic producers will not accept a lower price than P_w per unit, and domestic consumers cannot be charged any more than this price. Thus, with international trade the equilibrium price will be P_w.
3   With international trade, domestic consumers can buy as much as they want to at P_w. Similarly, domestic producers can always opt to sell into the world market at P_w, so they will not accept a lower price than this. Hence, the equilibrium price in the domestic market allowing for international trade will be P_w.
4   Of course, if the country is an exporter of the good, a tariff will have no effect.
5   This is akin to the effect of imposing a tax on producers where the supply curve is perfectly elastic.
6   Again, if the country is an exporter of the good, a quota will have no effect on limiting the quantity of imports.

PART VII

Economics in practice

CHAPTER 20

Some other markets

20.1 Introduction

So far in this book, our analysis of markets has concentrated on consumer goods (such as shirts, cupcakes and cars) and services (such as haircuts, transport and education). But the economic tools you have learned about in previous chapters can be used to give us insights into a range of different markets.

In this chapter we apply some of the tools of market analysis to several specific markets – namely the housing market, the labour market and the capital market. One of the key points of this chapter is that even though specific markets have their own idiosyncrasies, the economic tools outlined in this text are often very useful in analysing and understanding these markets and making accurate predictions.

20.2 The housing market

The housing market is an important market and, for many, buying a house is one of the biggest financial decisions that they will make in their lifetime. In that sense, the market for housing is a bit different from other markets because most people only buy one house (or apartment) at a time, if at all. Also, in previous chapters, we have referred to the supply side of the market as being made up of 'firms' – but in the housing market, a large component of supply is made up of individuals looking to resell their existing houses. Nevertheless, as we shall see, the demand and supply framework we have discussed previously is still a pretty good way to analyse what is going on in that market.

20.2.1 Demand for housing

As outlined in Chapter 6, we often assume that individuals have smooth demand curves, which implies that they can adjust how many units of a good

DOI: 10.4324/9781003376644-27

they consume by small amounts, either up or down. This is not really the case with housing. For most people the choice is either to have one house (or apartment) or none; we call this type of demand 'discrete'. Conveniently, however, it is often possible to derive a smooth market demand curve, even from discrete individual demand curves. Moreover, we are able to use the standard interpretation of demand when thinking about welfare.

> **Example.** To see why this is, consider the following example: Suppose there are four potential home buyers in a city: Anastasia, Syed, Jennifer and Vladimir. Each is thinking about buying at most one house. Anastasia values having a home at $1m. In other words, the MB of a home for Anastasia is $1m. Syed values a home at $800,000; Jennifer at $600,000; and Vladimir at $400,000. From these valuations we can derive the market demand curve. If the price of a house is more than $1m, no one buys and the quantity demanded is zero. If the price of a home is $1m, only Anastasia will buy and the quantity demand is one. This is also true for any price below $1m but more than $800,000. If the price is $800,000 Syed is prepared to enter the market, and the total quantity demanded will be two homes. The quantity demanded remains at two until the price drops to $600,000, which is the price at which Jennifer will be willing to buy a home. Finally, if the price is less than or equal to $400,000 Vladimir will also buy a home, and the total quantity demanded is four houses. While the demand curve is kinked, it is also (broadly) downward sloping. If we think that there are many potential home buyers in the city – not just four – the kinks will get closer and closer together, and demand can be approximated by a smooth curve. Note also that even when consumers have discrete demand, their demand is derived from their willingness to pay (MB) so we can interpret the area under the demand curve above the price line as consumer surplus.

Another important factor that affects demand for housing is interest rates. Most people have to borrow to pay for such a large purchase as a home. This means that the cost of borrowing – the interest rate that needs to be paid – will affect the price that someone is willing and able to pay for a house. Consequently, there is a relationship between the interest rate applicable to home loans (and the anticipated interest rates over the lifetime of the loan) and the level of demand for housing.

20.2.2 Supply of housing

The quantity of houses supplied will depend on many factors, including the number of builders and their opportunity cost of increasing the number of dwellings they construct. In some cases, the opportunity cost of making an extra house is increasing, meaning there is an upward-sloping supply curve. This could be because, as house prices rise, homeowners may be more inclined to put their house on the market. However, in other cases, the number of houses in a region might be fixed. This could arise if there is limited land in the city, which could be nestled between the coast and mountains

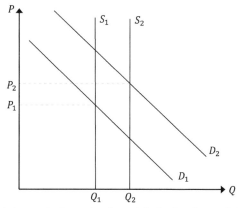

FIGURE 20.1 The effect of changes in demand and supply in the housing market

and when strict planning rules effectively prevent the construction of new dwellings. In those cases the supply curve for housing in the city will be perfectly inelastic.

In many crowded cities around the world, housing stock is very limited and getting access to new housing stock can be challenging. Figure 20.1 illustrates how the release of new housing stock can change the market equilibrium. In that market, there is a perfectly inelastic supply curve, such that the market quantity of houses at Q_1; the market-clearing price, given the demand curve D_1, is P_1. Suppose there is an increase in supply from S_1 to S_2; this could reflect a change in government policy, such as releasing a new tract of land for development or changing planning rules to allow for urban infill. Alone, the increase in supply results in a shift along the demand curve that results in a lower equilibrium price. But, in many cities around the world, demand for new housing is also growing, often due to population growth. So let's say that, over the same period of time, demand increases from D_1 to D_2. Now, in the new market equilibrium, prices are higher than they were previously at (P_2 rather than P_1). This shows that if demand is growing relatively more quickly than supply, prices will rise, which reflects the experience of many cities around the world.

20.2.3 Housing auctions

Houses can be different from each other. Some have extra features (additional space, additional bedrooms, a pool, and so on). Other dwellings have better access to amenities (transport, school, a beach, harbour views) than other places. Other things being equal, the prices for houses with more features will garner a higher price. But homes in a particular area are (more or less) substitutes for one another; prices for dwellings tend to move up (and down) together.

The uniqueness of particular homes is one reason why sellers might choose an auction to sell their house. In real estate, the type of auction typically used is an out-cry auction, also known as an English auction. This is where bidders call out their bids (in ascending order) until no one is willing to offer a higher price; the house is sold to the person who called out the highest (and final) bid at the price they called out. Auction theory is a field unto itself; however, one lesson for sellers is simple – the price they can sell their home for will be higher (on average) the more genuine bidders there are in the market. To see this, let us return to our example with Anastasia, Syed, Jennifer and Vladimir above. Let us assume that none of them currently have a home and they all turn up to a particular auction to hopefully buy somewhere to live. The bids will start low, and get higher. Once the bid price is above $400,000 Vladimir will drop out of the auction (and will stop bidding any further). Similarly, when the price exceeds $600,000, Jennifer will withdraw from bidding any further (the price exceeds her *MB*). Once the price gets just above $800,000, Syed too will stop bidding. Anastasia will win the auction with a bid just over $800,000 (or even $800,000, as Syed would not out bid an offer of that value). Now, assume that a new potential buyer, Khanh, moves to the city with hopes of buying a place. Khanh has a home valuation of $900,000, and she turns up at the auction. Given the same logic, Anastasia still wins the auction, but now she has to pay $900,000 or just a little bit more. Khanh's presence boosts the price by approximately $100,000.

20.3 The labour market

The labour market is one of the most important markets, and one that most people are involved in at some point. The product being traded and the participants in the market are different from those in a traditional consumer product market – but, even so, our tools of supply and demand apply.

In the labour market, the 'product' being traded is labour. The supply side is made up of individuals who supply labour, and the demand side is made up of firms that want to use the labour as part of their production process, reversing the traditional roles in the consumer goods market. In the labour market, the wage is the price of labour. To make things simpler let us think of the wage as being the hourly rate of pay, although we could use some other reference point.

20.3.1 Supply of labour

Individuals agree to supply their time, effort and know-how in exchange for a wage. For most jobs, the job market is reasonably competitive, so workers are more or less price takers, meaning that they cannot affect the going market wage. However, workers have some control over how many hours they want to work at the going wage rate. An individual will be willing to work an additional hour, provided the hourly wage is at least as much as the opportunity cost of her time. As argued in Chapter 8, the supply curve for an individual is (typically) upward sloping, reflecting the increasing opportunity cost for an individual to work longer hours; the first few hours of time might be easy to find, but eventually additional hours will need to be at night, at the weekend, at the expense of other plans, and so on. This means that an increase in the wage rate increases the quantity of labour supplied by the individual (the number of hours they are willing to work).

The market supply curve is the horizontal summation of the individual worker supply curves. Given that the individual supply curves are upward sloping (reflecting the increasing marginal cost of their time), the market supply curve will also be upward sloping and the law of supply will (generally) hold.

Note that the interpretations of the supply curve from Chapter 8 also hold here. Holding everything else constant, if there is a change in the wage rate there will be a movement along the supply curve. On the other hand, if there is a change in anything else that is relevant that affects the opportunity cost of potential workers' time, there will be a shift in the supply curve.

20.3.2 Demand for labour

A firm must decide how much labour they want to hire, which in our framework is measured in how many working hours. To do so, it will compare the cost of hiring an extra hour of labour (the hourly wage rate) and how much it will benefit in terms of revenue from that extra worker hour, often called the marginal revenue product (MRP). The MRP for a price-taking firm is how much extra output the worker will produce in the hour – the worker's marginal product (MP) – multiplied by the output price, which is the price that the good or service can be sold for to consumers. That is, the $MRP = MRP \times P$.

A firm's MRP is its demand curve for labour. It shows how many units of labour (how many worker hours) it wants to hire given the going wage rate. A firm will keep hiring workers (for more hours) provided that the MRP is at least as great as the wage rate. The firm will stop employing more labour when $MRP = w$.

Note here that the MRP curve is typically downward sloping. This is because of the law of diminishing MP (Chapter 7); each additional hour of labour adds less than the previous one. The short-run market labour demand curve is the horizontal summation of the individual firm labour demand (MRP) curves. Consequently, if the individual firm MRP curves are downward sloping, the short-run labour demand curve will also be downward sloping; that is, the law of demand holds.

As noted with supply, if there is a change in the wage rate, there will be a movement along the labour demand curve. If, for example, the wage rate falls, there is an increase in the quantity of labour demanded. If there is a change in anything else that is relevant, such as the output price of the good the firm is making, there will be a change (or shift) in labour demand.

20.3.3 Equilibrium and market predictions

An example of a labour market is illustrated in Figure 20.2. The short-run market labour demand curve is D_L. The short-run labour supply curve is represented by S_L. The labour market will be in equilibrium when the quantity supplied equals the quantity demanded. The market-clearing wage w^* equates the quantities demanded and supplied. In the usual way, if the wage is below w^* there will be pressure on it to rise. Conversely, if

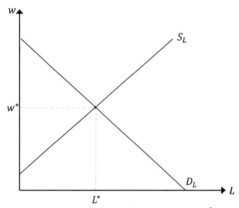

FIGURE 20.2 Equilibrium in the labour market. The equilibrium wage is w^* and the equilibrium quantity traded is L^*

the wage is about the market-clearing wage w^* there will be pressure on the wage to continue to fall until the market is back in equilibrium.

Note that in equilibrium, there is no unemployment because everyone who is willing to work at the going market wage is employed (for their desired number of hours).

One advantage of this model is that it can make clear predictions about how the market will respond to an exogenous change. For example, if there is an increase in the price of the good a firm is making, this will cause a shift in the demand curve to the right. The wage rate will rise, and in the new market equilibrium the quantity of labour hired (the hours of work) will increase.

20.3.4 Complications

The labour market has many complexities and nuances, and it is a market that is typically subject to regulation. Fortunately, however, often these complexities do not prevent us from getting realistic predictions about the labour market using the (relatively uncomplicated) competitive market model.

Some complications are worth noting, however. Firstly, as detailed in Chapter 16 many labour markets are subject to price regulation, notably minimum wages. This can result in an excess supply of labour and unemployment when the minimum wage is binding.

Secondly, there is not one labour market – there are many, each reflecting the supply of workers with particular skills, know-how and availability (geographically perhaps) and demand for workers from a particular sector or related industries.

Thirdly, in some industries a hiring firm or a supplier of labour (like a union) has market power. If, for example, a firm is the monopoly in the product market it will have to take into account that its selling price will fall as it increases output, which in turn will affect its labour demand curve (it will still be downward sloping, however). Or a union might realise that it can restrict the quantity of supplied labour to increase the wage. If there is a large employer and a powerful union, each with bargaining power, the negotiations and outcome could result from a bargaining process, as was studied in Chapter 5.

Fourthly, there is the possibility of a 'backwards-bending labour-supply curve'. Essentially this means that for some range, when the wage rate increases a worker decreases the quantity of labour they supply (the amount of work they are willing to do). The intuition for this could be that a worker would like a certain amount of money to spend on goods and services but also like their leisure time. If the wage rate increases, this would allow them to earn the amount of money they want with fewer hours of work. This is a real phenomenon, and some individuals make exactly these sorts of choices. However, when the actions of all workers in the market are aggregated to produce the market supply curve, the increase in quantity supplied from individuals opting to work more to take advantage of the higher wage tends to dominate the effect of some people working less. This means that at the market level the law of supply tends to hold.

Finally, workers are often of different abilities (they are not all the same) but this is often not immediately obvious to the firms wishing to hire. This difference in knowledge between the trading parties is called **asymmetric information**. Asymmetric information is one reason why firms sometimes go to a great deal of trouble to screen workers (interviews, aptitude tests, and so on) before hiring anyone. The more important it is to hire workers with the right skills (or the harder it is to immediately ascertain how good a potential worker is) the more resources a firm will be willing to spend on screening workers first. Similarly, individuals can exert efforts to demonstrate – or signal – to potential employers their abilities and skills; this is one of the reasons workers get qualifications and undertake education. It helps a productive worker differentiate themselves from others. There can also be hidden information once a worker is hired in that it might not always be possible for a boss to observe whether someone is working hard or not (that is, the effort an employee puts in might not be directly observable by a firm). This is one reason why firms offer their employees incentive pay and bonuses – it provides an incentive for workers to put in effort, even if their boss cannot directly see what they are doing.

These complications are all interesting, and sometimes these specific details and nuances are important. However, often the broader implications of the competitive market model are sufficient to provide the type of predictions required to understand the economic phenomena studied. Moreover, even if some of these nuances are present (asymmetric information, market power, and so on), the forces of supply and demand may well dominate any other factors at play.

20.4 The capital market

Another important market is the capital market. Again, much can be gained by applying the tools of supply and demand to this market. In the same way as we did with the labour market, let us assume that all participants are price takers.

The capital market broadly involves people saving and borrowing money. People who save effectively lend these funds to the people who want to borrow them (in this simplified framework, savers are lenders). Borrowers use these funds for any number of reasons, which could be to finance some investment, to pay for a large purchase such as a house or even for consumption. The price in the capital market is the interest rate. The quantity is the dollar amount of money (either lent or borrowed).

20.4.1 Supply of capital

The suppliers in the capital market are savers. Given the interest rate, these individuals will decide the quantity of funds they wish to save. For most people, there would be an increasing opportunity cost of saving more funds. This suggests that for an individual borrower their supply curve for funds (money) they are willing to lend will be upward sloping; that is, to be encouraged to save more requires a higher interest rate (which is the price paid on savings). The (short-run) market supply curve for the capital market is the horizontal summation of the individual supply curves. If the individual lenders have upward-sloping supply curves, the market supply curve will be upward sloping too, and the law of supply will hold.

20.4.2 Demand for capital

The demand side of the capital market is made up of individuals interested in borrowing funds. For an individual, their demand curve for borrowing funds will typically be downward sloping. The interest rate is the price an individual has to pay on the funds (or the quantity of money) borrowed. When deciding how much to borrow, an individual will think about the price (the interest rate) and the marginal benefit of funds; the lower the price, the more funds for which the MB exceeds the price. Hence there is a negative relationship between the price and the quantity demand for funds. If the borrower will use the funds for an investment opportunity a lower rate of interest encourages the investor to borrow more; there will be more investment opportunities for which the return or earnings (the MB) exceed the price of borrowing funds (the interest rate). As usual, the short-run market demand curve is the horizontal summation of the individual demand curves. If individual demand curves are downward sloping, the market demand curve will be too; the law of demand will hold.

20.4.3 Equilibrium and market predictions

As illustrated in Figure 20.3, the market equilibrium will be where the quantity of money supplied equals the quantity demanded, which is where the market demand (D_1) and supply (S_1) curves intersect. Here the equilibrium interest rate is r_1^* and the quantity of funds lent and borrowed is F_1^*. In the typical way, we can study the comparative statics (what happens in the shift to the new market equilibrium interest rate and quantity of money borrowed and lent) if there is some exogenous change that shifts one or other of the curves. Such a change might be something like a new tax on savings (shifting

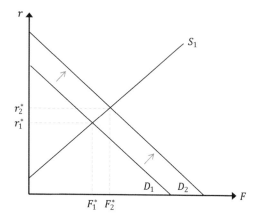

FIGURE 20.3 An increase in demand in the capital market

the supply curve) or an increase in the profitability of investment opportunities (shifting the demand curve). As an illustration, assume that some new profitable investment opportunities arise, shifting the money demand curve to D_2. There will be movement along the money supply curve S_1. In the new market equilibrium the quantity of funds borrowed and lent will increase to F_2^* at a higher interest rate of r_2^*.

20.4.4 Complications

As with any market, the capital market has its complications. Firstly, very often intermediaries – banks and financial institutions – play a key role in matching lenders with borrowers (or more usually pooling the deposits of savers and lending these funds to borrowers). These institutions charge for this service, so there is typically a wedge in the interest rate received by lenders and the one that borrowers must pay. If the role of banks is not the focus of our analysis, it is usually not such a bad approximation to assume that both sides of the market receive and pay (nearly) the same interest rate.

Secondly, many capital markets are regulated. Banks, and hence the financial system as a whole, are subject to the central bank's monetary policy. While monetary policy is part of a government's macroeconomic policy and beyond the scope of this text, for this discussion it suffices to note that monetary policy essentially relies on the arguments made above about how the capital market works; if the central bank would like to reduce economic activity it will increase interest rates (reducing the quantity of funds borrowed); on the other hand, if it wants to increase economic activity, the central bank will act to reduce the interest rate so as to encourage more borrowing (and spending).

Thirdly, this market is subject to *asymmetric information* in various forms. To assure lenders of the solvency of banks, governments regulate financial institutions with prudential requirements. Banks (and savers) might be worried that they will lend money to individuals or firms that either choose not to or cannot pay the money back. To avoid this, lenders screen customers and require borrowers to provide collateral that the bank can keep in the event of non-payment.

Fourth, there is, of course, more than one capital market. Indeed, there are many. Different types of borrowers include those seeking loans for personal consumption (holiday loans and the like), the home-loan market and various types of business loans. Each market comes with its own risks, and these risks will be reflected in the interest charged to the borrower. Other things being equal, the higher the risk (that is, the more likely the borrower will default and not pay back the loan) the higher the interest rate the lender will charge.

20.5 Concluding comments

In this chapter we discussed three specific markets. The underlying theme of the chapter is that any particular market will have its own special idiosyncrasies. Sometimes these special market features are what is of interest. In that case, we would need to build models that take account of the particular scenarios or regulations involved. At other times, as economists we are looking for more general insights that are driven mostly by the fundamentals of supply and demand. In this case, a simple competitive market might be sufficient to provide the insights required.

CHAPTER 21

Economic policy

21.1 Introduction

In this book so far, we have focused on describing what is happening in a market and identifying what market players (consumers, producers and governments) can do in response to those market conditions. This type of economics is sometimes called **positive economics** – economics that focuses on describing and explaining what is happening or what is possible in a market.

Economic policy is about the role of government in shaping and managing markets and the economy. It goes beyond looking at what governments *can* do and asks, what is it that they *should* do? This type of economics is grounded in **normative economics** – economics that focuses on value-based judgements about what ought to be or what should happen.

This chapter looks at how economic theory is used to inform economic policy.

21.2 Economic policy in practice: some examples

The best way to understand how economic theory gets turned into economic policy is to look at some examples where markets have benefited from government policies to address market failures.

21.2.1 Lowering transaction costs

In Chapter 17, we discussed the Coase Theorem, which states that provided property rights have been clearly assigned and there are no transaction costs, bargaining will lead to an efficient outcome, regardless of the initial allocation of property rights. In practice, however, the presence of transaction costs can

DOI: 10.4324/9781003376644-28

get in the way of parties coming to an agreement, preventing an efficient outcome from being reached.

The question for policy makers is whether and when the government should intervene to reduce or eliminate transaction costs – and, if so, how it should do so.

One example of government intervention to lower transaction costs is land ownership. In Australia, land ownership was historically established through deeds; every sale or mortgage of land was executed by deed (a document that recorded the transaction). To find out who owned land, you would have to examine a chain of deeds to trace ownership back to the original grant of land. If you were buying property, this was a costly and cumbersome way to verify that you were dealing with its true owner. In the late 1800s, government reforms to the land title system drastically simplified the way land ownership could be proved. Nowadays, almost all land interests in Australia are recorded in a centralised register (called the 'Torrens Title Register'), which is administered and maintained by the government. This register means that, for almost all land dealings, ownership can be verified by consulting the register, circumventing the need to examine a chain of deeds.

21.2.2 Managing common resources

In Chapter 18, we discussed common resources and the Tragedy of the Commons. Recall that common resources, because they are non-excludable but rivalrous, are liable to over-exploitation. In this context, a key policy question is whether a government should do anything to address the over-exploitation of common resources, and if so what.

One example of government policy relating to the use of common resources is fishing licences. Traditionally, anyone could fish in public waters, which led to over-fishing and the depletion of fish stocks. Around the world, many governments have introduced a requirement to obtain a fishing licence for certain fishing activities. In these cases, those governments have decided that steps should be taken to prevent the over-exploitation of fishing stocks, and they have chosen to do so by restricting access to fishing stocks to licence holders. This is typically supplemented by regulations about what fishing activities are permissible – for example, in some areas it may be acceptable to catch only certain types or sizes of fish. And in some cases, there are outright bans on certain types of fishing – for example, in most parts of the world, there is a ban on commercial whaling.

Here are some other examples of the common resource problem. You may like to think about what a government could or should do in response to these scenarios.

- A new source of fresh water has been discovered. Some local residents have been using that water for cleaning, and others have been taking water to irrigate their crops. As a result, the quantity and quality of the water available for use has declined.
- There has been a boom in local radio stations, all of which use radio signals to transmit their programmes. The radio signals have been interfering with each other, resulting in lower-quality transmissions.

- A road has been widened to accommodate increased traffic in a popular shopping area. But some drivers have been using the new lanes as free parking, preventing them from being used as road lanes by other drivers.

21.2.3 Competition policy

In Part IV, we discussed different types of markets. We saw that while some markets are very competitive, others are not – and that, in general, markets that are more competitive tend to have better market outcomes. Competition policy is about how governments can support or encourage markets to be more competitive and therefore more efficient.

Around the world, many governments have decided that they should play a role in promoting competition and stamping out anti-competitive behaviour. As such, competition laws (also called 'anti-trust laws' and 'trade practices laws') are common in developed economies, and are a key tool for those governments to give effect to their competition policies. These laws cover issues like:

- Whether agreements or practices that limit competition between firms (such as collusion and cartels) should be permitted.
- What sorts of uses of market power should be permitted (such as whether predatory pricing, price gouging or refusing to deal with other firms should be permitted).
- When firms should be allowed to merge with or acquire another firm.

A complication of competition policy is that market power can arise if one firm has lower costs than its rivals or when it offers a better product. This creates a tradeoff for policy makers between a more productive firm and the welfare losses generated by market power.

21.3 The Theory of Second Best

In Part V, we looked at several sources of market failure, including monopoly markets, externalities and public goods. These failures cause the market outcome to deviate from the efficient or surplus-maximising outcome, reducing the total surplus. We have also seen that government intervention (in the form of taxes, subsidies, quantity control, etc.) can address these market failures and increase welfare in the market.

However, in some cases, markets may be affected by more than one source of market failure – for example, a market may be affected by more than one externality. The **Theory of Second Best** posits that if there is a market failure that cannot be corrected, actions to correct other market failures may have the effect of decreasing the total surplus overall. What this means is that, in the presence of multiple market failures, it may be preferable not to address a single market failure on its own.

To understand how the Theory of Second Best works, consider the following example.

Example. Suppose the market for tractors is a monopoly. The market demand curve for tractors is given by the equation $P = 10 - Q$ and the marginal cost of producing tractors is \$2. However, suppose the production of tractors is also accompanied by a negative externality of \$4 per tractor.

The socially optimal outcome is given by setting the marginal social benefit equal to the marginal social cost (that is, $10 - Q = 2 + 4$), which yields an efficient quantity of $Q^* = 4$.

Consider the outcome in the monopoly market. In this case the profit-maximising monopolist sets marginal revenue equal to marginal cost, disregarding the negative externality (that is, $10 - 2Q = 2$), which yields a monopoly quantity of $Q^m = 4$; this quantity is actually the socially efficient outcome as $Q^m = Q^* = 4$. Thus, in this example, the monopolist maximises total welfare and there is no DWL in the monopoly market.

Now, suppose the government intervenes in the market to remove the monopoly power of the firm, so that the market becomes perfectly competitive, but it does nothing about the negative externality. The competitive market outcome after the policy intervention can be determined by setting marginal benefit equal to marginal cost, disregarding the negative externality (that is, $10 - Q = 2$), which yields a competitive level of output of $Q^c = 8$. Notice that in this example, the competitive market produces too much output relative to the socially efficient outcome ($Q^c > Q^*$), so a DWL results. Moreover, the outcome is worse than the monopoly market outcome without government intervention; here, the removal of one distortion (the monopoly power) without simultaneously addressing the other (the negative externality) reduces surplus, rather than making things better. Indeed, the surplus is higher if the government does nothing, rather than partially correcting the market failures in this scenario.

The intuition underlying the Theory of Second Best is that multiple market failures can counteract one another. In the above example, the monopoly power of the seller meant it would tend to underproduce relative to the socially optimal outcome, whereas the presence of a negative externality meant that the market outcome would tend to be too high. Overall, the combination of these market failures produced a higher surplus than when one or the other distortions were removed on their own. This idea potentially applies whenever there is more than one market failure present in a market.

This means that before intervening in a market, a policy maker needs to be well informed about the state of the market and the possible existence of other distortions before trying to correct or remove a market failure. Moreover, it suggests that good policy requires caution and careful implementation.

21.4 The policy cycle

In practice, there are several steps to making and developing economic policy and these steps are sometimes referred to as the **policy cycle**. This is depicted in Figure 21.1.

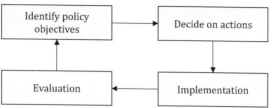

FIGURE 21.1 The policy cycle

1) The first step of the policy cycle is to identify the policy problem that needs to be solved. To do this, policy makers will need to understand the current state of play and pinpoint what market failures currently exist. This step also involves articulating policy objectives – that is, what the desired outcome is.
2) The next step is about deciding what should be done in response. Policy makers will consider the options for tackling the policy problem (including the option of doing nothing) and weigh the relative costs and benefits of each option. They will then need to decide what policy actions to proceed with.
3) The chosen policy actions will then be implemented. Effective implementation hinges on a range of factors – including questions about what needs to be done, who will be responsible for implementation, what time and resources are needed and how actions will be coordinated.
4) Finally, the policy and its implementation will be evaluated. This looks at whether the chosen policy actions were effective and appropriate for achieving the policy objectives. Evaluation can also help determine what works and what needs to be done differently. A decision will be made whether to terminate, renew or change the policy program. If changes are made, the policy cycle starts anew.

21.5 Concluding comments

In this chapter, we briefly discussed how economic policies are informed and shaped by microeconomic theory. Several further points are worth noting about how policy decisions are made in the real world.

The first is that economic efficiency is often not the only consideration that governments take into account when deciding what policy actions should be taken. Typically, economic policy is about balancing a range of different considerations including what is economically efficient, what is fair or just, what is sustainable, and so on. Sometimes political considerations, such as what is popular or palatable, also come into play when governments decide how to respond to a policy problem. This means that there is a bit of an art to policy-making; it is rare that a policy objective is as straightforward as simply maximising total welfare or eliminating deadweight loss.

The second is that developing and implementing policy responses takes time, effort and money – in other words, there is an opportunity cost. For this reason, there is a practical limit to how many and what economic policies a government can pursue at any given time. It also means that, for some policy problems (or market failures), finding and implementing solutions is not worth it.

Economics
and evidence

22.1 Introduction

Economic theory provides a framework for describing and understanding, in principle, the way markets and market participants behave. But to pin down what is happening, or what is likely to happen, in the real world, economists often supplement that theory with data and evidence.

For example, in Chapter 9, we covered how supply and demand interact to produce a market equilibrium. From this discussion, we know that the price of a good and the quantity sold in a market are determined by the shape of the demand and supply curves. But, in practice, how can economists know what the shapes of the demand and supply curves are? We could start by looking for information about consumer preferences, sales volumes, production costs, and so on.

Evidence is what enables economists to apply economic theory to real-world situations. This chapter gives an overview of some ways that economists draw on evidence to augment economic theory.

22.2 Econometrics and statistics

Econometrics refers to the application of mathematical and statistical methods to economic data. Typically, it involves using existing observational data to derive new insights about the relationship between two or more variables, though sometimes econometricians will also have a hand in creating new data sets.

At their core, econometric models are motivated by economic theory. That is to say, economic theory lets us know what questions need to be answered and econometric methods are the tools that can help us get towards the answer.

DOI: 10.4324/9781003376644-29

For example, in Chapter 10, we discussed inferior, normal and luxury goods. Recall that these terms refer to how responsive demand for a good is to changes in income. For some goods, you might intuitively know what sort of goods they are – such as bus travel, high-end fashion and take-away coffee. But for others, it might not be so obvious. For those, we could use data and econometrics to estimate the income elasticity of a good.

These can be important questions for businesses. A firm with some market power will be interested in whether it can make more profit if it raises the price of its goods slightly. As we saw in Chapter 13 the profit-maximising price for a monopolist depends on its own price elasticity of demand and its marginal cost. Again, the price elasticity of a good is an empirical question (as is its marginal cost). A firm is unlikely to know the full demand curve when it is making its pricing decision, but if it can have an estimate of the price elasticity around its current price, that will give a good sense of whether the price should be increased or decreased. If the firm makes gradual adjustments in price, continues to collect more sales data and reassess its pricing strategy, it should be able to iterate towards the profit-maximising price. Such a strategy is helpful too when there are (unobserved) shifts in demand.

Policy makers might be interested in how effective a particular policy is. For example, a government might want to know how a subsidy has affected the uptake of childcare services. This is an empirical question – how many families changed the quantity demanded for childcare services after they had access to the subsidy? The answer will inform governments how effective a policy is, allowing them to make choices about which policies to pursue and which programmes should be terminated (or reduced in size).

22.3 Experimental economics

Experimental economics refers to the use of experiments to answer economic questions. It enables economists to collect data about what choices people make in controlled settings, when external influences and confounding factors are removed.

Here are some questions we could look to answer using experimental economics.

- What is the demand for widgets? We could run an experiment where we offer participants the opportunity to buy widgets at different prices. The number they choose to buy at each price would give us information about their individual demand curves, which we could use to derive a market demand curve.
- How long does it take players to coordinate? As we discussed in Chapter 3, in a coordination game the players are trying to coordinate, but there is no dominant strategy for either player so there are sometimes coordination failures. We could run an experiment where the participants repeatedly play a coordination game to see what happens.

- How quickly do markets reach equilibrium? We could run an experiment where we have the participants act as buyers and sellers in a market. We could simulate demand or supply shocks and see how quickly the market adjusts to the new equilibrium in response.

In the context of economic policy, which we discussed in the previous chapter, a pilot programme or a policy trial can also be considered a form of experimental economics. This is because they can provide insights about what is likely to happen with and without a policy intervention.

22.4 Behavioural economics

Much of economic theory relies on the assumption that economic agents are **rational**, meaning that when they make a choice they will choose the thing that they like the best. **Behavioural economics** is about studying and testing the limits of that assumption. It recognises that sometimes decisions can be affected by psychological, cognitive, cultural and social factors – with the result that real-world behaviour sometimes deviates from what is predicted by classical economic theory.

Some areas of study by behavioural economists include:

- **Bounded rationality**, which explores the idea that economic agents do not always have the cognitive resources or 'computing power' to make optimal choices. This means that when individuals make decisions, they may choose an option that is satisfactory and not necessarily the one that is best. For example, imagine being presented with a large array of options – would you sometimes settle for an option that is good enough rather than searching for the very best?
- **Prospect theory**, which posits that individuals value gains differently to losses. A notable finding in this area is that individuals prefer to avoid losses over acquiring equivalent gains. In other words, individuals tend to prefer to avoid losing $100 over finding $100. These insights can be important when thinking about how individuals approach situations where there is some risk of a loss.
- **Nudge theory**, which looks at whether and how decisions can be influenced by changes to the way options or decisions are presented. For example, are consumers more likely to buy products if they are placed at eye level than if they were placed on higher or lower shelves? Are they more likely to use a service if they receive it by default than if they had to opt in? Are they more inclined to choose the first, second or last item in a series of options?

While these results from behavioural economics can be of academic interest, it is important to keep things in context. Often the observed behavioural results are specific to a time, place, experiment and even a particular individual. This means caution is required if we would like to generalise any particular finding to a broader context. For example, while we might observe bounded rationality in individual consumers (or ourselves), it is often when the actions of everyone in the market are aggregated that the insights from the more traditional economic models hold. Further to this, standard economic approaches are often sufficient to explain the behaviour of individual consumers or firms, even if there is an alternative behavioural explanation. In these cases, the standard approach is preferred because it requires fewer specific assumptions that perhaps only relate to the particular situation being studied.

22.5 Concluding comments

In this chapter, we have discussed some of the ways that evidence can be used to flesh out economic theory – including the insights that econometrics, experimental economics and behavioural economics can provide. But these are by no means the only types of evidence the economists use. Sometimes economists can use 'softer' forms of evidence, such as qualitative or descriptive evidence. This includes opinions, anecdotes and evidence that is obtained through observation or discussion.

PART VIII

Review

CHAPTER 23

Questions & answers

Chapter 1

1. What is opportunity cost?

2. Opportunity cost only includes explicit costs? Discuss.

3. What following activities involve an opportunity cost for a consumer?

   a. Having a meal tomorrow night that costs $20.
   b. Taking time next weekend to go for a walk.
   c. Sleeping tonight.
   d. Starting a new university degree next year.
   e. All of the above.

4. Which of the following is not a sunk cost?

   a. The tax a firm will need to pay if they sell one of its properties.
   b. An advertising campaign from last year.
   c. The non-refundable deposit already paid to secure a new factory.
   d. Time spent by senior management at an upcoming corporate retreat.

5. City University needs to find a new building for its business school. They have two options. First, they could locate the business school in a building the university owns on campus. Second, the University knows of a suitable site of land (without a building) just off of campus. Some of the University's administrators suggest that given that the University already owns the land on campus and doesn't need to construct a new building, the first option is preferable. Assess this decision and compare the two options.

6. On a Saturday night, Suzanne went to see a band play some music. If Suzanne had not gone to see the band, she would have gone to see a

DOI: 10.4324/9781003376644-31

movie. Her third preference was to do some studying for her new graduate diploma. Which statement is true?

a. The opportunity cost of seeing the band is missing the movie.
b. Because the movie is still running at the cinema, the opportunity cost of seeing the band was not studying.
c. The opportunity cost of seeing the band is the benefit of going to the movie, net of the benefit of studying.
d. With the above information it is not possible to determine the opportunity cost of going to the band.
e. The opportunity cost of seeing the band is the benefit of seeing the movie and studying.

7. Give an example of two variables that move together but are otherwise unrelated. Relate your answer to correlation and causation.

Chapter 2

1. A line passes through a point (40, 80), where q equals 40 and P is 80. It also passes through a point (180, 10). What is the equation for this line?

2. Differentiate $C(q) = 100 + 10q + 0.5q^2$.

3. Demand is given by $q = 100 - 2P$. What is the price elasticity of demand when $q = 20$?

4. Demand is given by $P = 120 - 2q$, where P is the price and q is the quantity demanded. Supply is given by $P = 2q$. Solve these simultaneous equations.

5. Profit for a firm π is given by $\pi(q) = 80q - 2q^2$, where q is the number of units produced and sold. Find the number of units that maximises profit.

Chapter 3

1. In a Nash equilibrium:
a. All players adopt their best strategies, given the strategies adopted by all other players.
b. Each player is doing the best they can, given the strategies of every other player and the possible payoffs.
c. There are no possible unilateral profitable deviations for any player in the game.
d. All of the above.
e. Total surplus is maximised.

2. Two supermarkets, Coles and Woolworths, simultaneously choose the price of a litre of milk for the coming week. The options for each supermarket are HIGH and LOW. If both choose to price HIGH the payoffs are 15 to each firm. If both firms opt for LOW each firm gets a payoff of 4. If Coles chooses LOW and Woolworth opts for HIGH, the payoffs are 4 to Coles and 8 to Woolworths. If Coles

chooses HIGH and Woolworths LOW, the payoffs are 8 and 4 to Coles and Woolworths, respectively. Finally, if both firms choose LOW, each gets 7. Considering the Nash equilibrium of the game, which statement is true? (The first strategy in the parentheses is Coles' strategy; the second strategy is Woolworths'.)

a. The Nash equilibrium is (HIGH, HIGH); this game is not a prisoner's dilemma
b. The Nash equilibrium is (LOW, HIGH); this game is not a prisoner's dilemma
c. The Nash equilibrium is (HIGH, LOW); this game is a prisoner's dilemma
d. The Nash equilibrium is (LOW, LOW); this game is a prisoner's dilemma
e. The Nash equilibrium is (HIGH, HIGH); this game is a prisoner's dilemma

3. Coke and Pepsi are in a market together in which they can each make the following sequence of moves. First, Coke decides whether to launch a SPORTS drink or an ENERGY drink. Second, Pepsi observes Coke's choice then chooses SPORTS and ENERGY. If ENERGY is chosen by both firms, Coke gets 20 and Pepsi 60. If Coke chooses ENERGY and Pepsi SPORTS the payoffs are 50 and 30 to Coke and Pepsi, respectively. If Coke opts for SPORTS and Pepsi opts for ENERGY the payoffs are 50 and 30 to Coke and Pepsi. Finally, if both choose SPORTS the payoffs are 30 to Coke and 50 to Pepsi. In the subgame perfect (or credible) equilibrium, what do we observe each firm do?

a. Coke opts for ENERGY and Pepsi SPORTS.
b. Coke opts for SPORTS and Pepsi ENERGY.
c. Coke opts for SPORTS and Pepsi SPORTS.
d. Coke opts for ENERGY and Pepsi ENERGY.
e. None of the above.

4. In a dominant strategy equilibrium:

a. Each player reduces the surplus of the other player with the strategy that they adopt.
b. Total surplus (the sum of the payoffs to every player) is not maximised.
c. The best strategy for each player does not depend on the strategies of the other players in the game.
d. Total surplus is maximised.
e. None of the above.

5. On a peaceful Sunday afternoon, Vlad and Guillaume each simultaneously decide whether to go to Bondi (B) or Potts Point (PP). If both choose to go to Bondi they get −5 each. If both go to Potts Point they each get a payoff of −1. If Vlad chooses Bondi and Guillaume Potts Point the payoffs are 3, 2 to Vlad and Guillaume, respectively. If Vlad goes to Potts Point and Guillaume Bondi, the payoffs are 0 for each party. What are the Nash equilibria of this game?

6. Australia and Japan are negotiating a free trade agreement. At the final stages of these negotiations there are only two 'stages' remaining. First, Japan can agree to include beef IN the free trade agreement, or to leave beef OUT. Following Japan's choice of IN or OUT regarding beef, this choice is observed by Australia and they can choose to either AGREE or NOT agree with the proposal. The payoffs are as

follows: if Japan chooses IN and Australia chooses AGREE the payoffs are (90, 100), where the first payoff is for Japan and the second is Australia's payoff. If Japan chooses IN and Australia NOT to agree the payoffs are (20, 20). If Japan opts for OUT and Australia still AGREEs with the proposal, the payoffs are (100, 50). Finally, if Japan chooses OUT and Australia chooses NOT to agree the payoffs are (20, 20). What are the actions observed in the subgame perfect (or credible) equilibrium outcome in this game?

7. Australia and Japan are negotiating a free trade agreement. At the final stages of these negotiations there are only two 'stages' remaining. First, Japan can agree to include beef IN the free trade agreement, or to leave beef OUT. Following Japan's choice of IN or OUT regarding beef, this choice is observed by Australia and they can choose to either AGREE or to NOT agree with the proposal. In the case that Australia chooses NOT, it will be free to sign up for a free trade agreement with Korea (with the payoffs for Australia detailed below). The payoffs are as follows: if Japan chooses IN and Australia chooses AGREE the payoffs are (90, 100), where the first payoff is for Japan and the second is Australia's payoff. If Japan chooses IN and Australia NOT to agree the payoffs are (20, 60). If Japan opts for OUT and Australia still AGREEs with the proposal, the payoffs are (100, 50). Finally, if Japan chooses OUT and Australia chooses NOT to agree the payoffs are (20, 60). What are the actions observed in the subgame perfect (or credible) equilibrium outcome in this game?

8. Martin and Jim, two legendary guitarists, must simultaneously choose to play 'On' the beat, or 'Off' the beat. If both guitarists play On the beat, each gets a surplus of 10. If Martin plays On and Jim plays Off, the payoffs are 50 to each player. On the other hand, if Martin plays Off and Jim On, the payoffs are 40 to each player. Finally, they both get 5 if both decide to play Off. What are the Nash equilibria in the game?

9. Malcolm and Angus are two other guitarists who have to simultaneously decide to play 'Lead' or 'Rhythm'. If both play Lead, the payoffs are 2 to each player. If both opt for 'Rhythm', each player gets 10. If Angus plays Lead and Malcolm Rhythm, the payoffs are 100 to Angus and 120 to Malcolm. If Angus plays Rhythm while Malcolm opts for Lead, the payoffs are 80 to both players. What are the Nash equilibria of the game?

Chapter 4

1. Draw the production possibility curve for an economy that can produce either tractors or bicycles.
    a. Show a point at which the economy is not producing efficiently.
    b. Show a point that is unattainable given the current state of technology.
    c. Show a point where the economy is producing efficiently.
    d. Relate shifts along the production possibility curve to the concept of opportunity cost.

2. There are two countries, Australia and the Rest of the World, that can produce either good A or good B. Australia is more productive at producing both goods. Which statement is *not* true?

   a. Australia has an absolute advantage in producing both goods.
   b. The benefits of trade accrue to the country that does not have an absolute advantage in the traded good.
   c. Comparative advantage determines the patterns of production between the countries.
   d. The opportunity cost of producing good A is good B.

3. Bob can produce either good x or good y. In one hour he can produce 4 units of good x. Alternatively he can produce 2 units of good y in that hour. Suzie can produce either 6 units of good x in an hour or 2 units of good y in an hour.

   a. What is absolute advantage? Who has the absolute advantage in producing x and which party has the absolute advantage in producing good y?
   b. What is comparative advantage? Which party has the comparative advantage of producing good x and good y?
   c. If each party has 10 hours in which they can work, draw the production possibilities frontier for each party. What does the slope of each production possibilities frontier represent?
   d. What is the maximum price that Bob is willing to pay for a unit of good x? What is the minimum price that Suzie would be willing to sell a unit of good x for? What is the minimum price that Bob would be willing to sell a unit of good y for? What is the maximum price that Suzie would be willing to pay for a unit of good y?

4. Now reinterpret question 3 with Bob and Suzie: rather than both parties producing goods x and y, instead consider the situation in which Bob and Suzie undertake tasks x and y at a workplace. Which party should do task x? Which party should perform task y? What is different about this case than if we are considering two goods (or services) being traded in the market?

5. Australia can produce two goods – coffee and TVs. Consider two ways in which the Australian economy can grow: through an increase in population and through technological progress. Illustrate both of these changes on a PPF. What is the advantage of the second type of growth over the former?

6. Take an economy with two workers, Romi and Debra. There are two goods that can be made: Toys and Balls. Each person works an 8-hour day. Romi can produce a toy in 20 minutes and a ball in 2 hours. Debra can make 1 toy in 4 hours. It takes Debra 2 hours to make one ball. Initially, both Romi and Debra spend half of their time making toys and half of their time making balls. Each person consumes what they make.

   Now consider the following trade: Romi spends six hours making toys, and the remainder of her time making balls. Debra spends all her time making balls. They then trade – Romi trades 3 toys for 1 ball from Debra. Show that the total production of both goods increases following trade and both are better off with trade than without it. Explain your answer.

Chapter 5

1. Consider the following bargaining situation between a potential car buyer, called Davo, and a car dealer, Shazza. Shazza has a Falcon for sale that Davo values at $20,000. Shazza values the car at $0. The bargaining scenario is as follows: Shazza makes a proposal to Davo that he buy the Falcon for a particular price. If Davo accepts Shazza's proposal, trade takes place at the suggested price. If Davo refuses Shazza's offer, negotiations immediately breakdown between the two parties. Instead, Davo walks across the road and begins negotiating with another car dealer, Maggie. Maggie has a Corolla for sale that Davo values at $4,000; Maggie values the Corolla at $0. Negotiations between Maggie and Davo proceed as follows: Davo makes an offer to buy the car for a particular price. If Maggie accepts, trade takes place at that price. If Maggie rejects the offer, no trade takes place and bargaining between the parties ends. Without a new car Davo's utility is $0. If Maggie does not sell the Corolla to Davo her payoff is $0.

    a.   Illustrate this bargaining scenario in a diagram. How do you work out the outcome of this bargaining situation and why?

    b.   Assume that bargaining reaches the stage at which Davo is bargaining with Maggie. What is the price that Davo offers? What is Maggie's response?

    c.   Now consider when Shazza is bargaining with Davo. What happens and why?

    d.   What is the outcome of this bargaining situation? Compare the surplus that accrues to the buyer and seller in this outcome with the surplus maximising outcome.

2. Ansett, a bankrupt airline, and its administrator have to sell the company assets. The scrap value for the assets (the planes, its spare parts inventory, and so on) is $100M. Ansett has only one potential buyer for the airline as an on-going concern – Singapore Airlines – and negotiations must be completed by the close of business in two days. This is enough time for two rounds of offers. Negotiations proceed as follows: Ansett makes an offer that Singapore can accept or reject. If Singapore accepts, trade takes place at that price. In this case Ansett has a payoff of the agreed price and Singapore has a payoff of its value ($350M) minus the price. If Singapore rejects the offer, the company representatives go back to their hotels for the night. The following day Singapore Airlines gets to make an offer that Ansett can accept or reject. If Ansett accepts, trade takes place at that price. If Ansett rejects, no trade takes place between the companies because they have reached the bargaining deadline. In this case Singapore Airlines gets a surplus of $0 and the Ansett company is scrapped, so Ansett gets a payoff equal to its scrap value. Singapore values the Ansett company at $350M minus the price it has to pay.

    a.   Draw a game tree to represent these negotiations.

b. Assume that negotiations reach the second day. If this is the case, what would happen?

c. Now consider what happens on the first day of negotiation. What is the subgame perfect outcome of this bargain between Ansett and Singapore?

3. Bazza has invented a new drug K and holds the patent for the drug for the next two years. Bazza, not having any marketing skills, values the patent at $0 in each of the two years. Raelene, on the other hand, can make $100 in the first year if she holds the patent and $80 in the second year if she holds the patent. Without the patent Raelene gets a payoff of $0 each year. The two parties enter into negotiations with each other regarding the possibility of Raelene buying the patent off Bazza. The negotiation process is as follows: At the start of year 1 Bazza gets to make an offer to Raelene regarding the price of the patent. If Raelene accepts, she buys the patent at the asking price, and gets to use it for the next two years. If Raelene rejects the offer, negotiations are put on hold for a year. At the start of year 2 Raelene gets to make an offer to Bazza for the patent. If Bazza accepts, trade takes place at that price and Raelene gets to use the patent for year 2 only. If Bazza rejects the price offer, negotiations cease and both parties receive a payoff of $0.

What is the outcome of this bargaining game?

4. Consider the following bargaining model: two firms in different countries – A and B – are considering trading with one another. Firm A has an input of production (i.e. a computer chip) that Firm B would like to use in its new plant. A values the computer at 0; if B gets the computer it is worth $25 for each year that it gets to use it. There are two years (after which the computer is worth $0 to everyone).

The negotiating situation proceeds as follows: executives of firms A and B meet at the start of the first year, and firm A makes an offer to firm B. B can either accept or reject the offer. If the offer is accepted, A gets the agreed price and B pays the price and gets to use the computer for two years. If B rejects the offer, the executives part company and do not meet until the start of the second year.

Solving backwards, determine the initial price offer by A and argue whether or not it will be accepted by B.

Chapter 6

1. Why is a typical consumer's demand curve downward sloping?

2. What causes a movement along a demand curve (or a change in the quantity demanded)?

a. An unanticipated announcement of the health benefit of the good.

b. A change in the price of the good itself.

c. A change in consumers' income.

d. An increase in the price of a substitute product.

3. A consumer's marginal benefit curve is given by $MB = 10 - q$, where q is the quantity consumed. What is the consumer's demand curve? What is the maximum

price this consumer is willing to pay for the first unit? What is the maximum price she is willing to pay for the 7th unit?

4. What causes a change in demand (or a shift in the demand curve)?

   a. An unanticipated announcement of the health benefit of the good.
   b. A decrease in the price of a complementary product.
   c. A change in consumers' income.
   d. An increase in the price of a substitute product.
   e. All of the above.

5. What is the market demand curve if there are 3 consumers in the market each with individual demand curves of $P = 20 - q$?

6. What is the market demand curve if there are 5 consumers in the market each with individual demand curves of $P = 10 - 2q$?

Chapter 7

1. Which statement is true?

   a. Marginal cost intersects the maximum of average variable cost from above.
   b. Marginal cost insects average total cost at the minimum of marginal cost.
   c. Marginal cost intersects the minimum of average fixed cost from below.
   d. The relationship between marginal cost and average total cost cannot be determined without specific knowledge of the particular production process.
   e. Marginal cost intersects the minimum of average variable cost from below.

2. Arthur is considering becoming chair of a company board that will pay $200,000 a year. Taking this position will require Arthur to give up another directorship that pays $75,000 a year. The job will involve travel anticipated to have an out-of-pocket cost of $20,000 a year. It will also require Arthur to buy $150,000 of shares in the company (which he must sell back to the company for $150,000 when he ceases to be chair of the board); currently Arthur has the money invested in the bank, earning an interest rate of 10% per year. What is Arthur's anticipated economic profit in the business's first year of operation?

   a. $80,000
   b. $90,000
   c. −$25,000
   d. $110,000
   e. −$40,000

3. Sascha, a bank teller who works Monday to Friday, is considering buying a new lounge. Sascha can get the lounge from AllenKey Inc. for $150, but this lounge needs to be delivered (an extra $30) and then assembled by Sascha. The only time Sascha has to assemble the lounge is on a Sunday afternoon. It would take Sascha 3 hours to build the lounge, during which time she would otherwise watch the Aussie rules footy; Sascha loves her footy and would pay up to $100 to see the game. Sascha's hourly wage at the bank is $50 an hour. From experience, Sascha

also expects to experience a personal disutility (or cost) from frustration of $40 and anticipates that she will most likely break her partner Alex's favourite vase (replacement cost $75) in the process of putting the lounge together.

As an alternative, Sascha could buy an identical lounge from LazyBones Inc., which comes fully constructed, delivered and installed at one price. What is the minimum price of the lounge on sale at LazyBones for which Sascha will choose to buy from AllenKey Inc.?

a. $295
b. $445
c. $545
d. $395
e. None of the above.

4. Which statement is true?

a. Marginal cost intersects average total cost when marginal cost is at its maximum.
b. Marginal cost intersects average total cost when marginal cost is at its minimum.
c. Marginal cost intersects average variable cost when average variable cost is at its maximum.
d. Marginal cost intersects average total cost when average total cost is at its minimum.
e. Marginal cost intersects average fixed cost when average fixed cost is at its minimum.

5. Explain why in the long run, there are no fixed costs; a firm's long-run average cost is the lower envelope of its possible short-run average total cost curves; and a firm's long-run marginal cost cannot be higher than its short-run marginal cost.

6. A firm's cost curve is $TC(q) = 250 + 10q + 2q^2$, q is the quantity produced. What is the firm's marginal cost (MC), average variable cost (AVC) and its average total cost (ATC)?

7. Draw the typical short-run cost curves for a competitive firm, noting in particular the relationship between average variable costs, average total costs and marginal costs. Explain the shape of each curve. What is the difference between the long run and the short run? Again using a typical firm, show how to derive its long-run average total cost curve and show examples of economies of scale, diseconomies of scale and constant returns to scale on your diagram. Finally, for a given level of output (and assuming constant prices and technology), can a firm's costs ever be higher in the long run than in the short run?

Chapter 8

1. A firm's supply curve is its marginal cost curve. True or false?
2. Explain why a typical firm's supply is upward sloping.

3. Which change will cause a movement along the supply curve (or a change in the quantity supplied)?

    a.   An increase in the price of a key input.
    b.   A change in the production technology.
    c.   A change in the anticipated price of an input next year.
    d.   None of the above.

Chapter 9

1. Consider the markets for corn chips and potato chips, two substitutes. We observe the following facts:

    – The price rises and the quantity demanded falls in the corn chip market
    – The price rises and the quantity demanded rises in the market for potato chips

Which of the following could explain these observations?

    a.   Dry conditions in potato-growing areas hinder the cultivation of potato crops.
    b.   Frost in corn-growing areas hinders the growing of corn.
    c.   Good rains assist potato cultivation.
    d.   Damp conditions and warm weather assist corn production.
    e.   None of the above.

2. Beer and potato chips are complementary products that are both sold in a competitive market. Barley is an essential ingredient in the production of beer; potatoes are an input into making chips. We observe that price increases and the quantity traded decreases in the beer market; and both the price and the quantity traded decrease in the chip market. Which of the following scenarios is consistent with the observation in the two markets, outlined above?

    a.   An increase in irrigated lands has allowed for an increase in the supply of potatoes.
    b.   A bumper year with perfect conditions in the grain-growing regions increase yields of barley.
    c.   Low rainfall reduces barley yields in grain-growing regions.
    d.   A health campaign by the federal government has the effect of curtailing beer consumption.
    e.   Floods in potato-growing regions reduce potato production.

3. Consider the world markets for lamb and beef. Assume that in both markets the laws of demand and supply hold. What will be the effect of the discovery of mad-cow disease (which can be transmitted to humans by eating infected products)?

    a.   The quantity of lamb sold in the market increases; the price of beef decreases.
    b.   The quantity of lamb sold in the market decreases; the price of beef rises.
    c.   The quantity of lamb sold in the market decreases; the price of beef decreases.
    d.   The quantity of lamb sold in the market increases; the price of beef increases.
    e.   None of the above.

4. Consider a market in which the laws of demand and supply hold. Which of the following would result in an increase in equilibrium price and an ambiguous change in equilibrium quantity?

   a.   An increase in supply and an increase in demand.
   b.   An increase in supply and a decrease in demand.
   c.   A decrease in supply and an increase in demand.
   d.   A decrease in supply and a decrease in demand.
   e.   None of the above.

5. Consider a perfectly competitive market with a demand curve given by $P = 100 - q_d$, where P is the market price and q_d is the quantity demanded. The market supply curve is given by $P = 3q_s$, where q_s is the market quantity supplied.

   a.   Calculate the market equilibrium price and quantity. Illustrate your answer using a diagram.
   b.   What is Consumer Surplus (CS)? What is Producer Surplus (PS)? Calculate the CS and PS and the total surplus generated in the competitive market, again illustrating your answer using a diagram. How does this competitive market equilibrium compare to the outcome that maximises total surplus? Provide some intuition for your answer.

6. In a market, demand is given by $P = 21 - q$ and supply by $P = 2q$. In the competitive-market equilibrium, what are the CS and PS?

Chapter 10

1. Which statement is true?

   a.   The cross-price elasticity for complementary goods is positive.
   b.   The party with the lowest opportunity cost has a comparative disadvantage in producing a good.
   c.   The price elasticity of demand is constant along a linear demand curve.
   d.   The price elasticity of demand is equal to 0 if the demand curve is perfectly elastic.
   e.   The cross-price elasticity for substitute goods is positive.

2. Which statement is true?

   a.   If a market demand curve is linear (a straight line), revenue in the market is maximised when the price elasticity of demand is unit elastic.
   b.   If a market demand curve is linear (a straight line), the price elasticity of demand is constant along the length of the demand curve.
   c.   If a market demand curve is linear (a straight line), the price elasticity of demand can be either elastic or inelastic along the whole curve, depending on the slope of the curve.
   d.   If a market demand curve is linear (a straight line), revenue is maximised when the demand curve intersects the price axis.

e. If a market demand curve is linear (a straight line), revenue is maximised when the demand curve intersects the quantity axis.

3. For good Y, when the price is $P_1 = \$60$ the quantity demanded is $q_1 = 10$ units. When the price falls to $P_2 = \$40$ it is determined by the formula that the elasticity is -3 according to the initial point elasticity method. What is the quantity demanded, q_2, when the price is $40.

    a. $q_2 = 0$.
    b. $q_2 = 20$.
    c. $q_2 = 30$.
    d. $q_2 = 40$.
    e. None of the above.

4. In a market, demand is given by $P = 100 - 2q_d$, where P is the price and q_d is the quantity demanded. The supply curve is given by $P = 2q_s$, where q_s is the quantity supplied. At market equilibrium, what is the elasticity of supply?

    a. 0.
    b. $\frac{1}{2}$.
    c. 1.
    d. 2.
    e. 3.

5. In a market, demand is given by $P = 100 - 2q_d$, where P is the price and q_d is the quantity demanded. The supply curve is given by $P = 2q_s$, where q_s is the quantity supplied. At market equilibrium, what is the price elasticity of demand?

6. A consumer always spends one-third of her income on computing services. Using the point method, in this case the income elasticity of demand for computing services is:

    a. 0.
    b. 0.33.
    c. 1.
    d. 3.
    e. None of the above.

7. In a market when the price increased, the total expenditure on the good also increased. Is demand elastic, inelastic or unit elastic in this region? Explain your answer.

Chapter 12

1. In a perfectly competitive industry, each firm has a total cost function of $TC = 400 + 10q + q^2$ and a marginal cost curve of $MC = 10 + 2q$ if it produces a positive quantity of output q. If a firm produces zero output it has no costs. The market price is $50. Which statement is true?

    a. Each firm produces 20 units of output; the industry will require entry to reach its long-run equilibrium.

b. Each firm is producing 25 units; as the firm is making short-run profits, the industry is not at its long-run equilibrium.

c. Each firm is producing 25 units; the firm is covering its variable costs, but making a short-run loss.

d. Each firm is producing 20 units; the firm will continue producing in the short run, but will consider exiting in the long run as it is not covering its total costs of production.

e. Each firm produces 20 units of output; the market is in its long-run equilibrium.

2. Which statement is true?

a. In the long run, if the long-run supply curve in a competitive industry is horizontal, the supply curve for each individual firm in the industry is also horizontal.

b. The long-run supply curve in a constant-cost industry is horizontal at the minimum of average total cost; individual firm supply curves are upward sloping, being their marginal cost curves when price is above the minimum of average total cost.

c. The supply curve of a competitive firm in the long run in a constant cost industry is horizontal.

d. Both b and c are correct.

e. None of the above.

3. The short-run marginal and average variable cost curves for a competitive firm are given by $MC = 8 + 8Q$ and $AVC = 8 + 4Q$, respectively. The profit-maximising level of output (Q) is 2 and the total fixed cost (TFC) is $64. Which of the following must be true about the firm?

a. The firm is charging a price of $40 and covering its average variable cost, hence it should continue operating in the short run.

b. The firm is charging a price of $40 and making a short-run loss, and hence the firm must shut down immediately.

c. The firm is charging a price of $24 and making a zero profit, and hence the firm should shut down eventually.

d. The firm is charging a price of $24, covering its average variable costs, but in the long run at this price it should exit.

e. None of the above.

4. Which statement is true?

a. Marginal cost intersects average fixed cost when average fixed cost is at its minimum.

b. In the short run, a perfectly competitive profit-maximising firm that has not shut down is not operating on the upward-sloping portion of its AVC.

c. A perfectly competitive profit-maximising firm whose long run economic profit is exactly zero should expand production to try to earn a positive profit.

d.   It is possible for average variable cost to be greater than average total cost at high levels of output.

e.   None of the above.

5. Consider the Sydney taxi market. Assume that the market is competitive with free entry. Further, assume that each firm has an increasing marginal cost curve and u-shaped average variable cost and average total cost curves. The market is initially in long-run equilibrium.

a.   Using a diagram, show and explain a firm's long-run supply curve. What will the price be in the long run and what profits will the firm make? Explain your answer.

b.   Due to an increase in population, there is an increase in market demand for taxis. What will happen to the price, the quantity the firm sells and its profit in the short run? Use a diagram to help explain your answer.

c.   Following this demand increase, the NSW government does two things: it bans any new firms (taxis) from entering the market – that is, there are no more taxis allowed; and, to raise revenue, it starts charging taxi owners for the right to have a taxi (often called a 'licence fee'). With no new entry, what will be the market price and the quantity sold by each firm? What would be the maximum licence fee a firm would be willing to pay for the rights to drive a taxi in this market with no new entry?

6. Which statement is true?

a.   In the long run in a constant-cost industry, a firm has a perfectly elastic supply curve.

b.   In the long run in a constant-cost industry, firms have an upward-sloping supply curve and face a downward-sloping demand curve.

c.   In the long run in a constant-cost industry, firms have an upward-sloping supply curve and the industry supply curve is the horizontal summation of the supply curves of firms currently in the industry.

d.   In the long run in a constant-cost industry, firms have a perfectly elastic supply curve and the long-run industry supply curve is horizontal.

e.   In the long run in a constant-cost industry, firms have an upward-sloping supply curve and the industry supply curve is perfectly elastic.

7. Assume a constant-cost industry with free entry is initially at its long-run equilibrium. Following an unanticipated increase in demand:

a.   In the short run, firms currently in the market face a higher price, make short-run profits; in the long run, entry reduces price somewhat, but positive economic profits for the firms initially in the market remain.

b.   In the short run, firms incur higher marginal costs for the last good produced but make positive economic profits; in the long run, firms maximise profit by selling a quantity so that MC for the last unit sold is the same as it was in the original long-run equilibrium (before the increase in demand).

c. In the short run, firms do not change the quantity they sell, but they earn positive economic profits; in the long run economic profits are zero.

d. In the short run, each firm increases the output it sells and makes positive profits; in the long run, entry causes profits to return to zero but each firm in the industry sells a higher quantity than in the initial long-run equilibrium (before the increase in demand).

e. All firms continue to make zero profits in both the short and long run.

Chapter 13

1. A monopolist has a constant $MC = 20$ per unit produced, has no fixed costs and faces a demand curve of $2q = 100 - P$. If the monopolist sells at a single price, which statement is true about the monopolist's profit-maximising quantity and price and its profit?

2. Consider a monopolist with $MC = 2q$ and a fixed cost of $FC = \$50$, facing a market demand curve of $P = 40 - q$. What is the profit of a single-price monopolist?

3. Which statement is FALSE?

    a. A monopolist changing a linear (or single) price raises the price above the MB of the final good sold.

    b. A monopolist regulated with marginal-cost pricing regulation produces no deadweight loss (assuming it produces, and does not exit the industry).

    c. A monopolist charging a linear (single) price sets its profit-maximising quantity where $MR = MC$.

    d. A monopolist regulated by average total cost pricing regulation, ensuring that it earns zero profits, produces no deadweight loss.

    e. A monopolist with positive marginal costs and facing a linear demand curve always sets a quantity (or price) such that it sells on the elastic section of the demand curve.

4. Consider a monopoly market with a demand curve of $P = 60 - q$. The monopolist has a marginal cost of production of $MC = q$. If the monopolist charges a linear price (a single-price monopolist), what is the DWL of monopoly?

    a. 0.

    b. 80.

    c. 100.

    d. 120.

    e. 160.

5. A scientific research lab has invented a new cancer drug. The lab is willing to sell the patent for the drug to the highest bidder, and the holder of the patent will have a monopoly for the drug. The drug costs $40 to produce per unit (that is, $MC = \$40$ per unit) and the demand curve for the medication is $1/2q = 200 - P$. What would be the maximum amount that a firm would be willing to pay for the patent?

    a. 8800.

b.   12,800.
c.   16,000.
d.   6400.
e.   4800.

6. A scientific research lab has invented a new cancer drug. The government is willing to buy the patent and make it publicly available, so that any firm can produce the drug (that is, there will be a competitive market in the production of the new drug). The drug costs $40 to produce per unit ($MC = \$40$ per unit) and the demand curve for the medication is $1/2q = 200 - P$. What would be the maximum that the government would be willing to pay for the patent? (Hint: the government would like to maximise the total surplus of producers and consumers generated by the trade of this product in the market.)

a.   6400.
b.   12,800.
c.   19,200.
d.   12,400.
e.   25,600.

7. Consider a market with a demand curve given by $P = 100 - q_d$, where P is the market price and q_d is the quantity demanded. Assume that there is only one firm selling in this market, and that this monopolist has a marginal cost curve of $MC = 3q$ and has no fixed costs. The monopolist charges a linear price (or a single price) to all customers.

a.   What is the monopolist's marginal revenue (MR) curve, and its profit-maximising price and quantity? Explain the monopolist's MR, and illustrate your answer on a diagram. What is the monopolist's profit?

b.   Compare the total surplus in the competitive market with the monopoly outcome. Using economic intuition (and a diagram where appropriate) explain the differences between the two market outcomes.

8. Consider Donna, a monopolist, selling to a market with a demand curve $P = 20 - q$, where P is the market price and q is the quantity demanded. Donna has a constant marginal cost of production of $2 per unit and a fixed cost of $20.

a.   If Donna charges a linear price (or a single price), what is the profit-maximising price and quantity, Donna's profit and any deadweight loss that arises? Explain your answer with the help of a diagram.

b.   What is first-degree price discrimination? Assuming the demand curve given above is the demand curve for one consumer, if Donna can engage in first-degree price discrimination using a two-part tariff, what price, quantity, profit and deadweight loss will result? Again, explain your answer with the help of a diagram.

9. Which of the following is an example of second-degree price discrimination?

a.   A theatre that offers lower prices for children.

b. A computer firm that offers a computer and a printer in a package at a lower price than it would cost to purchase both separately.

c. A rail service offering lower priced tickets to students than non-students.

d. All of the above.

10. Consider a monopolist producing a good with zero marginal costs and $20 fixed costs. There are two consumers in the market. Consumer 1 has a demand curve $q_1 = 10 - P$, where q_1 is the quantity demanded and P is the per-unit price. Consumer 2 has a demand curve $q_2 = 15 - P$, where q_2 is the quantity demanded by consumer 2. If the monopolist perfectly price discriminates between two consumers using a two-part tariff.

a. The monopolist will charge a fixed fee of $100 to consumer 1 and a per-unit fee of $0; and the fixed fee of $225 to consumer 2 and a per-unit fee of $0.

b. The monopolist will charge a fixed fee of $12.5 to consumer 1 and a per-unit fee of $5; and a fixed fee of $25 to consumer 2 and a per-unit fee of $5.

c. The monopolist will not produce as it makes negative profits if it does.

d. The monopolist will charge a fixed fee of $100 to consumer 1 and a per-unit fee of $0; and the fixed fee of $112.5 to consumer 2 and a per-unit fee of $0.

e. None of the above.

Chapter 14

1. Consider the following statements. Which statements are characteristics of a monopolistic competitive industry?

a. In the long run, all firms in the industry make zero economic profits.

b. Firms sell differentiated products.

c. There is free entry in the long run.

d. All of the above.

2. The entry and exit of firms in a monopolistically competitive market guarantees that:

a. In the long run, economic profits and economic losses are driven back to zero.

b. Economic profits can survive in the long run, but no firm can make an economic loss.

c. A firm can have economic losses in the long run, but not a positive economic profit.

d. Both economic profits and economic losses will exist in the long run.

3. Jon runs one of many restaurants in the industry in a city. This industry is monopolistically competitive and it is initially in its long-run equilibrium.

a. Assume that Jon has typical u-shaped average cost curves. Draw a diagram illustrating Jon's profit-maximising output, price and profit. Explain your answer.

b. On your diagram, show the consumer surplus generated, and any *DWL*. Explain your answer.

c.   The government is contemplating regulating the industry so that prices must equal marginal cost. What would Jon's response be to this regulation in the long run?

4.   Because the average total cost of a firm is not minimised in the long run if the market is monopolistically competitive, the level of entry is too high and it is inefficient. Discuss.

Chapter 15

1.   Consider the following game: Amazon can choose to either Enter or Not Enter into the market for e-books. If Amazon chooses Not Enter then the payoffs are $1 to Amazon and $6 to Apple. If Amazon chooses to Enter then Apple observes this and chooses to either Punish or Accommodate. If Apple chooses to Punish the payoffs are $1 to Apple and −$1 to Amazon. If Apple Accommodates the payoffs are $2 to each party. What are all of the Nash equilibria in this game?

   a.   (Enter, Accommodate).
   b.   (Not Enter, Punish).
   c.   (Enter, Punish).
   d.   (Not Enter, Punish) and (Enter, Accommodate).
   e.   (Not Enter, Punish), (Not Enter, Punish) and (Enter, Accommodate).

2.   Consider the following game: Amazon can choose to either Enter of Not Enter into the market for e-books. If Amazon chooses Not Enter then the payoffs are $1 to Amazon and $6 to Apple. If Amazon chooses to Enter then Apple observes this and chooses to either Punish or Accommodate. If Apple chooses to Punish the payoffs are $1 to Apple and −$1 to Amazon. If Apple Accommodates the payoffs are $2 to each party. What are all of the subgame perfect equilibria in this game?

   a.   (Enter, Accommodate).
   b.   (Not Enter, Punish).
   c.   (Enter, Punish).
   d.   (Not Enter, Punish) and (Enter, Accommodate).
   e.   (Not Enter, Punish), (Not Enter, Punish) and (Enter, Accommodate).

3.   Consider the following market. Chrome can choose when launching its new product either to do it LARGE or as NICHE. After Chrome has chosen its action, Firefox observes Chrome's choice and then can choose to ADAPT to RETAIN its own product. After Firefox has chosen its action, the game ends and the payoffs are made. The payoffs are as follows: If Chrome chooses LARGE and Firefox ADAPT, the payoffs are 25 and 40 to Chrome and Firefox, respectively. If Chrome goes LARGE and Firefox RETAINS the payoffs are 30 and 50 to Chrome and Firefox. If Chrome plays NICHE and Firefox ADAPTS, the payoffs are (40 Chrome, 30 Firefox) and if Chrome plays NICHE and Firefox RETAINS the payoffs are (20, 20) for Chrome and Firefox, respectively.

a. What is a Nash equilibrium? Outline the Nash equilibrium or equilibria in the game, and explain your answer.

b. What is a subgame perfect (or credible) equilibrium and how would you find such an equilibrium? What is the outcome in the subgame perfect equilibrium in this game? Explain your answer.

c. Does the subgame perfect equilibrium (or credible equilibrium) result in the outcome that maximises total surplus? If it is, explain why. If not, is there some transfer between the two parties that can help achieve the surplus-maximising result? Explain your answer.

4. Sonia the Terrible lands her ship and crew of scurvy-pirate raiders on a foreign beach. Up on the headland is a village, led by Jen the Brave. At this point, Sonia has a choice: she can SLASH her water barrels, eliminating her water supplies; or she can NOT SLASH, which keeps her water supplies completely intact. Having seen the action taken by Sonia, Jen can choose to CHARGE or to WAIT. The payoffs are as follows: if Sonia the Terrible chooses to SLASH and Jen CHARGEs, the payoffs are (100, 20) to Sonia and Jen, respectively. If Sonia SLASHes and Jen WAITs, the payoffs are (10, 30). On the other hand, if Sonia chooses to NOT SLASH and Jen CHARGEs, the payoff is (20, 15). If Sonia opts to NOT SLASH and Jen chooses to WAIT, the payoffs are (40, 10), respectively. What is the subgame perfect (or credible) equilibrium outcome?

a. Sonia the Terrible chooses to SLASH; Jen the Brave chooses to CHARGE.

b. Sonia the Terrible chooses to NOT SLASH; Jen the Brave chooses to WAIT.

c. Sonia the Terrible chooses to NOT SLASH; Jen the Brave chooses to CHARGE.

d. Sonia the Terrible chooses to SLASH; Jen the Brave chooses to WAIT.

e. None of the above.

5. Consider the following game involving Sony and Nintendo. Each has to decide on a new platform for its new generation of games. The two choices are Platform 1 and Platform 2. If both firms choose Platform 1 the payoff is 20 to each firm. If both firms choose Platform 2, the payoff is 30 to each firm. If Sony chooses Platform 2 and Nintendo Platform 1 the payoffs are 8 to Sony and 2 to Nintendo. Finally, if Sony opts for Platform 1 and Nintendo for Platform 2, the payoffs are 5 to Sony and 7 to Nintendo. What is Sony's preferred outcome? What is Nintendo's preference? What are the Nash equilibrium or equilibria of the game? Explain your answer.

6. Define Nash equilibrium. Give an example of a prisoners' dilemma in a business context. Explain why your game is a prisoners' dilemma.

7. Consider the following game between firm A and firm B. In each period firms A and B each decide at the same time whether to advertise (Adv) or not advertise (NA). The payoffs in each period are: if both firms advertise they each get a pay-off of 2; if one firm advertises and the other chooses NA the payoffs are 6 to the advertiser and 1 to the firm that did not advertise; and, finally, if they both choose to not advertise each gets 5.

a. If the game only goes for one period, what is the Nash equilibrium.

b. Now assume that there are three periods; that is, the two firms play the adv/NA game three times in a row. What is the Nash equilibrium?

Chapter 16

1. Consider two markets for haircuts: Sydney and Melbourne. Supply in both cities is perfectly elastic and at the same price. Demand in Sydney is relative inelastic compared with demand for haircuts in Melbourne, in the relevant range. The federal government introduces a tax of t in both markets. Which statement is true?

   a. The deadweight loss created by the tax is larger in Sydney than in Melbourne; the reduction in quantity is larger in Sydney than in Melbourne.

   b. The deadweight loss created by the tax is larger in Sydney than in Melbourne; the reduction in quantity is larger in Melbourne than in Sydney.

   c. The deadweight loss created by the tax is larger in Melbourne than in Sydney; the reduction in quantity is larger in Sydney than in Melbourne.

   d. The deadweight loss created by the tax is larger in Melbourne than in Sydney; the reduction in quantity is larger in Melbourne than in Sydney.

   e. None of the above.

2. Which statement is true?

   a. A positive tax always creates a deadweight loss.

   b. A tax that does not raise any revenue has zero deadweight loss.

   c. If a tax is imposed on a market, the economic incidence of the tax depends on who legally has to pay for the tax.

   d. If demand is downward sloping and supply is perfectly inelastic, consumers pay for all of the tax.

   e. None of the above.

3. In a market the demand curve is given by $P = 30 - 2q_d$, where P is the price and q_d is the quantity demanded. Supply is given by $P = q_s$. The government imposes a per-unit tax to be legally paid by suppliers of $6 per unit. Following the imposition of the tax, which statement is true?

   a. Consumers pay $4 more than without the tax; producers receive $2 less with the tax than before it was imposed.

   b. Consumers pay $16 with the tax; producers receive a price of $10 with the tax.

   c. Producers receive $4 with the tax; consumers pay $10.

   d. Consumers pay $12 with the tax; producers receive a price of $6 after the tax is imposed.

   e. Producers pay for all of the economic incidence of the tax.

4. In a market the demand curve is given by $P = 30 - 2q_d$, where P is the price and q_d is the quantity demanded. Supply is given by $P = q_s$. The government imposes a per-unit tax to be legally paid by suppliers of $6 per unit. Following the imposition of the tax, what is the DWL?

5. In a market the demand function is given by $q_d = 100 - P$, where q_d is the quantity demanded and P is the price. Supply is perfectly elastic at $P = \$40$. The government implements a subsidy to producers of $10 a unit. With the subsidy, what is the DWL?

6. The deadweight loss from a per-unit tax in a product market is:
   a. Positively related to the (absolute) elasticity of demand, but is not affected by the elasticity of supply.
   b. Negatively related to the (absolute) elasticity of demand and to the (absolute) elasticity of supply.
   c. Positively related to the (absolute) elasticity of demand and to the (absolute) elasticity of supply.
   d. Positively related to the (absolute) elasticity of supply and not affected by the elasticity of demand.
   e. It depends on which side of the market the tax is levied on.

7. Consider the following market: Demand is given by $q_d = 150 - 2P$, where q_d is the quantity demanded and P is the price. Supply is given by $q_s = P$, where q_s is the quantity supplied.
   a. What is the market equilibrium?
   b. The government implements a tax of $30 per unit to be paid by consumers. What is the new market equilibrium? What is the economic incidence of the tax (that is, who pays for the tax)? How would your answer change if the government implemented a production tax of $30 per unit instead?
   c. With the aid of a diagram, calculate the deadweight loss that arises as a result of the tax. Provide intuition for the result.

Chapter 17

1. The government issues tradeable pollution permits to deal with an externality. With tradeable pollution permits:
   a. The cost of reducing pollution is minimised, regardless of its initial distribution amongst polluting firms.
   b. The firms that are allocated permits will continue to emit more pollution than firms with fewer, or zero, permits.
   c. Although the price of permits reflects the opportunity cost of polluting, this only applies to firms without permits.
   d. The firms that are allocated permits will trade all their permits to other firms, and keep the money.
   e. The cost of reducing pollution is minimised, although firms receiving permits will emit more pollution than other firms.

2. Consider a market for sport in which the private marginal benefit (PMB) is given by $PMB = 120 - 2q$, where q is the quantity consumed. The marginal cost of providing

the service is given by $MC = q$. In this market there is also a positive consumption externality of $30 per unit consumed.

a. Define externality.

b. For this market, compare the market outcome with the socially efficient outcome. What is the deadweight loss, if any? With the aid of a diagram, provide some intuition for your answer.

c. In this market, the government is restricted in that it cannot by law subsidise or tax consumers, but it can legally tax or subsidise producers. Can the government intervene in the market to achieve the surplus-maximising outcome? Again, explain your answer.

3. What is the Coase Theorem? Why might the Coase Theorem fail?

4. Consider a market in which there is a demand curve of $q_d = 10 - P$, where q_d is the quantity demanded and P is the price. The market supply curve is given by $q_s = P$, where q_s is the quantity supplied. There is, however, a negative production externality of $2 per unit produced. What is the deadweight loss (the loss of surplus) in the market outcome?

a. $1.

b. $2.

c. $3.

d. $4.

e. It is not possible to ascertain with the information provided.

5. The private demand for education is given by $q_d = 500 - 5P$. The supply of education is given by $q_s = 5P$.

a. What is the market equilibrium?

b. Education generates a positive externality of $5 a unit. What is the social optimum? What is the deadweight loss?

c. Outline a possible intervention in the market by the government that could improve the market outcome.

6. There has been some debate about the use of single-use plastic bags.

a. If there is a negative consumption externality, compare the welfare effects of a ban on plastic bags with the market outcome. Is there a level of externality for which a zero level of output is efficient?

b. What is an alternative policy to a banning plastic bags?

7. The costs of reducing each unit of pollution for firm A are $10 for the first unit of pollution abated (or reduced), $20 for the second unit abated, $30 for the third, $40 for the fourth, $50 for the fifth, $60 for the sixth and $70 for the seventh unit of pollution that is not emitted. For firm B the costs of reducing pollution are $5 for the first unit not emitted, $15 for the second unit abated, $25 for the third unit, $35 for the fourth unit, $45 for the fifth unit, $55 for the sixth unit not emitted and $65 for the seventh unit not emitted. The government imposes a tax of $37 for each unit

of pollution emitted. What is the total level of abatement (or the total reduction) in pollution after the tax has been implemented?

8. Consider an externality between a beekeeper (and her bees) and almond production from an almond orchard. It costs the beekeeper $25 to maintain each beehive. If the beekeeper places her hives near the almond orchard, almond production increases by $10 per hive. The benefit to the beekeeper from placing her hives near the almond orchard is $50 for the first hive, $40 for the second hive, $30 for the third hive, $20 for the fourth hive, $10 for the fifth hive and $0 for any subsequent hives. If the almond orchard buys the beekeeping operation (that is, the two activities are performed by the same firm) what is the number of hives that will be placed near the almond orchard? Explain your answer in the context of the literature on market mechanisms to deal with externalities.

Chapter 18

1. Consider a public good that has a marginal benefit for consumer 1 of $MB = 20 - q$ and a marginal benefit for consumer 2 of $MB = 30 - 1.5q$. If the marginal cost of provision is $10 per unit, what is the socially optimal level of output?

2. A public good is

   a. non-rival and excludable.
   b. a private good that benefits many people.
   c. rival in consumption, but not excludable.
   d. non-rival and non-excludable.
   e. None of the above.

3. The local council is considering providing access to a public good. Beth, Cathy and David are the only potential users of the good. Their willingness to pay for the good is as follows: $P_{Beth} = 10 - Q$; $P_{Cathy} = 30 - 3Q$; and $P_{David} = 20 - 2Q$, where a total of Q units are provided. If there are no fixed costs, and the marginal cost of providing the good is given by $MC = 20 + 2Q$, what is the optimal quantity?

Chapter 19

1. Suppose that the federal government imposes a tariff on imported cars to protect the Australian car industry from foreign competition.

   a. Assuming that Australia is a price taker in the world car market, use a diagram to help analyse the welfare effects of the policy.
   b. Who is going to be opposed to the removal of the tariff? Who is going to be in favour of the removal of the tariff? Why might reducing tariffs be a potentially difficult political issue?

2. What is an import quota? Using a diagram, analyse the impact of a binding import quota. Show that a quota can produce the same effect on local production and on the number of imports as a tariff set a given rate. What is the value of the import licences?

3. Guyana, a small country, is considering opening up its aluminium market to international trade – that is international trade is currently not permitted. The government knows that the world price for aluminium is higher than the price that is prevailing in the domestic market. Knowing little else, the government hires you as a consultant. The government asks you the following questions:

   a. If international trade is allowed, what will be the effect on domestic prices, domestic production and domestic consumption? Use a diagram to help explain your answer.

   b. Again using the assistance of a diagram, explain what happens to PS and CS if international trade is allowed. What happens to the total surplus?

   c. Is the policy of not allowing international trade in aluminium Pareto efficient? Explain your answer.

4. Critically assess the arguments for protecting a domestic industry from international trade.

5. Consider the market for bottled water in Australia (a small country). The quantity demanded in Australia q_d is given by $q_d = 90 - P$, where P is the market price. The domestic quantity supplied q_s is given by $q_s = 2P$. The world price for bottled water is $10.

   a. With the aid of a diagram, calculate the change in consumer surplus, producer surplus and overall welfare if Australia removes a ban on the international trade of bottled water. Is the original ban on international trade in bottled water efficient? Give reasons for your answer.

   b. After the Australian government has removed the ban on international trade, it then implements an import tax of $10. Again, with the help of a diagram, calculate the change in quantity demanded, domestic quantity produced, imports and exports and the change in consumer surplus, producer surplus and government revenue. Make sure you explain the economic intuition behind your working and your answer.

   c. The government, instead of the import tax, considers implementing a $10 per unit production subsidy for domestic producers. What are the implications for the market, in particular, the change in consumer, producer surplus and tax revenue and the impact on overall welfare? Compare the outcome to that in part b. Make sure you explain the economic reasoning behind your answer.

   d. You are hired as an economic consultant by the Australian government. What is your ranking of the three alternative policies outlined in parts a, b and c (that is free trade, a tariff and a production subsidy)? Which policy would you recommend and why?

Chapter 20

1. Assume that the market for housing in a region is competitive, except for the fact that there is not free entry (due to government restrictions on land release and

development). Discuss the short- and long-run implications given that demand is growing (due to population growth).

2. Using supply-and-demand analysis, show how prices in the housing market can fall over time, even if the population is growing, if the government can release sufficient land for development.

3. Assume that the (competitive) domestic capital market is in equilibrium. Now assume that the government opens the capital market to international competition so that domestic borrowers and savers (lenders) can trade on the international market. Assume that the country is small and that the world interest rate is below the domestic interest rate (prior to opening up the capital market to international competition). Outline what happens to domestic savers and borrowers given the change to allow for international trade.

4. Olivia wants to sell her luxury north shore apartment. What happens in expectation of the auction price for her home when there is net migration away from the north shore?

5. How can it be that an individual's labour supply curve can be backwards bending, but not the market supply curve? Use diagrams to aid your answer.

6. Consider the labour market for fruit picking. The market is competitive, although there are two notable seasons: the winter (low-demand) period and the summer (high-demand) period. The government sets a minimum wage at just above the winter period equilibrium wage. Analyse with the help of diagrams what happens over the year in this labour market.

Chapter 21

1. In a market domestic supply is given by $q_s = P$ and domestic demand by $P = 50 - q_d$. An almost perfect substitute product is available from overseas at a world price of $2 per unit; however, there is a negative consumption externality associated with the imported good. What is the optimal policy?

   a.   A tax on domestic producers of $3 per unit.

   b.   A tariff (an import tax) of $3 per unit.

   c.   A consumption tax levied on consumers of $3 per unit.

   d.   It does not matter if the per-unit of $3 is levied on consumers or producers.

   e.   None of the above.

2. Consider Donna, a monopolist, selling to a market with a demand curve $P = 20 - q$, where P is the market price and q is the quantity demanded. Donna has a constant marginal cost of production of $2 per unit and a fixed cost of $20.

   a.   If Donna charges a linear price (or a single price), what is the profit-maximising price and quantity, Donna's profit and any deadweight loss that arises? Explain you answer with the help of a diagram.

   b.   Now consider that there is a negative production externality of $10 per unit. What is the deadweight loss generated by the market outcome? What is an optimal policy response by the government? Explain your answer.

2. 'Economic policy contains both positive and normative economics.' Discuss.

3. 'Given markets are efficient, there is no role for government intervention in the economy.' Evaluate this statement.

4. Do you agree or disagree with the following statement? 'The only valid goal of economic policy is efficiency.' Provide reasons for your answer.

Chapter 22

1. 'Econometric (statistical) evidence without theory shows correlation not causality.' Evaluate this statement.

2. Experimental evidence from lab experiments repeatedly fails to be replicated both in the real world. Why might this be the case?

3. 'Given people are not rational, economic models that assume full rationality tell us little about the real world.' Evaluate this statement.

Selected answers

Chapter 1

1. Opportunity cost of an activity is the next best forgone opportunity.

2. Opportunity cost is the next best forgone opportunity – this includes both explicit and implicit costs (for example, what a person might alternatively do with their time).

3. e. All of the activities listed involve tradeoffs.

4. d.

5. Just because the University already owns the building on campus, it does not mean it is a sunk cost. The opportunity cost is not using it for something else (renting it, selling the land and building or using it for a different purpose). Alternatively, if the University opts to move their business school off campus they will face the explicit costs of purchasing the land and constructing the building. Of course, these explicit costs will have an opportunity cost as well; for example, the resources could have been put to a different use (like funding the chemistry department).

   Without knowledge of the University's preferences, it is impossible to further assess the choice between the two sites; however, it may be the case that the University is better off moving the business school off campus. Certainly, the administrators' comment is not valid or a sensible criterion for making this decision.

6. a.

Chapter 2

1. $P = 100 - 0.5q$.

2. $C'(q) = \frac{dC}{dq} = 10 + q$.

3. $\varepsilon_d = -4$.

4. $q = 30, P = 60$.

5. $q^* = 20$ units.

Chapter 3

1. d.

2. a.

3. c.

4. c.

5. (PP, B) and (B, PP), where the first term in each bracket is Vlad's strategy and the second term is Guillaume's strategy.

6. Japan chooses OUT, and Australia AGREE.

7. Japan chooses IN and Australia AGREE.

8. (On, Off) and (Off, On), where the first strategy in each parenthesis is Martin's and the second is Jim's. The first Nash equilibrium produces higher total surplus. The two guitarists might know to play this equilibrium from experience practicing and playing together in the past.

9. (Lead, Rhythm) and (Rhythm, Lead).

Chapter 4

2. b is not true.

3. a. The party that is more productive has the absolute advantage. Suzie has the absolute advantage in x, no one has the absolute advantage in y.

   b. Comparative advantage means having a lower opportunity cost. Bob has the comparative advantage in y – his opportunity cost is two units of x compared with Suzie's opportunity cost of 3 units of x. Suzie has the opportunity cost in producing x – her opportunity cost is $\frac{1}{3}$ unit of y compared with Bob's opportunity cost of $\frac{1}{2}$ unit of y.

   c. The slope of the PPF represents the opportunity cost for each individual changing production from one good to the other.

   d. Each individual will only be willing to trade if they can either buy a good for a lower price than their opportunity cost, or if they are selling a good, they must receive a price that is at least as large as their opportunity cost. The maximum price Bob is willing to pay for x is $\frac{1}{2}$ a unit of y. The minimum price Suzie will accept for selling a unit of x is $\frac{1}{3}$ a unit of y. The minimum price that Bob would sell y for is 2 units of x. The maximum price that Suzie would pay for a unit of good y is 3 units of x.

   Together, these minima and maxima give the range of prices between which trade is mutually beneficial.

4. In this case, Bob still has a comparative advantage in task y. Suzie has a comparative advantage in task x. To maximise the output of the firm Bob should specialise in

task y and Suzie in task x. (Examples of this abound from real firms. For instance, a lawyer might be both better at providing legal advice and doing the filing than her assistant, but the total output of the firm might be greater if she lets the assistant do the filing while she concentrates on providing legal advice to clients.)

In this way, the idea that it is someone's relative opportunity cost (their comparative advantage) that determines what they should specialise in, and not their absolute advantage; this also applies to the allocation of tasks within a firm, as well as to trading patterns we observe in the market.

There are several things different when we are considering internal organisation of production as opposed to trade in markets. Here are a few of the important differences: first, task allocation in a firm is chosen by the manager – they are not determined by voluntary trading choices of individuals in the market. That is, there is nothing automatic in regards to the decision as to task allocation in a firm – it is up to a clever manager to see her workers' opportunity costs and allocate jobs accordingly. Second, we are abstracting in this argument about the balance between tasks required and the output mix that a firm would want to produce (that is, which goods they want to sell on the market). But to the extent that profits will be increased by a firm that is able to produce more output with the same (or fewer) inputs, comparative advantage is a key driver in how a successful firm will allocate tasks amongst its employees.

5. Both increase in population and technological progress shift the PPF to the right.

The advantage of technological progress is that it leads to an increase in the per-worker (or per-person) consumption.

Imagine an economy that produced only coffee. Increasing the number of workers who can spend time producing coffee would increase coffee production. This would not necessarily increase the consumption of coffee per person. (In principle, it could if the new workers were relatively more productive than the old workers, but let's assume that this is not the case.) Alternatively, if technological progress occurred and machines became more efficient, then the economy could produce more coffee with the same number of workers. This would lead to an increase in per-person consumption of coffee.

This example illustrates the idea that living standards are determined by productivity.

Chapter 5

1. a.   To work out the outcome of these negotiations we work backwards. By solving backwards we capture the fact that these bargaining agents are forward looking; they will all take into account possible future actions or events when thinking about what to do (in the present).

   b.   Maggie's payoff if she rejects the offer is 0, so she will accept any offer greater or equal to 0. Knowing this (working backwards) Davo offers Maggie a price for the Corolla of 0 (or an offer very close to zero). So at this stage of the negotiations (if reached), Davo offers a price of $0 and Maggie accepts that offer.

c. Davo in a sense has an outside option – he can always reject Shazza's offer, start bargaining with Maggie and end up with a payoff of $4000. As a result, Davo will not accept any offer that gives him less surplus than $4000. In other words 20,000 minus the price must be ≥ 4000. Hence, the maximum price Davo is willing to accept will be $16,000; that is, Davo will accept any offer from Shazza of 16,000 or less. Shazza knows this, so she offers the highest price that Davo will accept; Shazza offers $16,000. In summary, Shazza offers a price of $16,000 and Davo accepts this offer.

d. In this bargaining outcome Shazza gets $16,000 surplus, Davo gets $4000 surplus and Maggie gets $0. Thus the total surplus is $20,000. The maximum possible surplus in this situation is $20,000 (when Davo ends up with the Falcon). As Davo does buy the Falcon here, the total surplus is maximised.

2. b. Singapore offers a price of $100 and Ansett accepts.
   b. Ansett offers a price of $100, and Singapore accepts; Singapore gets a net payoff of $350 - 100 = \$250M$, and Ansett $100M.

3. Bazza offers a price of $100 and Raelene accepts. Trade takes place immediately in the first year. Note here that there is a cost of delay. Bazza knows that if Raelene rejects the offer the potential gains from the patent in year 1 will be forgone. This gives Bazza some bargaining power – in fact, he captures the potential gains from using the patent in year 1.

4. Solving backward. At the very beginning of the game, A offers a price of $25 and B accepts this offer.

Chapter 6

1. Due to the consumer's diminishing marginal benefit for the good or service.

2. b.

3. $MB = 10 - q$ is the consumer's demand curve, although it is usually written as $P = 10 - q$. The maximum price for the first unit (for a very small unit) is 10 – the intercept of the P-axis. The maximum price a consumer is willing to pay for the 7th unit is 3.

4. e.

5. $P = 20 - \frac{1}{3}Q$.

6. $P = 10 - \frac{1}{5}Q$.

Chapter 7

1. e.

2. b.

3. d.

4. d.

6. $MC = 10 + 4q$, $AVC = 10 + 2q$ and $ATC = 250/q + 10 + 2q$.

Chapter 8

1. True. Notwithstanding a few nuances regarding the short and long run, if a firm is going to produce a positive level of output its marginal cost curve is its supply curve.

2. A firm's supply curve is its MC curve. It is upward sloping in the short run due to its diminishing marginal product.

3. d.

Chapter 9

1. b.

2. c.

3. a.

4. c.

5. a. $q^* = 25$, $P^* = 100 - 25 = 75$.

   b. Consumer surplus: MB minus the price paid for each unit consumed. It measures the net benefit a consumer receives from consuming a good, as they perceive it.

   Producer surplus: is the difference between the price received by a firm for selling a good and the minimum price they would have accepted to sell the good, for every good sold. It is the difference between the price received and the marginal cost of producing a good for every good sold: $CS = (100 - 75)(25)/2 = \$625$; and $PS = (25)(75)/2 = \$937.5$.

   The competitive market outcome maximises surplus as all trades for which $MB \geq MC$ take place. In a competitive market, consumers keep buying provided $MB \geq P$, and firms keep selling as long as $P \geq MC$; thus all mutually beneficial trades take place (when $MB \geq MC$) and all the gains from trade are realised.

6. $CS = \$24.5$; $PS = \$49$.

Chapter 10

1. e.

2. a.

3. b.

4. c.

5. -1.

6. c.

Chapter 12

1. e.
2. b.
3. d.
4. e.
6. e.
7. b.

Chapter 13

1. q_m = 20 units, P_M = 60, π = 800.
2. π = \$150.
3. d.
4. c.
5. b.
6. e.
7. a. $MR = 100 - 2q$; profit maximisation when MR = MC. $q_M = 20$ and $P_M = 100 - 20$.

   A monopolist charging a single price must drop its price to all infra-marginal consumers in order to sell an extra unit. Hence, $MR < P$ (for all units but the very first unit). Like all firms it will maximise profit by continuing to sell when $MR \geq MC$, so it maximised profit here when $MR = MC$.

   b.   Surplus is maximised when all trades for which $MB \geq MC$. Here this means that 25 units are traded. This is the same as the competitive market outcome (as all trades for which $MB \geq MC$ take place with that market structure).

   For a monopolist, profit is maximised when $MR = MC$ – here at 20 units. As the monopolist's $MR < P$, this quantity will be less than the quantity required so that $MB = MC$ for the last unit traded. That is, in this case between an output of 20 and 25 units, the MB of a good is greater than its MC of production – there are potential gains from trade (surplus could increase), but these potential gains are forgone due to the monopolist restricting output. A DWL (or loss of potential surplus) of \$50 results in this case.

8. a. $MR = 20 - 2q$; $P^M = 11$, $q_m = 9$, $\pi = 61$, $DWL = 40.5$.
   b.   Fixed fee $F = 162$, per-unit price $p = 2$; $\pi = 142$.
9. b.
10. d.

Chapter 14

1. d.
2. a.
4. *ATC* is not minimised in the long run in a monopolistically competitive firm. In the long run the firm equates *MR* and *MC*, and makes zero profit. This requires $P = ATC$. As $P > MC$, *ATC* is not minimised.

   However, as the firms in a monopolistically competitive industry are not selling identical products (as they are in perfect competition), each new firm offers a new product to consumers. As consumers appreciate this variety, entry by new firms can increase the surplus.

   As a consequence, it is not immediately obvious that just because *ATC* is not minimised the entry is excessive.

   Note that a firm will enter a market if its (variable) profit covers its fixed costs. In terms of society's welfare, the increase in fixed costs from entry must be outweighed by the increase in surplus (both to the entering firm and to consumers). These two objectives do not necessarily coincide.

   In comparison to total welfare, there can be excessive or too little entry into a market that is monopolistically competitive. Moreover, there are two effects that influence total welfare and the number of firms in the market. First, the product variety effect suggests that there will be too little entry. Because a firm increases product variety, that increases consumer surplus; to the extent that this increase in surplus is not captured by the entry firm, there is too little incentive to enter. Second, an entering firm steals business from existing firms, providing it with an incentive to enter but not actually increasing overall surplus; this effect suggests excessive entry.

   Hence, one effect suggests too little entry (or the number of firms in the market); the other suggests excessive entry. Which of these effects dominate will determine whether there are too many or too few firms in the market with respect to maximising total welfare.

Chapter 15

1. d.
2. a.
4. c.
5. The Nash equilibria are Platform 1, Platform 1 and Platform 2, Platform 2.

   This is a coordination game – the parties like to coordinate their actions. More generally, you can think of firms wanting to do the same thing (as in this example, where they want compatible platforms) or wanting to do different (or opposite) things, for example you might want to locate your restaurant where your rival is not (or Sony might want to make their system incompatible with Nintendo's). Note that even though both firms prefer the equilibrium Platform 2, Platform 2, there is no unilateral incentive to deviate out of the Platform 1, Platform 1 if that's where the firms find themselves.

7. a. (Adv, Adv)

   b. The NE is: (Adv, Adv), (Adv, Adv) and (Adv, Adv). In other words, play Adv in every period.

Chapter 16

1. d.

2. e.

3. a.

4. $6.

5. $50.

6. c.

7. a. $P^* = \$50$, $q^* = 50$.

   b. Producers receive $30 per unit; consumers pay $60 per unit; quantity with the tax is 30 units.

   Incidence of the tax: Consumers pay for $10; producers pay $20 per unit for the tax (note, in total they pay for the entire tax $30 per unit).

   If the tax was implemented on the production side the economic incidence of the tax would be identical (as would the quantity bought and sold).

   The intuition for this is that the burden of the tax depends on the relative elasticities of supply and demand (the side of the market that is relatively more inelastic paying more of the tax), not who legally is required to pay the tax to the government. Thus, the economic incidence of the tax is the same as with a consumption tax. Further, the gap between the consumer and producer price is required to be equal to the size of the tax – this means that the quantity sold in the market needs to be reduced just enough so that the gap between S and D is equal to the tax. It does not matter, therefore, who legally has to pay for the tax as the market output ends up being the same regardless of whether it is a consumption or a production tax.

   c. The tax effectively shifts the demand curve vertically down by the size of the tax. This is because consumers cannot reduce the tax they must pay to the government from the MB they received from each unit they consume – it is as if their MB was reduced by the size of the tax for each unit they consume.

   The new equilibrium quantity is where the new demand curve with the tax intersects the supply curve – in this case, $q_t = 30$ units.

   A DWL arises because the tax places a wedge between the MB of the last unit consumed and the MC of the last unit produced. Because the consumer has to 'cover' the tax, they need to receive at least enough MB from any good they buy to cover the price plus the tax. That means that the last good bought has the characteristic that $MB - T = MC$. Beyond this level of consumption, the consumer does not receive enough benefit from purchasing a unit to cover the price plus the tax (the full cost of buying a unit).

This wedge between *MB* and *MC* means that not all the gains from trade are realised. Between q_t and q^*, each extra unit would provide a greater benefit than it costs to produce – there are unrealised potentially mutually beneficial trades that are not made. The DWL is the total loss in surplus from these unrealised gains from trade as a result of the tax.

Chapter 17

1. a.

4. a.

5. a. $P = 50, q = 250$ units.
   b. $q^* = 262.5$ units; $DWL = 31.25$.
   c. The government could implement a subsidy for education of $5 a unit. This means the private benefit from education equals the benefit from the education itself, plus the $5 subsidy from the government. In this case, the private incentives to get education are $MB = 105 - q_d/5$, which aligns society's and the individual's incentives to get education.

6. a. With a negative externality e per unit, the SMC curve is shifted down from the MPB curve by e per unit. The efficient quantity is q^* below q_m.
   b. In order for zero level of output to be the efficient quantity, the externality needs to be sufficiently large so that the SMB curve and the MSC curve never intersect. That is, the negative externality e must be at least as large as the gap between the MPB and MSC at zero level of output.

7. Firm A reduces emission when the cost of abatement is less than the tax, so Firm A reduces emissions by 3 units.

   Firm B reduces emissions by 4 units.

   Total reduction is 7 units.

   The general principle is that a firm will try to minimise the negative impact – they will reduce emissions when that is less costly than the tax. When the loss to the firm from reducing emissions is greater than the tax, a firm will choose to pay the tax (and continue to emit that unit of pollution).

8. 4; participants in trade have an incentive to maximise surplus (if they can) because with a larger surplus at least one person can be made better off without making anyone worse off (or everyone can be made better off) – refer to Coase Theorem.

Chapter 18

1. 16 units.

2. d.

3. $Q^* = 5$.

Chapter 19

3. a.   Prior to international trade, equilibrium is determined by the intersection of domestic supply and demand. After international trade is allowed, domestic price immediately rises to be equal to the world price P_w. At this higher price, domestic quantity supplied increases, and domestic quantity demanded decreases. The difference between domestic quantity supplied and domestic quantity demand is exported.

   b.   Trade has made producers better off and consumers worse off. Part of this is a transfer from consumers to producers, but trade has increased the total surplus (the gains to the winners exceed the losses to the losers).

   c.   Pareto efficiency – an outcome is Pareto efficient if it is not possible to make one party better off without making any other party worse off.

   The outcome without trade is not Pareto efficient. Trade increases the total surplus, so it makes it possible for the winners by allowing the change to adequately compensate the losers for any losses they may incur. As international trade increases total surplus, it is possible to fully compensate producers, plus have some extra surplus remaining.

5. a.   No international trade: Price $30, $q = 60$.

   At world price (with trade): $P = 10$, $q_d = 80$, $q_s = 20$.

   Consumer surplus increases by $1400; producer surplus falls by 800; overall surplus increases by $600 with international trade. The original ban is not efficient.

   b.   With tariff domestic price is $P_t = 20$; $q_d^t = 70$, $q_s^t = 40$. Imports are 30 units.

   Consumer surplus falls by 750; producer surplus increases by 300, Government revenue is 300; total welfare falls with the tariff by 150.

   c.   With a production subsidy, the domestic price remains at the world price. But now effectively domestic producers receive 20 for each unit sold. Hence $q_d^s = 80$, $q_s^s = 40$.

   CS is unchanged from free trade. PS increases by 300. Government expenditure (a minus) is 400. So total welfare falls by 100.

   With a production subsidy there is no consumption DWL, there is just the production DWL. So a production subsidy results in higher welfare than the tariff (but less than free trade).

   d.   If maximising total surplus is the objective, free trade is the best policy, followed by the subsidy, the tariff, then the ban on international trade. Remember, with more total surplus it is possible to fully compensate the losers from a policy change and still make others better off.

Chapter 21

1. b.

2. a. $P^M = 11$, $q^M = 9$ units.

b. The efficient quantity is where $MB = MSC = 12$; the efficient quantity is $q^* = 8$. Hence the monopoly output is still too high, so a tax of \$2 per unit will induce the efficient level of output, because $MR = MC + t$, or $20 - 2(8) = 2 + t$, hence $t = 2$. Note that the monopolist reduces the level of output compared with a competitive industry, so a smaller tax is required. If this were a competitive industry (with price-taking behaviour), the tax would need to be \$10 per unit.

Index